Persons, Situations, and Emotions

SERIES IN AFFECTIVE SCIENCE

Series Editors
Richard J. Davidson
Paul Ekman
Klaus Scherer

The Nature of Emotion
Fundamental Questions
edited by Paul Ekman and Richard J. Davidson

Boo!
Culture, Experience, and the Startle Reflex
by Ronald Simons

Emotions in Psychopathology
Theory and Research
edited by William F. Flack, Jr., and James D. Laird

What the Face Reveals
Basic and Applied Studies of Spontaneous Expression
Using the Facial Action Coding System (FACS)
edited by Paul Ekman and Erika Rosenberg

Shame
Interpersonal Behavior, Psychopathology, and Culture
edited by Paul Gilbert and Bernice Andrews

Affective Neuroscience
The Foundations of Human and Animal Emotions
by Jaak Panksepp

Extreme Fear, Shyness, and Social Phobia
Origins, Biological Mechanisms, and Clinical Outcomes
edited by Louis A. Schmidt and Jay Schulkin

Cognitive Neuroscience of Emotion
edited by Richard D. Lane and Lynn Nadel

Anxiety, Depression, and Emotion
edited by Richard J. Davidson

Persons, Situations, and Emotions
An Ecological Approach
edited by Hermann Brandstätter and Andrzej Eliasz

Persons, Situations, and Emotions

An Ecological Approach

Edited by
Hermann Brandstätter
& Andrzej Eliasz

OXFORD
UNIVERSITY PRESS

2001

OXFORD

UNIVERSITY PRESS

Oxford   New York
Athens   Auckland   Bangkok   Bogotá   Buenos Aires   Calcutta
Cape Town   Chennai   Dar es Salaam   Delhi   Florence   Hong Kong   Istanbul
Karachi   Kuala Lumpur   Madrid   Melbourne   Mexico City   Mumbai
Nairobi   Paris   São Paulo   Singapore   Shanghai   Taipei   Tokyo   Toronto   Warsaw

and associated companies in
Berlin   Ibadan

Copyright © 2001 Oxford University Press

Published by Oxford University Press, Inc.
198 Madison Avenue, New York, New York 10016
http://www.oup-usa.org

Oxford is a registered trademark of Oxford University Press

Library of Congress Cataloging-in-Publication Data
Persons, situations, and emotions : an ecological approach / [edited by] Hermann
Brandstätter, Andrzej Eliasz.
p.   cm. — (Series in affective science)
Includes bibliographical references and index.
ISBN 0-19-513517-2
1. Emotions.   2. Context effects (Psychology)   3. Personality.   4. Temperament.
I. Brandstätter, Hermann.   II. Eliasz, Andrzej.   III. Series.

BF531 .P47   2001
152.4—dc21   99-036503

1 3 5 7 9 8 6 4 2

Printed in the United States of America
on acid-free paper

Foreword

Klaus R. Scherer

This book is an important contribution to the Affective Science series since it illustrates several of the aims pursued by the editors. One of its major assets is the insistence of the authors that affective experience can only be understood as a result of a transaction between person and situation. In other words, an emotional reaction cannot be understood without taking into account the characteristics of a person, such as temperament, personality, motivation, attitudes, or values, and the characteristics of the situation, its constraints, and affordances. This important assumption echoes Lazarus's insistence on explaining stress and emotion in transactional terms, taking both the significance of the event and the coping potential of the person into account. Brandstätter and Eliasz, together with the authors contributing to this volume, provide ample evidence for the need to adopt such a complex approach to the study of mood and emotion in everyday situations (using time-sampling diary studies)—almost all of the empirical results they report consist of interaction effects between person and situation factors (for example, temperament, motivation, and values on the one hand and different types of work or life situations on the other). An important aim of this book is to demonstrate that affective science research can be conducted in the field, stressing ecological validity, by examining real-life changes in moods and emotions as they are experienced by "normal" people (as compared to the college undergraduates that tend to be studied in laboratory research). A corollary of this approach is the firm link established to applied issues such as well-being, health, organizational behavior, work satisfaction, unemployment, and so on, which demonstrates the important role that affective science research can play in these areas. Last but not least, this volume also bridges some of the European and American research traditions in this field, highlighting the contributions of classic and current European perspectives, published in many different languages, by integrating them with up-to-date reviews of the Anglo-American literature.

Acknowledgments

When we, the editors of this book, met for the first time at the Symposium on Social Psychology and Emotions, jointly organized by Serge Moscovici (Maison des Sciences de l'Homme, Paris) and Robert B. Zajonc (Research Center for Group Dynamics, Institute for Social Research, Ann Arbor) in January 1987, we realized that we share not only a general interest in research on personality and emotions in social contexts, but also the belief in the fruitfulness of an ecological approach. It was a long way from this meeting to the start of a common research project and, finally, to the editing of this book. Our efforts in cooperation across borders which had separated Europe for more than forty years were supported by the research foundation of the Austrian National Bank, the Polish Academy of Sciences, and the Austrian Ministery of Science. We are indebted to Andrea Abele-Brehm, Ann Elisabeth Auhagen, Peter Becker, Monika Bullinger, Stefan Hormuth, Andreas Krapp, Philipp Mayring, Urs Schallberger, Ulrich Schiefele, Peter Schwenkmezger, and Dieter Zapf for reviewing the authors' contributions. Their highly appreciated critical comments greatly helped to clarify theoretical issues as well as methodological problems and to enhance the legibility of the chapters that were thoroughly revised according to the peer reviews. Since the native languages of the authors and editors are German, Hungarian, Italian, Polish, and Slovak, we are grateful for the assistance of Deborah Preece-Brocksom and Charlotte Strümpel, as native speakers of English, for checking the drafts for idiomatic English. For standardizing the chapters' format and for carefully editing the manuscripts, we are particularly grateful to Helga Brandstätter. Finally we want to thank Richard J. Davidson, Paul Ekman, and Klaus Scherer, the editors of the Series in Affective Science, as well as Oxford University Press, in particular Joan Bossert, Philip Laughlin, and Jennifer Rozgonyi, for their encouragement and support.

Altenberg, Austria   H. B.
Warsaw, Poland   A. E.
September 2000

Contents

Foreword by Klaus R. Scherer   v

Contributors   ix

Part I   Emotions in Perspective: The Ecological Approach   1

1   Persons' Emotional Responses to Situations   3
Hermann Brandstätter and Andrzej Eliasz

2   Time Sampling Diary: An Ecological Approach to the Study
of Emotions in Everyday Life Situations   20
Hermann Brandstätter

Part II   Temperament and Emotions: Focus on Congruence   53

3   Temperament, Type A, and Motives: A Time Sampling Study   55
Andrzej Eliasz

4   Self-Regulatory Abilities, Temperament, and Volition
in Everyday Life Situations   74
Magdalena Marszał-Wiśniewska

5 Value-Motive Congruence and Reactivity as
Determinants of Well-Being   95
Anna Zalewska and Hermann Brandstätter

6 Personal Resources and Organizational Well-Being   113
Tatiana Klonowicz

Part III   Experiencing Work, Family Life, and Unemployment   131

7 Extraversion and Optimal Level of Arousal in High-Risk Work   133
Alois Farthofer and Hermann Brandstätter

8 Time Sampling of Unemployment Experiences by Slovak Youth   147
Jozef Džuka

9 Everyday Life of Commuters' Wives   163
Christa Rodler and Erich Kirchler

Part IV   Well-Being during an International Summer School   185

10 Correspondence Analysis of Everyday Life Experience   187
Tiziana Mancini and Paola Bastianoni

11 Freedom as Moderator of the Personality-Mood Relationship   199
Gyöngyi Kiss, Erika Dornai, and Hermann Brandstätter

Index   215

Contributors

Paola BASTIANONI
University of Bologna, Italy

Hermann BRANDSTÄTTER
University of Linz, Austria

Erika DORNAI
Hungarian Academy of Sciences,
Hungary

Jozef DŽUKA
University of Prešov, Slovakia

Andrzej ELIASZ
Warsaw School of Advanced Social
Psychology and Polish Academy of
Sciences, Poland

Alois FARTHOFER
University of Linz, Austria

Erich KIRCHLER
University of Vienna, Austria

Gyöngyi B. KISS
Hungarian Academy of Sciences,
Hungary

Tatiana KLONOWICZ
Warsaw School of Advanced Social
Psychology and Polish Academy of
Sciences, Poland

Tiziana MANCINI
University of Parma, Italy

Magdalena MARSZAŁ-WIŚNIEWSKA
Warsaw School of Advanced Social
Psychology and Polish Academy of
Sciences, Poland

Christa RODLER
University of Vienna, Austria

Anna M. ZALEWSKA
University of Łódź, Poland

PART 1

EMOTIONS IN PERSPECTIVE

The Ecological Approach

1

Persons' Emotional Responses to Situations

Hermann Brandstätter & Andrzej Eliasz

When Csikszentmihalyi at the University of Chicago (Csikszentmihalyi, Larson, & Prescott, 1977) and Brandstätter (1977), then at the University of Augsburg, independently started their research on emotional experience in everyday life situations with different kinds of time sampling techniques, emotions were not yet as important a topic of psychological research as they have become in the past 15 years. However, the coincidence of the onset of these two research programs is probably not purely accidental, but somehow indicative of a more general uneasiness about the long-standing neglect of emotions in psychological research.

Measures of Life Satisfaction

Subjective well-being, measured as summary ratings of satisfaction with specific life domains (e.g., work, family, economic situation) or with life in general, has been routinely assessed for several decades in surveys on the quality of life (cf. Campbell, Converse, & Rogers, 1976; for an overview of the theoretical perspectives and methodological problems in research on subjective well-being see Diener, 1984; Diener, Suh, Lucas, & Smith, 1999). There has been, however, some concern about how current mood affects those satisfaction judgments (Forgas, 1995; Rusting, 1998; Schwarz & Clore, 1983; Schwarz & Strack, 1991), and about the influence of social desirability on these same judgments (Sudman, Greely, & Pinto, 1967, quoted by Diener, 1984, p. 551).

What ratings of satisfaction with life as a whole or with the different domains of life really measure is still not fully understood. Are people comparing their living conditions (e.g., income, housing, work, social relationships) with some standards (e.g., their previous standing or that of others; cf. Michalos, 1980) before they give an answer to the life satisfaction questions? This might mean that they look outwards, focusing on the (external) resources of need fulfillment and eventually saying to themselves "I earn more than others, I can afford better housing, a more expensive car, a better education for my children; I know more people I can rely upon, my work entails more freedom and independence, I have fewer health problems. Therefore I am better off, which means that I am (or have to be) satisfied with my life."

In a quite different way, people might try to remember how often they have felt good or bad in different types of situations during the past weeks, months, or years, whatever their time horizon might be (Diener, Larsen, Levine, & Emmons, 1985; Schimmack & Diener, 1997; Tversky & Griffin, 1991).

A third possibility is to answer life satisfaction questions simply according to emotions conditioned to the words "my life," "my family," "my work," and so on in the course of daily experience. A person who often enjoys being with his or her spouse would not make a kind of frequency count but would "read" the satisfaction score from the emotional response conditioned to the image and word of "my spouse."

Whatever the process resulting in life satisfaction judgments may be—probably somehow all three routes are used with different weights, depending on the circumstances and on personality characteristics (for some other aspects of the problem see Abele & Becker, 1994)—one wants to know how the moment-to-moment emotional experience relates to the cognitively accentuated, rather abstract judgments of satisfaction.

Finding out about what is going on in people's everyday life when they judge it as more or less satisfying is one of the reasons for conducting time sampling studies of emotional experience. Another reason is rooted in the research tradition of environmental or ecological psychology. Here again, using attitude scales in assessing how rural or urban environments, housing, neighborhoods or workplaces, and so on are perceived and evaluated, leaves some doubts about what people really feel during work and leisure time spent in those different environments. Time samples of emotional experience including information on activities, places, other persons present, affected motives, and (subjective) causal attributions of emotions is expected to give better insight into what really matters, that is, what really makes people feel good or bad, this showing also a better way to necessary changes in the environment.

The Concept of Emotion and Mood

We all know from our daily experience: Moving from one situation to another, our mood is modulated up and down, slowly or quickly, in dark or bright "colors," by memories, observations, and expectations, while we are pursuing our goals in a physical and social environment that may support or obstruct our desires and intentions.

Emotions offer the most immediate feedback on how successful a person is in pursuing his or her goals, which are a confluence of motives, perceived opportunities, incentives provided by the environment, and beliefs about one's task-specific capabilities. The intensity of emotions varies with the intensity of the actualized motives (cf. Smith & Lazarus, 1990). The quality of emotions varies with the motives involved and with the experience and causal attribution of successes and failures. Emotions have a central integrative function; they link cognitions to action impulses, at a level of evolution that is higher than yet somehow analogous to the instinctive and less flexible coordination of sensation and motion in animals.

With respect to the central integrative function of emotions, one can find a remarkable correspondence between past phenomenological ideas (e.g., Klages, 1950; Lersch, 1970; Vetter, 1966) and recent conceptions of emotions. Dörner (1985), for example, conceives emotions as guiding spirits that tell us not only that something important has happened, but also in which direction we should move and how we can regulate our actions (p. 163).

We speak of mood and emotions as if each of these words referred to a different phenomenon. Many scholars in the field of emotions indeed differentiate very clearly between these two concepts, saying that emotions are responses to remembered, perceived, or expected events that focus a person's feeling on objects, whereas mood lacks this object reference or intentionality (cf., for example, Ekman & Davidson, 1994).

According to Forgas, differences between moods and emotions concern intensity, enduring affective states, and cognitive content. Emotions are "more intense, short-lived and usually have a definite cause and clear cognitive content" (Forgas, Johnson, & Ciarrochi, 1998, p. 157).

We do not deny that this distinction can make sense in both ordinary and scientific language. Nevertheless, we prefer to deal with mood and emotions as one complex affective phenomenon. To us, mood is also somehow intentional, being related not to single events (of short duration), but to a person's more comprehensive and more stable life situation. Mood implies a global evaluation of one's situation. We can reasonably assume that each (event-related) emotion is a modulation of mood, its short term elevation or depression, whatever the specific quality of mood and emotions may be. Virtually the same event is supposed to be experienced differently depending on the basic affective "tuning", that is, depending on a person's mood. Also, each emotion leaves behind some residues that change the basic tuning more or less deeply, in a more or less enduring fashion (a similar view can be found in Brebner, 1998).

These interconnections between mood and emotions, that is, between two levels of the affective system, are interdependent. We assume that these mutual relations are susceptible to and in turn influence the broader system of personality within and across different situations. Relations of this kind are called transactional (Pervin, 1976). This line of reasoning also corresponds with the concept of temperament as an element of the stimulation control system of transactional relations (Eliasz, 1990).

Personality and Emotions

A person's emotional experience in every-day life situations is a very important, if not the most important, source of personality research, including research on

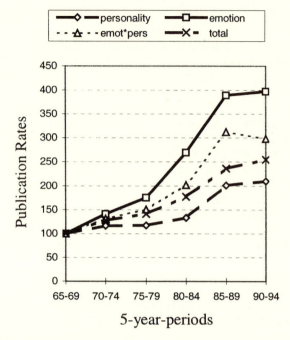

Figure 1.1. Publication rates from 1965 to 1994 in the fields of personality, emotion, personality combined with emotion and all PsychLit documents together (1965 = 100%).

individual differences in structures and processes of motivation and cognition. What someone regularly feels when confronted with highly demanding tasks, with people needing help, or with opportunities to exert power or to interact with friends, tells us much about what she or he desires and expects to happen, whenever he or she enters one of these different situations.

Since the idea of person-environment fit (Brandstätter, 1994b; French, Rodgers, & Cobb, 1974; Holland, 1997) was recognized as an important, possibly the most important, condition of happiness, right from the beginning of the Time Sampling Diary (TSD) research, the taking of individual differences in temperament, personality structure, motives, and values into account has been accepted as a promising research strategy. The growing interest in the relationship between personality and emotions also shows up in the sheer number of publications on the subject that have appeared in the psychological literature (PsychLit). The number of journal articles on the effects of personality on emotions has increased sharply over the past thirty years, remarkably more than the general publication rates, as a frequency count of such publications documented in PsychLit shows (Figure 1.1).

The idea that personality differences imply individual differences in the quality, intensity, frequency, and variability of emotions can, of course, already be found in the time-honored concept of the four temperaments, which originated in the writings of Hippocrates (fifth-fourth century B.C.) and, centuries later, was elaborated by Galenus (second century A.D.). Various interpretations and refor-mulations of the four temperaments can be found in the writings of philosophers of the eighteenth and nineteenth centuries (cf. Stern, 1911, pp. 187). Individual differences in people's emotions were also recognized as essential features of per-sonality structure by a number of psychologists in the late nineteenth and early twentieth centuries (cf. Pongratz, 1967, p. 286).

Looking at the research of the past decades, we find several attempts, some of which apply time sampling techniques, to relate personality dimensions or per-sonality structure to emotional experience, (Diener, Smith, & Fujita, 1995; Em-mons & Diener, 1985; Heady & Wearing, 1989; Rusting & Larsen, 1997; Suls, Green, & Hillis, 1998), others rely on day-to-day retrospective diaries (Wessman & Ricks, 1966) or on traditional self-reports on remembered frequencies or inten-sities of emotions (Argyle & Lu, 1990; Costa & McCrae, 1980; Furnham & Brewin, 1990; Hotard, McFatter, Whirter, & Stegall, 1989; McFatter, 1994; Meyer & Shack, 1989; Watson & Clark, 1992). In particular, extraversion and neuroticism were related to subjective well-being, mostly with the finding that extraversion corre-lates mainly with measures of positive emotions, and neuroticism with measures of negative emotions (see Argyle & Lu, 1990; Bolger & Schilling, 1991; Brand-stätter, 1994a; Costa & McCrae, 1980; DeNeve & Cooper, 1998; Diener et al., 1985; McFatter, 1994; Rusting & Larsen, 1997, for a discussion of the alleged indepen-dence of frequencies or intensities of positive and negative emotions).

All chapters of this book deal with interindividual and intraindividual varia-tion of mood related to personality dimensions or personality types, on the one hand, and environmental dimensions or types of environments, on the other. In addition to the concept "personality," the reader will often encounter the term "temperament" in the book. The distinction between temperament and person-ality needs some clarification (cf. Eliasz, 1985; Strelau 1983, 1987). Temperament concerns biologically rooted individual differences that appear already in in-fancy, characterize all mammals, and relate to formal characteristics of behavior. In contrast, personality is formed mainly by social processes and gradually de-velops during childhood and adolescence. Personality is characteristic of only human beings and concerns the content of behavior (Strelau, 1983, 1998; Strelau and Zawadzki, 1995). According to Strelau, the temperament-personality differ-ence resides also in the kind of regulative functions that are supposed to be a component of the structure of personality. This point of view was questioned by Eliasz (1990). The commonly accepted differences between temperament and personality involve the biological roots and the style-versus-content aspect of be-havior. Those differences are emphasized by scholars of temperament indepen-dent of their theoretical framework—on the one hand, Strelau (1983) and, on the other, Thomas and Chess (1977). Some authors do not distinguish temperament from personality, whereas others treat temperament as a subset of personality (cf. Matthews & Deary, 1998, pp. 64–66). Recently, Strelau (1998) too has concep-tualized temperament as a special part of personality, but he still stresses the specific characteristics of temperamental traits previously mentioned. Thus, tem-perament is understood as a person's mostly inherited general "reactivity" (sensitivity) of the nervous and endocrine system. Personality is rooted in the temperament but developed and differentiated under the influence of the per-son's experience with the physical and social environment. Whereas temperament refers to the characteristic style of a person's experience and behavior (e.g., arousable, energetic, mobile), the personality construct refers more to the kinds of behaviors that characterize a person (e.g., respecting norms in social encounters, being self-confident in competing with others, following one's feelings more than one's reflections in making important decisions) in particular social situations. Some personality dimensions, like extraverson and emotional stability, have deeper roots in temperament than others (e.g., conscientiousness or dominance), which may be influenced more by experience, particularly experience in early childhood.

The Ecological Approach to Emotions

The chapters in this book share not only the theoretical focus on emotions as joint and interactive functions of the characteristics of the persons and of the behavior settings, but also the ecological approach. Emotions can be and are often studied in the laboratory with the advantage of experimental control and improved conditions for causal inferences in hypotheses testing. What happens to people in their daily lives and how they feel about it, however, can better be found out by having them report their experience each evening retrospectively for the day or for the moment of self-observation several times a day.

When we, the editors of this book, met for the first time during an international conference on emotions in Paris in 1987, we realized that we share an interest in the effects of personality on emotions in the context of everyday situations. Later, we started to exchange our ideas and to coordinate our research. All chapters of this book report on studies performed with the Time Sampling Diary (TSD) designed by Brandstätter (1977), and all chapters deal also with individual differences in emotional responses to everyday situations. The chapters of part 2 of the book examine in particular some basic dimensions of temperament (cf. Eliasz, 1990; Strelau, 1983) and their manifestations in emotions.

The ecological approach enables researchers to assess how personality dimensions operate in various situations (cf. the special issue on "Personality and Daily Experiences" in the *Journal of Personality*, 1991, 59). According to Mischel (1990), personality variables are characterized by a structural as well as a functional aspect. The authors of this book consider both aspects. With respect to personality structure, we look, for example, for internal structure of Type A and volitional properties. Also, some aspects of the "architecture" of personality, that is, some configurations of personality variables or patterns of personality and temperamental variables, were studied. Personality structure can be better understood if the functional aspect of the temperament and personality variables is taken into account. Cross-situational consistency versus inconsistency, for example, can be understood only from a functional perspective. The TSD gives an opportunity to study psychological processes, mainly emotional and motivational, across various situations and personality variables.

With their focus on person-environment interaction, the chapters of this book refer to the controversial debate on personality traits. Mischel, one of the promoters of this debate (Mischel, 1968), no longer questions the existence of personality variables any more, but tries to identify the conditions that foster various degrees of cross-situational consistency of behavior (Mischel, 1990, 1998). Shoda (1998) uses the term "behavioral signature" to depict the "idiographic nature" of personality variables, which are thought to develop from a person's interaction with the specific contexts of his or her life. The term "behavioral signature" corresponds to the notion of "coherent stability" (Endler, 1977). By and large, these terms refer to an individual's characteristic inconsistentcy of cross-situational behavior, which is stable over time. Both behavioral signature and coherent stability allow us to predict individual behavior. Cross-situational inconsistency of behavior is neglected very often by researchers who aggregate data from various situations in order to arrive at an average level of frequency and intensity of behavior, which then is conceived of as a personality trait. This method carries the risk of overgeneralization. Data collected with the TSD are a warning against such unwarranted generalizations.

Bermudez (1998) points out that psychological studies on mental health are insufficient if they are limited to personality characteristics. According to him, the trait approach has to be supplemented by the process approach. Within the process approach attention is focused on cognitive, affective, and motivational processes displayed in specific circumstances. This conclusion is in line with the approach to the emotional experience that we have chosen in this book. These two approaches—the structure (trait) approach and the process—in the past have often been separated but are now more often integrated within the unitary theoretical framework of a Cognitive-Affective Personality System (see, for example, Shoda, 1998).

An Overview of the Book Chapters

The TSD method, its merits and shortcomings, are described in detail by *Brandstätter* in chapter 2, in which he also gives an impression of the versatility and usefulness of the TSD-technique in basic personality and emotions research as well as in the context of organizational psychology. Studies briefly reported in this chapter refer to (a) individual's emotions as they interact with other people, (b) motivational person-environment-fit as a condition of subjective well-being, (c) the quality of the relationship of married couples as it appears in their TSD-records, (d) the TSD as a means of measuring organizational climate, (e) individuals' attribution of their emotional experiences during their first six months at a new workplace, and (f) the emotional vocabulary of women and men. Finally, the advantages and the shortcomings of the TSD are discussed. The appendix of chapter 2 contains instructions for keeping the diary and coding the diary entries.

Chapters 3 to 6 (part II of the book), empirically based on a very large data set collected from Polish bank employees who kept the diary over 10 days in each of their first, second, third, and sixth months at their new workplace, theoretically center around the concept of temperament.

Eliasz, in chapter 3, analyzes the motivational and emotional consequences of congruence and incongruence between (predominantly inherited) temperament and Type A that are developed under the strong influence of socialization agents. Type A combined with low reactivity is assumed to be congruent, whereas Type A combined with high reactivity is conceived of as incongruent, causing emotional problems in those striving for high achievement in situations perceived as competitive. It is predicted and found that high reactive Type A persons (compared to low reactive Type A persons) more often actualize motives for control over the environment, motives induced by low self-confidence and motives relating to the state of organism, in order to cope with the demands of work situations. This is interpreted as a way of coping with stress characteristic of high reactive Type A persons in work situations. High reactive Type A individuals are also less able than low reactive Type A persons to adjust their actualizations of motives and goals to changing situations, that is, to moving from highly demanding work in the bank ("work-in") to less demanding work situations outside the workplace ("work-out"). Thus, the TSD reveals quite clearly some of the problems caused by incongruence between temperament and Type A behavior.

Marszał-Wiśniewska, in chapter 4, speaks of "temperament-volition coherence" and focuses on another aspect of intrapersonal congruence, that between temperament and state versus action orientation in the sense of Kuhl and Beckmann (1994). Again, by analogy to the relationship between temperament and Type A behavior that is analyzed by Eliasz in this volume, temperament is conceived of as predominantly genetically influenced, while characteristics of volition are thought to be subject to the influence of socialization agents. Incoherence is inherent in the combination of low reactivity and state orientation as well as high reactivity and action orientation. Whenever the participants in the TSD-study were pursuing a goal in the moment of self-observation, they recorded which of their abilities or lack of abilities was a cause of successful or unsuccessful goal striving. Of particular interest were self-regulatory abilities defined in the following way:

- Ability to focus attention on goal-relevant aspects of the situation (active attentional selectivity)
- Ability to prevent emotions from interfering with goal enactment (emotion control)
- Ability to pursue goals persistently by thinking about the positive consequences of goal attainment and the negative consequences of giving up (motivation control)
- Ability to make decisions quickly (parsimony of information processing)
- Ability to get social support (environmental control).

For groups differentiated with respect to temperament (reactivity and mobility) and orientation, (action versus state), the author explored how frequently people refer to these action control abilities and how frequently these abilities are associated with success and failure. Thus, individual differences of action control processes can be analyzed in a theoretically meaningful way.

Incoherence (incongruence) between temperament (mobility and reactivity) and orientation (state versus action) entailed less frequent and less efficient motivation control, which also means less efficiency in goal striving at the workplace. The advantage of action orientation over state orientation appears in a higher ability-demand fit in all four classes of situations (leisure at home, leisure out of home, work at home, work out of the home). It was the intention of the author to show that temperamental and volitional traits influence people's sub-

jective experience and behavior in their daily lives. Since traits and current experience are measured in completely different ways—traditional questionnaires,
on the one hand, and time sampling dairy, on the other hand—this is of special
interest from both a theoretical and a methodological perspective.

How the congruence between values and motives influences daily emotional
experience in interaction with a person's temperament (reactivity) is the central
topic of chapter 5, written by *Zalewska and Brandstätter*. Values are conceived
of as cognitively reflected evaluations of broadly defined life states (goals),
whereas motives, actualized in everyday life and assessed through time sampling,
are more impulsive and affective forces initiating and directing a person's actions.
The actualization of motives entails immediate positive or negative emotions in
the case of success or failure in goal striving. The three value and motive domains
considered in the chapter are achievement, affiliation, and power. The values
were measured using an adaptation of Super's Work Values Inventory (Seifert &
Bergmann, 1983). Motive strength was operationalized as the relative frequency
by which a person referred to the specific motive in the TSD. Incongruence between values and motives was assumed to be a source of internal stimulation,
which in combination with high or low reactivity (implying low or high need for
stimulation, respectively) results in optimal, under- or overarousal and influences
the current mood in a positive or negative direction. The results are in agreement
with the optimal arousal hypothesis in the domain of power. In the affiliation and
predominantly also in the achievement domain, value-motive congruence tends
to foster more positive emotions than value-motive incongruence, irrespective of
reactivity. The optimal arousal hypothesis seems to be promising in explaining
complex interactions between temperament (reactivity), value-motive congruence, and specific motives. This interaction varies with the behavior setting
(workplace or elsewhere), although there are still some inconsistencies with respect to the achievement domain.

In chapter 6, *Klonowicz* studies subjective well-being, conceived of as an indication of person-environment fit, by relating personal resources (temperament
as an "energetic" resource and intelligence, measured with Raven's progressive
matrices, as a "structural" or cognitive resource) to the rather high demands of a
new workplace. Variability of mood and psychosomatic complaints are highest,
while the level of mood ("mood balance") is lowest in a cluster of persons characterized by low personal resources (low intelligence, low mobility, and high
reactivity). Optimally adjusted is a cluster of persons characterized by average
intelligence, high mobility, and low reactivity, whereas, in terms of adjustment
(measured as subjective well-being), the cluster that exhibits "high intelligence,
average mobility, and low reactivity" is situated between these two clusters,
somewhat closer to the optimally adjusted cluster. This may indicate that persons
with particularly high intelligence missed having demanding tasks and were,
therefore, only moderately happy. Again, the data support the general hypothesis
that subjective well-being is a function of personality-environment fit.

Whereas all the chapters in part II are based on the very rich data set obtained
from the Warsaw sample of bank employees, each chapter in part III reports on
a TSD study done with a different sample—an Austrian sample of steel workers,
a Slovakian sample of short- and long-term unemployed youth, and an Austrian

sample of housewives (with at least one child under 15 years of age) whose husbands were either (a) working in the neighborhood of their residence, (b) commuting daily, or (c) commuting weekly to a distant workplace.

The person-by-situation interaction as an explanation for mood is the central problem in the study of *Farthofer and Brandstätter* on extraversion and optimal arousal in risky work, described in chapter 7. The chapter takes a look at how crane-drivers and steel-processing operators experience their stressful and highly responsible work, which is characterized by health risks for workers and high material losses.

Following Eysenck (1967), the authors assume that extraverts have a higher need for arousal than introverts. Situations perceived as risky were assumed to be highly arousing and, therefore, to favor extraverts. The authors find, as predicted, that in high-risk work situations like those encountered by crane drivers and operators in a steel company, extraverts feel better than introverts who under highly stimulating risk are supposedly over-aroused. Previous research, briefly discussed in the chapter, has shown that emotions influence information processing and decision making. Therefore, paying attention to personal and situational conditions of optimal arousal is an important issue in personnel selection and training for dangerous work settings.

In *Džuka*'s study, described in chapter 8, the TSD revealed that long-term (more than 12 months) unemployed Slovak youth, compared to short-term unemployed (less than 7 months), experienced negative emotions more often. Also, within each unemployment status, the highest frequency of negative emotions was found among unstable introverts. The lowest frequency occurred not, as one might expect, with stable extraverts but with stable introverts. Stable introverts seem to suffer less than stable extraverts from inactivity imposed by unemployment. Quite often, as Brandstätter (1998) has shown, the effects of personality dimensions on mood are not additive but multiplicative, indicating interactions between the personality dimensions.

In rural areas, people often have to commute over long distances between home and workplace. *Rodler and Kirchler*, as described in chapter 9, looked at differences in the emotional experiences of three groups of married women who stayed at home with at least one child under 15 years of age while the husband (a) went to work near the home, (b) commuted daily 70–100 km, and (c) commuted weekly 70–100 km and thus was with his family for weekends only. The authors analyzed in detail how frequently the women in these three groups (husbands not commuting, husbands commuting daily, and husbands commuting weekly) were at different places, performed different activities, were together with different kinds of people, talked about different topics, related their emotional experiences to different classes of motives, and attributed their emotional experiences to different causes. The authors also compared the average mood in these classes of situations and attributions. The most important result they report is a low level of well-being among the wives of daily commuters, particularly in the presence of their children. They suggest that these commuters may have been exhausted from work and traveling and were therefore unable to give the support their wives desired in child care and housework.

Unexpectedly, the authors found no significant linear correlation between emotional stability and extraversion and general mood score. Possibly, a closer look at the data would have revealed non-linear effects of single dimensions and interaction effects between different dimensions.

Both chapters in part IV of this book are based on a data set generated by a class of graduate students participating in a workshop on the ecological approach to the study of emotions conducted by the editors of this book within a summer school run by the European Association of Experimental Social Psychology at Serock (Poland) in 1994. The participants kept the diary during the two weeks of the workshop and for the week that followed their return home.

Chapter 10, written by *Mancini and Bastianoni* is of special interest for methodological reasons. Multiple Correspondence Analysis (MCA) is an efficient way to visualize the interconnections between the various categories (places, activities, persons present, and motives involved) used in characterizing the situation in each moment of self-observation and to show the relationship of these categories to negative, neutral, and positive mood. Although personality dimensions were not included in this analysis, the position of each person in the two-dimensional space (work vs. leisure and home vs. out-of-home as axes) was depicted. Thus, individual differences in preferences for places, activities, and interaction partners, as well as the kinds of actualized motives and the quality of emotions, become clearly visible. This opens the possibility of using the technique in counseling by feeding back the TSD results to individual participants and supporting them in the reflection on and interpretation of their data.

The second chapter in part IV, by *Kiss, Dornai, and Brandstätter*, deals with perceived situational freedom, that is, external freedom from social pressures and internal freedom from the demands of one's own conscience. The authors show that personality characteristics and values influence mood most when internal freedom is high while external freedom is statistically controlled for. Individuals perceive themselves as externally and/or internally free if they can leave the present situation or do something else in the situation without being blamed by significant others (external freedom) and/or without violating their personal norms (having a guilty conscience) in doing so. It was predicted and found that one's emotions reflect value priorities and other personality dispositions (in terms of the global 16PF dimensions) to a greater extent in situations where internal freedom is high than when it is low. It may well be that some of the moderator effects concerning the personality differences in the influence of situations on emotions reported in this volume and elsewhere can be better understood by taking perceived internal and external freedom into account.

Can we gain any new insights from the studies reported in this book? Some of the results, of course, support plausible and theoretically well-founded hypotheses and are therefore, as an anonymous reviewer expressed it, "comforting but not particularly exciting." However, there is also quite a number of less obvious but nevertheless theoretically derived hypotheses that find support in the data which could scarcely have been found without the Time Sampling Diary, thus adding to our knowledge and understanding of the conditions of subjective well-being in everyday life situations. These hypotheses concern the effects on well-being of congruence/incongruence between (a) temperament and Type A (chapter 3), (b) temperament and action orientation (chapter 4), and (c) values and motives (chapter 5). Congruence in this sense (as a characteristic of personality structure) is an essential aspect of (internal) personality integration, which, although hitherto widely neglected in research on personality and emotions, has a remarkable explanatory power (for a recent discussion of the effects on subjective well-being of pursuing self-concordant vs. self-discordant goals see Sheldon & Elliot, 1999). The issue of person-environment fit, that is, between personal resources and situational demands (chapter 6) and between arousability and stimulation (chapter 7) is not trivial, either, because P-E-fit hypotheses, to our knowledge, were never tested with time sampling of emotions in work settings over such long periods of self-observation. In the unemployment study (chapter 8), stable introverts and not, as one would expect from prevailing opinions, stable extraverts came up with the lowest frequency of negative emotions. This points to the existence of interaction effects, which are often overlooked, between a person's emotional stability and extraversion on the one hand, and opportunities and demands of the situation on the other hand. The remaining chapters, too, present results that are neither trivial nor redundant. Even if interviews with the wives of commuting husbands had produced the same results for spouses of daily and of weekly commuters, deriving such findings from time sampling diaries (TSD) is more convincing, because it is less susceptible to retrospective cognitive biases and to responses influenced by social desirability (chapter 9). Multiple Correspondence Analysis, applied for probably the first time to TSD data (chapter 10), may prove particularly useful in future studies. The distinction between perceived external and internal freedom and their effect on how personality characteristics and value orientations influence subjective well-being is unique to the final chapter 11. Only TSD techniques can get hold of such moderator effects.

Conclusions

This book developed from a close cooperation between two research groups, one established at the Institute of Psychology of the Polish Academy of Sciences, Warsaw, the other at the Johannes-Kepler-University of Linz in Austria, each with connections to colleagues involved in emotions research at other universities. Both groups used the time sampling diary as the principal method of collecting data on people's emotional experience in everyday life situations, and both groups adopted the central concept of person-environment interaction in explaining the intraindividual and interindividual variation of mood. However, the personality constructs and personality measures used by the two groups were different, since each group followed its own tradition in personality research: basic dimensions of temperament, in particular reactivity and mobility, on one hand, global 16PF personality dimensions such as extraversion and emotional stability on the other.

With respect to the influence of temperament on mood, the idea of intrapersonal congruence or coherence between different subsystems of personality proved particularly useful. Congruence between biologically based temperament characteristics and personality traits developed in interaction with the social and cultural environment turned out to be of crucial importance for subjective well-being in a variety of situations. This congruence is an issue in relating reactivity to Type A (Eliasz), reactivity to action control (Marszał-Wiśniewska), temperament to values and motives (Zalewska & Brandstätter), and energetic resources (temperament) to intellectual resources (Klonowicz). Even if some higher-order interactions between the characteristics of the individual and the characteristics of the circumstances were unexpected and as yet not easily amenable to a theoretical interpretation, they make us think about possible routes for future research. Using empirical research based on a theory, that is, on some kind of integrated and logically consistent previous knowledge about the phenomenon of interest, is a good research strategy. Being open to unexpected observations that might suggest new questions and a new approach to answering these questions is a good strategy, too.

If we assume that temperament is more biologically rooted than personality, parents as well as caregivers should be careful not to shape the children's and youngsters' personalities in ways that are incompatible with their temperaments. Otherwise, a mismatch between temperament and personality will cause problems later at the expense of the child's subjective well-being and health.

The idea of integration of the different structures and functions within the "architecture" of the personality has been convincingly elaborated by Philipp Lersch (1970), who pointed also to the roots of this idea in the thinking of ancient Greek philosophers and, of course, in the writings of Sigmund Freud. If Metcalfe and Mischel (1998) speak of the "hot" and the "cool" systems of personality, the coordination and integration of these two systems obviously is a central issue, too. It seems that, in personality research, thinking in terms of personality structures and patterns of functions, and not only in terms of linear combinations of personality dimensions, has once again become more common.

The studies reported in this volume share a focus on the person-situation interaction in explaining inter- and intraindividual variation of mood. They relate abilities to demands, motives and individual values to incentives and social rewards, temperament (reactivity) to stimulation intensity, self-knowledge (including goals and task-specific self-confidence) to situational knowledge (perception of possibilities and incentives). This knowledge, however, may be more or less accurate. Initiating an action follows partly the person's conscious cognitive representations of self and the world around the self, and partly subconscious desires, impulses, and response patterns over which the person has only very limited control. Whether an action or a sequence of actions leads to positive feelings of success or negative feelings of failure, whatever the motives and goals involved might be, depends very much on the *real* capabilities of a person and on the *real* opportunities (or barriers) and incentives provided by the environment, and not only on a person's self-and world schemata, which may be incorrect and therefore inefficient.

One of the shortcomings of the TSD is the fact that it generates very rich data on people's experience, that is, on their cognitions and emotions, but not on their real abilities (in solving different kinds of social and non-social tasks), not on the real difficulties they have to cope with, and not on the real rewards and punishments provided by the environment. Laboratory research can systematically vary the difficulty of tasks, but these tasks are hardly representative of the situational demands people encounter in their daily lives. In future studies researchers will have to analyze both self-observations and observations by others. A step in this direction has already been taken by Kirchler (1988) and by Brandstätter and Wagner (1994), who collected observations from the partners of the target persons in addition to their self-reports.

There is another problem that deserves more attention in the future. TSD data, collected from many persons in a variety of situations on many occasions, contain complex dependencies of observations to which the statistical models commonly used in analyzing the TSD data may not be optimally adjusted. It remains to be shown whether more recent methodological developments such as multi-level regression analysis (Goldstein, 1995) or some other new models designed for analyzing interdependent data (Kenny & Judd, 1996; cf. also Wickens, 1998) are better suited to clarify the relationships within and between the different units of observation and analysis (single observations, situations, persons, organizations). The usefulness of Multiple Correspondence Analysis in analyzing TSD data has been shown by Mancini and Bastianoni (in this volume). This technique may prove quite valuable in future research on patterns of personal and situational characteristics.

We hope that this book will encourage researchers on personality and emotions to approach the phenomena of their interest more often from an ecological perspective and to use methods that give more valid information about people's experience in their daily lives. Traditional attitude scales are short-cut measures of individuals' satisfaction with different life domains; they tap predominantly respondents' global cognitive evaluation of their emotional experiences. There can be no doubt that the time sampling diary provides the most immediate access to people's everyday lives; although it demands a greater investment of time and effort on the part of the participants as well as of the researcher, it is a valuable supplement to attitude scales and retrospective self-reports in emotions research.

References

Abele, A., & Becker, P. (Eds.). (1994). *Wohlbefinden. Theorie—Empirie—Diagnostik* [Subjective well-being: Theory—empirical research—assessment] (2nd ed.). Munich: Juventa.

Argyle, M., & Lu, L. (1990). The happiness of extraverts. *Personality and Individual Differences, 11,* 1011–1017.

Bermudez, J. (1998, July). *Personality and health-protective behavior.* Keynote address at the Ninth European Conference on Personality, Guildford, Great Britain.

Bolger, N., & Schilling, E. A. (1991). Personality and the problems of everyday life: The role of neuroticism in the exposure and reactivity to daily stressors. *Journal of Personality, 59,* 355–386.

Brandstätter, H. (1977). Wohlbefinden und Unbehagen. Entwurf eines Verfahrens zur Messung situationsabhängiger Stimmungen [Positive and negative mood. The design of a study for measuring mood changing with situations]. In W. H. Tack (Ed.), *Bericht über den 30. Kongreß der DGfPs in Regensburg 1976* (Vol. 2, pp. 60–62). Göttingen: Hogrefe.

Brandstätter, H. (1994a). Alltagsereignisse und Wohlbefinden [Daily events and subjective well-being]. In A. Abele & P. Becker (Eds.), *Wohlbefinden. Theorie—Empirie—Diagnostik* (2nd ed., pp. 191–225). Munich: Juventa.

Brandstätter, H. (1994b). Well-being and motivational person-environment fit: A time-sampling study of emotions. *European Journal of Personality Psychology, 8,* 75–93.

Brandstätter, H. (1998, July). *Personality influences on emotions in everyday life situations.* Paper presented at the Ninth European Conference on Personality, Guildford, Great Britain.

Brandstätter, H., & Wagner, W. (1994). Erwerbstätigkeit der Frau und Alltagsbefinden von Ehepartnern im Zeitverlauf [Employment status of the wife and subjective well-being in everyday life of married couples]. *Zeitschrift für Sozialpsychologie, 25*, 126–146.

Brebner, J. (1998). Happiness and personality. *Personality and Individual Differences, 25*, 279–296.

Campbell, A., Converse, P. E., & Rodgers, W. L. (1976). *The quality of American life.* New York: Russell Sage Foundation.

Costa, P. T. Jr., & McCrae, R. R. (1980). Influence of extraversion and neuroticism on subjective well-being: Happy and unhappy people. *Journal of Personality and Social Psychology, 38*, 668–678.

Csikszentmihalyi, M., Larson, R., & Prescott, S. (1977). The ecology of adolescent activity and experience. *Journal of Youth and Adolescence 6*, 281–294.

DeNeve, K. M., & Cooper, H. (1998). The happy personality: A meta-analysis of 137 personality traits and subjective well-being. *Psychological Bulletin, 124*, 197–229.

Diener, E. (1984). Subjective well-being. *Psychological Bulletin, 95*, 542–575.

Diener, E., Larsen, R. J., Levine, S., & Emmons, R. A. (1985). Intensity and frequency: The underlying dimensions of positive and negative affect. *Journal of Personality and Social Psychology, 48*, 1253–1265.

Diener, E., Suh, E. M., Lucas, R. E., & Smith, H. L. (1999). Subjective well-being: Three decades of progress. *Psychological Bulletin, 125*, 276–302.

Diener, E., Smith, H., & Fujita, F. (1995). The personality structure of affect. *Journal of Personality and Social Psychology, 69*, 130–141.

Dörner, D. (1985). Verhalten, Denken und Emotionen [Behavior, thinking, and emotions]. In L. H. Eckensberger & E. D. Lantermann (Eds.) *Emotion und Reflexivität* (pp. 157–181). Munich: Urban & Schwarzenberg.

Ekman, P., & Davidson, R. J. (Eds.). (1994). *The nature of emotion. Fundamental questions.* New York: Oxford University Press.

Eliasz, A. (1985). Transactional model of temperament. In J. Strelau (Ed.), *Temperamental bases of behavior: Warsaw studies on individual differences* (pp. 41–78). Lisse: Swets & Zeitlinger.

Eliasz, A. (1990). Broadening the concept of temperament: From disposition to hypothetical construct. *European Journal of Personality, 4*, 287–302.

Emmons, R. A., & Diener, E. (1985). Personality correlates of subjective well-being. *Personality and Social Psychology Bulletin, 11*, 89–97.

Endler, N. S. (1977). The role of person-by-situation interactions in personality theory. In I. E. Uzgiris & F. Weizman (Eds.), *The structuring of experience* (pp. 343–369). New York: Plenum Press.

Eysenck, H. J. (1967) *The biological basis of personality.* Springfield, IL: Thomas.

Forgas, J. P. (1995). Mood and judgment: The affect infusion model (AIM). *Psychological Bulletin, 117*, 39–66.

Forgas, J. P., Johnson, R., & Ciarrochi, J. (1998). Mood management: The role of processing strategies in affect control and affect infusion. In M. Kofta, G. Weary, & G. Sedek (Eds.), *Personal control in action. Cognitive and motivational mechanisms* (pp. 155–195). New York: Plenum Press.

French, J. R. P. Jr., Rodgers, W., & Cobb, S. (1974). Adjustment as person-environment fit. In G. V. Coelho, D. A. Hamburg, & J. E. Adams (Eds.), *Coping and adaptation* (pp. 316–333). New York: Basic Books.

Furnham, A., & Brewin, C. R. (1990). Personality and happiness. *Personality and Individual Differences, 11*, 1093–1096.

Goldstein, H. (1995). *Multilevel statistical models* (2nd ed.). London: Arnold.

Heady, B., & Wearing, A. (1989). Personality, life events, and subjective well-being: Toward a dynamic equilibrium model. *Journal of Personality and Social Psychology, 57*, 731–739.

Holland, J. L. (1997). *Making vocational choices* (3rd ed.). Englewood Cliffs, NJ: Prentice Hall.

Hotard, S. R., McFatter, R. M., McWhirter, R. M., & Stegall, M. E. (1989). Interactive effects of extroversion, neuroticism, and social relationships on subjective well-being. *Journal of Personality and Social Psychology, 57*, 321–331.

Kenny, D. A., & Judd, C. M. (1996). A general procedure for the estimation of interdependence. *Psychological Bulletin, 119*, 138–148.

Kirchler, E. (1988). Marital happiness and interaction in everyday surroundings: A time sample diary approach for couples. *Journal of Social and Personal Relationships, 5*, 375–382.

Klages, L. (1950). *Grundlegung der Wissenschaft vom Ausdruck* [Foundations of the science of expression] (7th ed.). Bonn: Bouvier.

Kuhl, J., & Beckmann, J. (1994). *Volition and personality. Action versus state orientation.* Göttingen: Hogrefe.

Lersch, Ph. (1970). *Aufbau der Person* [Structure of the person] (11th ed.). Munich: Barth (1st ed. 1938 under the title *Aufbau des Charakters* [Structure of the character], Leipzig: Barth.

Matthews, G., & Deary, I. J. (1998). *Personality traits.* Cambridge: Cambridge University Press.

McFatter, R. M. (1994). Interaction in predicting mood from extraversion and neuroticism. *Journal of Personality and Social Psychology, 66*, 570–578.

Metcalfe J., & Mischel, W. (1998, July). *A hot-system cool-system analysis of delay of gratification.* Paper presented at the Ninth European Conference on Personality, Guildford, Great Britain.

Meyer, G. J., & Shack, J. R. (1989). Structural convergence of mood and personality: Evidence for old and new directions. *Journal of Personality and Social Psychology, 57*, 691–706.

Michalos, A. C. (1980). Life satisfaction and happiness. *Social Indicators Research, 8*, 385–422.

Mischel, W. (1968). *Personality and assessment.* New York: Wiley.

Mischel, W. (1990). Personality dispositions revisited and revised: A view after three decades. In L. A. Pervin (Ed.), *Handbook of personality: Theory and research* (pp. 111–134). New York: Guilford Press.

Mischel, W. (1998, July). *Toward a unified cumulative science of personality.* Keynote address at the Ninth European Conference on Personality, Guildford, Great Britain.

Pervin, L. A. (1976). Performance and satisfaction as a function of individual-environment fit. In N. S. Endler & D. Magnusson (Eds.), *Interactional psychology and personality* (pp. 71–89). New York: Wiley.

Pongratz, J. L. (1967). *Problemgeschichte der Psychologie* [History of psychological problems]. Bern: Francke.

Rusting, C. L. (1998). Personality, mood, and cognitive processing of emotional information: Three conceptual frameworks. *Psychological Bulletin, 124*, 165–196.

Rusting, C. L., & Larsen, R. J. (1997). Extraversion, neuroticism, and susceptibility to positive and negative affect: A test of two theoretical models. *Personality and Individual Differences, 22*, 607–612.

Scherer, K., Walbott, H. G., & Summerfield, A. B. (1986). *Experiencing emotion: A cross-cultural study.* Cambridge: Cambridge University Press.

Schimmack, U., & Diener, E. (1997). Affect intensity: Separating intensity and frequency in repeated measured affect. *Journal of Personality and Social Psychology, 73*, 1313–1329.

Schwarz, N., & Clore, G. L. (1983). Mood, misattribution, and judgments of well-being: Informative and directive functions of affective states. *Journal of Personality and Social Psychology, 45*, 513–523.

Schwarz, N., & Strack, F. (1991). Evaluating one's life: A judgment model of subjective well-being. In F. Strack, M. Argyle, & N. Schwarz (Eds.), *Subjective well-being* (pp. 27–47). Oxford: Pergamon Press.

Seifert, K.-H., & Bergmann, C. (1983). Deutschsprachige Adaptation des Work Values Inventory von Super [A German adaptation of Super's Work Values Inventory]. *Zeitschrift für Arbeits- und Organisationspsychologie, 27*, 160–172.

Sheldon, K. M., & Elliot, A. J. (1999). Goal striving, need satisfaction, and longitudinal well-being: The self-concordance model. *Journal of Personality and Social Psychology, 76*, 482–497.

Shoda, Y. (1998, July). *Personality coherence: Behavioral signatures and features of situations*. Paper presented at the Ninth European Conference on Personality, Guildford, Great Britain.

Smith, C. A., & Lazarus, R. S. (1990). Emotion and adaptation. In L. A. Pervin (Ed.), *Handbook of personality. Theory and research* (pp. 609–637). New York: Guilford Press.

Stern, W. (1911). Differentielle Psychologie in ihren Grundlagen [Foundations of differential psychology]. Leipzig: Barth.

Strelau, J. (1983). *Temperament—personality—activity*. London: Academic Press.

Strelau, J. (1987). The concept of temperament in personality research. *European Journal of Personality, 1*, 107–117.

Strelau, J. (1998). *Temperament: A psychological perspective*. New York: Plenum Press.

Sudman, S., Greely, A. M., & Pinto, L. J. (1967). The use of self-administered questionnaires. In S. Sudman (Ed.), *Reducing the cost of surveys* (pp. 46–57). Chicago: Aldine.

Strelau, J., & Zawadzki, B. (1995). The formal characteristics of Behaviour-Temperament Inventory (FCB-TI): Validity studies. *European Journal of Personality, 9*, 207–229.

Suls, J., Green, P., & Hillis, S. (1998). Emotional reactivity to everyday problems, affective inertia, and neuroticism. *Personality and Social Psychology Bulletin, 24*, 127–136.

Thomas, A., & Chess, S. (1977). *Temperament and development*. New York: Brunner/Mazel.

Tversky, A., & Griffin, D. (1991). Endowment and contrast in judgments of well-being. In F. Strack, M. Argyle, & N. Schwarz (Eds.), *Subjective well-being* (pp. 10–118). Oxford: Pergamon Press.

Vetter, A. (1966). *Personale Anthropologie* [Anthropology of the person]. Freiburg: Alber.

Watson, D., & Clark, L. A. (1992). On traits and temperament. General and specific factors of emotional experience and their relation to the five-factor model. *Journal of Personality, 60*, 441–476.

Wessman, A. E., & Ricks, D. F. (1966). *Mood and personality*. New York: Holt, Rinehart, & Winston.

Wickens, T. D. (1998). Categorical data analysis. *Annual Review of Psychology, 48*, 537–558.

2

Time Sampling Diary

An Ecological Approach to the Study of Emotions in Everyday Life Situations

Hermann Brandstätter

Following the flow of a person's daily activities over a long period of time is not just difficult, it is virtually impossible. A person moving around all the time, pursuing simultaneously several goals, entering inaccessible private settings, protecting thoughts and feelings against unwanted detection by partners in interactions or from observers—, all this makes observation and recording extremely cumbersome. As a viable substitute, we may rely on people's narratives, accepting their reconstruction of their experience from memory. No doubt, narratives are important sources of information on people's lives. They can extend over long periods of time, are flexible with respect to the variety of topics and settings, and provide a structure of personal meaning by relating single events and actions to the world-view, leading strivings, and action plans of a person. There is, however, a long way from real life to the subjects' narratives and from there to the researcher's reconstruction of a life history or some part of it. Much imaginative and creative transformation is going on, the conditions and rules of which are not well understood yet (Berscheid, 1994).

Are we closer to what is really happening if we choose a more narrow time frame and simplify the task for the participants (and the researcher) by asking our subjects to keep a retrospective diary, entering late in the evening the events, thoughts, feelings, and actions just of the past day? Yes, we are, but still we would like to come closer to the time when events actually occurred and when the person had an experience he or she may not find worthwhile reporting later. Then, self-report time-sampling of experience in situ is a real choice, giving access to any kind of situation, providing representative data, and keeping the effort for the participant and the researcher at a tolerable level.

I designed the Time Sampling Diary (TSD) in the mid-1970s at the University of Augsburg (Brandstätter, 1977), when Mihalyi Csikszentmihalyi at the University of Chicago (Csikszentmihalyi, Larson, & Prescott, 1977) independently started a similar research program, as we found out some years later. From 1984 on, Ed Diener was also and is very active in this field of research with his collaborators at the University of Illinois and elsewhere, publishing mainly in the *Journal of Personality and Social Psychology* (for the first publications of this research group see Diener, 1984; Diener, Larsen, & Emmons, 1984; the most recent overview is given by Diener, Suh, Lucas, & Smith, 1999). In 1991 a special issue (No. 3 of Vol. 59) of the *Journal of Personality* focused on the influence of personality on daily experience, highlighting a variety of different approaches and methodological reflections (cf. Tennen, Suls, & Affleck, 1991).

The Basic Assumptions

There are some basic assumptions behind the TSD-approach to the study of emotions. First, emotions offer the most immediate feed-back on how successful a person is in pursuing his or her goals, which are a confluence of motives, perceived opportunities (incentives) or barriers in the environment, and beliefs about one's capabilities. Motives, personal strivings (Emmons, 1986, 1996), and action goals are related, but different concepts. Motives are conceived of as a person's basic needs for survival as an organism, for establishing and maintaining essential social relationships, and for developing one's potential in a personally meaningful life, just to mention a few very broad and abstract categories of motives. The level of personal strivings is conceptually more concrete, since it takes into account the person's life situations. Still more concrete and specific, as well as cognitively elaborated, are the action goals. These elements are linked in a hierarchical relationship: personal strivings grow out of motives and general self and world schemata. Action goals are specific and hierarchically structured operationalizations of personal strivings according to a person's specific situational schemata (how one relates one's capabilities to the environmental opportunities and demands).

A person pursuing his or her goals continuously receives an emotional feed-back of success (approaching or reaching the goal) or failure (being blocked by some internal or external obstacles). Goal-directed behavior is emotionally neutral only, if the progress toward the goal follows a well established routine, and there are no obstacles that unexpectedly hinder the progress or cause relief when surmounted (Dörner, 1985). The intensity of emotions varies with the intensity of the actualized and affected motives. The quality of positive or negative emotions depends on a person's attributions of success and failure (compared to the aspirations) as well as on the kind of motives involved. Thus, internal attribution of failure has an affinity to feelings of fear or sadness, whereas external attribution of failure protects against negative feelings or is connected with anger if others are perceived as deliberately impeding one's goal attainment. Within the positive emotions connected with success and the negative emotions connected with failure—I speak of success and failure of any motive, not only of the achievement motive (cf. Heckhausen, 1991)—the quality of emotions also depends on the motive affected. Thus, triumph is a strong positive emotion indicating an extraordinary success that satisfied the power motive, whereas pride mirrors the fulfill-ment of the achievement motive.

The integrative function of emotions is a central notion of otherwise quite different theoretical approaches to the study of emotions. A basic idea of Klaus Scherer's *component process model* of emotions is, for example, that emotions are complex responses of the organism to a particularly relevant internal or ex-ternal stimulation and that emotions are synchronized and integrated responses of the different subsystems of the person involved in adapting to critical changes of internal states or external conditions (Scherer, 1990).

The integration of cognition and action (motion) via emotions is stressed also by Dörner (1985), who conceives of emotions as guiding spirits that tell us not only that something important happened but also in which direction we should move and how we can regulate our actions (p. 163). Thus, the feeling of trusting one's (epistemic or heuristic) competence suggests an action strategy that is dif-ferent from the strategy imposed by anxiety and fear. Suggesting a strategy means that there is more or less freedom to follow the suggestion or to resist the emo-tional impulses by deliberate and voluntary counteraction.

These and some other ideas of contemporary motivation and emotions re-search (e.g., Cantor, 1994; Emmons, 1986, 1996; Forgas, 1992; Frijda, 1986; Klin-ger, 1977, 1996; Oatley & Jenkins, 1996; Scherer, 1990) remind me of basic con-cepts developed about 50 years ago within German phenomenological psychology, for example by Philipp Lersch (1970) and,—from an explicit per-spective of a cultural history and philosophical anthropology,—by August Vetter (1966). This approach, labeled *geisteswissenschaftlich*, was heavily criticized by those who favored behaviorism and/or who were convinced that accumulation of scientific knowledge could be achieved only by statistical hypotheses tested in highly controlled experiments. If there is some correspondence between past phe-nomenological ideas (e.g., Lersch, 1970; Vetter, 1966) and contemporary cognitive or information processing theories of emotions, this is the case not because there is still an explicit phenomenological tradition but rather because the specific "nat-ural" qualities of emotional phenomena and of emotion language cannot be over-looked in any comprehensive theoretical reconstruction and explanation of emo-tions.

The TSD focuses a person's attention on her or his feelings in the moments of randomized self-observations. These feelings appear in a concrete situational con-text characterized by time, place, activities, and persons present (cf. Eckes & Six, 1984), and the participants indicate the perceived causes of the emotions and the affected motives. Thus, the TSD of emotional experience tells us very much about what people strive for, what kind of situations are freely chosen or imposed, what makes them happy or unhappy, and how characteristics of the person, assessed by traditional personality questionnaires, interact with characteristics of the cir-cumstances in producing satisfaction or frustration of motives.

To give an impression of the versatility of the TSD-technique, I will select six examples of how the TSD can be used to analyze people's emotional experiences in everyday life situations. The first example relates emotions to the social roles of people present in the moment of observation. The second deals with motiva-tional person-environment correspondence as a condition of well-being. The third shows how husbands and wives are interdependent in their subjective well-being.

The fourth compares the motivational and emotional climate of five very different organizations. The fifth follows the adjustment process during the first six months at a new workplace. The sixth takes a look at sex differences in the language of emotion.

Method

Diary Format and Questionnaire

At the first meeting the participants are thoroughly informed of the procedure they should follow: They are told to make notes in a booklet on their momentary experience about four times a day over a period of 30 days. The random time samples are different for each day and each person. There are seven questions to answer each time:

1. Is my mood at the moment rather negative, indifferent, or rather positive?
2. How can I describe my momentary mood state using one or two adjectives?
3. Why do I feel as I have indicated?
4. Where am I?
5. What am I doing?
6. Who else is present?
7. To what extent do I feel free to choose to stay in or leave my present activity?

The detailed diary instructions are given in Appendix A.

Before leaving the first meeting, the participants answer a German version of Cattell's 16PF questionnaire (Schneewind, Schröder, & Cattell, 1983) and the 16PA (Brandstätter, 1988). After two days' experience with the diary, the participants meet again with the experimenters or are called by phone to discuss their problems with the method. The following day they start recording in the diary, which has to be kept for 28 consecutive days or, if the study extends over a longer period of time, for 10 days each in the first, second, third, and sixth month (of unemployment or adjusting to a new job or to studies at the university). At the end of the recording time period, the participants answer the 16PF and 16PA questionnaires a second time, as well as a questionnaire on their attitudes toward the study. Except for minor modifications and some variations in the additional questionnaires, the procedure has been virtually the same in all 20 studies run over the past 20 years with the TSD, partly in my research groups, partly elsewhere.

Time Sampling

The schedule for time sampling, printed on a sheet of paper and handed out to the participants, is generated by a computer program by dividing the 24 hours of the day into six segments of four hours each and choosing randomly one point of time within each segment. In the booklet a separate page is provided for each of the 180 scheduled observation times (6 per day over 30 days). The participants have to set the alarm of a wrist watch to go off at the next observation time. Assuming 8 hours of sleep on average, the expected number of records per day is 4, resulting in a total expected number of 120 records per person over 30 days. The actual number varies between days and persons owing to variations in hours of sleeping and in frequencies of omissions. In case a scheduled time point has been forgotten, the participants are instructed to take their notes just for the moment they become aware of their omission. Since there are also times for recording scheduled during the night, the participants have to mark those that were within their hours of sleep when they awaken the next morning.

Coding the Diary Records

In order to make sure that the participants trust our promise that all data will be completely anonymous and confidential, and to preserve the personal structuring of experience, the diary notes are coded by the participants themselves (see the coding instructions in Appendix A). The list of categories is designed or, if a prior study provides suitable categories, revised in cooperation with the participants, who then are trained in using the coding scheme.

There are categories for the following aspects of situations:

a. Time of note
b. Mood state (negative, indifferent, positive)
c. Time perspective (present mood state attributed to a past, present, or future event)
d. Sources of satisfaction and dissatisfaction (e.g., other persons, objects, weather)
e. Affected motives (e.g., achievement, affiliation, power)
f. Behavior setting (e.g., living room, shop, office)
g. Activities (e.g., working, cooking, watching TV)
h. Other persons present (e.g., spouse, children, colleagues)
i. Perceived freedom
j. Adjectives describing the mood state

Lists of categories of places, activities, persons, and attributions can be found in Brandstätter (1983).

In coding the sources of satisfaction/dissatisfaction or, as we may also call them, the "casual attributions" (category d), the participants, after looking at the specific record, have to answer the following questions for each observation time: Who or what, was the source of my mood state at that particular moment, and who or what made me feel happy or unhappy? Participants have a list of sources comprising various classes of persons (e.g., self, husband, children) and objects (e.g., work equipment, clothes, mass media) at hand. The most important source has to be put in first place; sources of minor importance can be added in second or third place.

The list of 19 motives consists of statements indicating the frustration or satisfaction of the respective motives (see Appendix B). For each page of their diary, corresponding to one point of time, they have to mark at least one and no more than three motives. Examples of those statements are:

I feel rather bad because (a) what I have achieved in my work is not good enough (achievement), (b) my surroundings are monotonous and boring (sentience), and (c) I am lonely and/or have difficulties in making contacts (affiliation); I feel rather good because (a) I experience success in my work (achievement), (b) there are varied and novel experiences (sentience), and (c) I am enjoying the company of people I like (affiliation). The 19 motives were classified by the author (cf. Brandstätter, 1983, p. 876) into six broader categories: Sentience/Activity, Achievement, Physical Comfort, Affiliation, Power, and "Higher" Motives (comprising need for knowledge, order, esthetics, morality, and religion).

The adjectives used for describing the quality of mood and emotions are usually not coded by the participants but are literally transferred from the diary. In one of the most recent studies (Kiss, Dornai, & Brandstätter, this volume), the participants, coming from different European countries and describing their emotions in their native languages, did code the adjectives by choosing from Russell's (1980) list of 24 adjectives making up the affect circumplex the one that in its meaning came closest to the set of (one, two or three) adjectives freely generated by the participant for describing the momentary mood. The adjectives of the circumplex, represented in the two-dimensional space of arousal (ordinate) and valence (abscissa), are (counter-clockwise, beginning with the upper right quadrant):

- glad, pleased, happy, delighted, excited, astonished, aroused,
- tense, alarmed, angry, afraid, annoyed, distressed, frustrated,
- miserable, sad, gloomy, depressed, bored, droopy, tired,
- sleepy, calm, relaxed, satisfied, at ease, content, serene.

The Experience Sampling Method (ESM) (Csikszentmihalyi, Larson, & Prescott, 1977; Csikszentmihalyi & Larson, 1987) and the Time Sampling Diary (TSD), the methods used most frequently (for other variants of the technique, see Wheeler & Reis, 1991), are different in some remarkable aspects. What seems to be particularly important is the fact that with TSD *the participants do their codings of the diary entries themselves*, thus structuring their experience according to their personal understanding of situations. No less important is the free answer format in describing the specific qualities of emotions. The *participants generate their own adjectives* and thus give a more idiographic picture of their individual emotional experiences and their individual ways of speaking about emotions. The explicit reference to *attributions* (subjective explanations of emotions) and affected *motives* is also noteworthy as a special characteristic of the TSD. On the other hand, ESM gives more direct information on the importance of the current goals and on how the participant perceives his or/her task specific skills.

Consistency and Stability of TSD-Measures

It is not the intention here to give a comprehensive account of the reliability of TSD-measures (cf. Hormuth, 1986). Only examples of reliability checks are presented here in order to show that internal consistency and temporal stability are mainly a function of the level of aggregation of the observations, which is actually a rather trivial fact. Event-related emotional responses, but also state measures of mood, the causal attributions of emotions and mood states (to external or internal sources), the actualization of motives, and the characteristics of the situation (place, activities, and persons present) are expected to vary across situations and time points of observation. Only if we go beyond the actual moment of experience in an attempt to describe a person's characteristic responses, that is, if we move from state to more or less situation-specific traits, do consistency of multiple indicators of a trait construct, generalizability across different situations, and temporal stability of the measures become an issue.

The following reliability estimates are based on the data of Brandstätter and Gaubatz (1997) who studied office workers' emotional experience during the first 10 days of the first, second, third, and sixth month after they joined a new organization. There, the correlation of the momentary mood scores (from -2 = very bad to $+2$ = very good) between two time points of observation was on the average $r = .23$. The average correlation between the average mood scores of two days, each day comprising about four observations per person, was $r = .54$. This is exactly what one would expect according to the Spearman-Brown formula estimating the reliability of a test made of 4 items if the reliability of the single items is $r = .23$. The average test-retest-correlation between the average mood scores obtained for two periods of 10 days each (the first 10 days of the first, second, and third month of work at the new workplace) was $r = .91$, which also comes close to the Spearman-Brown estimation of $r = .92$ for a test made of 40 items with an item-reliability of $r = .23$.

The median consistency (coefficient alpha) across four classes of situations (leisure alone, leisure with others, work alone, work with others), calculated for each of the four observation periods of 10 days, is $\alpha = .78$, with a median average correlation (between two situations within an observation period) of $r = .46$.

The median stability (coefficient alpha) across four observations periods (first 10 days of the first, second, third, and sixth month each after organizational entry) is .69, with a median average correlation (between two periods within a specific class of situations) of $r = .35$.

As expected, the consistency coefficients are higher than the stability coefficients. The cell frequencies (30 persons $\times$ 4 situations $\times$ 4 periods result in 480 cells), for which the average mood scores were calculated on which the consistency and stability analyses are based, vary in a range from 0 to 29, with a median cell frequency of 8.

The mood scores of participants were also differentiated according to classes of motives affected, classes of attributions, or some characteristics of the situation (e.g., places or kind of persons present), and cross-situational consistency coefficients for the average mood scores of these categories were calculated. This yielded coefficients in the magnitude to be expected according to the Spearman-Brown-function of reliability,[1] taking into account the number of observations for which the mean mood scores are calculated. The stability coefficients are usually somewhat lower than the consistency coefficients, which, of course, are dependent also on the degree of psychological heterogeneity in the situations.

The Versatility of the TSD Illustrated with
Six Different Applications

The primary purpose of this chapter is to show what kind of hypotheses or questions can be tested or answered with the TSD-technique. Therefore, I will not report *in extenso* on a specific study, but instead give a number of quite different examples of empirical results that have been published in detail elsewhere.

Example 1: Emotions in Interacting with Other People

The emotions experienced in the presence of other people reveal something of the general quality of a person's social relationships. For the moment, however, we will disregard individual differences and focus on social situations in general. To show that people generally experience different emotions when they are with their partner, with relatives/friends, with acquaintances/strangers or when they are alone is rather trivial, but it nevertheless gives an idea of the validity of self-reports on emotions. Table 2.1 gives an impression of how emotions, described by the participants in adjective terms that later were rated by judges on the dimensions valence and activation, are related to the kind of people present.

There are four broad categories of emotions (cf. Russell, 1980; Russell & Carroll, 1999) derived from the two basic dimensions of valence and activation (arousal):

Positive active:	Joy and activation
Positive passive:	Relaxation and satiation
Negative active:	Anger and fear
Negative passive:	Fatigue and sadness

We see that, on the average, positive active emotions (joy and activation) are prominent with relatives/friends, while negative passive emotions (fatigue and sadness) are most frequent when the person is alone (Table 2.1). Of course, the effects of other persons on the participants' mood are somehow confounded with the effects of the places where of the encounter took place and of the activities performed alone or with others. However, with large data sets, one can show that the kind of other persons present makes a difference in the frequency distribution of classes of emotions, even if activities (e.g., leisure vs. work) and places (e.g., home, out of home) are controlled.

Example 2: Motivational Person-Environment Fit (PEF)
as a Condition of Well-Being

The first example was purely descriptive, the second implies hypothesis testing. Here, the central assumption is that to feel good in social situations, people's motives (goals) must correspond to the gratifications provided by the social setting (Brandstätter, 1994a). This is not just a semantic explication of the concept of happiness, but a hypothesis that should and can be tested empirically, if the person's motive structure and the setting's reward potential can be measured independently. The TSD allows one to analyze in a unique way how people's well-being varies with their everyday life situations—whether they are alone or with

Table 2.1 Relative Frequencies of Five Classes of Emotions Dependent on Four Social Situations

Valence	Arousal	Alone (%)	Family (%)	Relatives/ Friends (%)	Acquaintances/ Strangers (%)	N
Unclassified		19.3	*15.2*	*16.0*	**20.9**	3505
Positive	Active	*18.1*	24.2	**34.6**	25.7	5038
Positive	Passive	21.9	**30.6**	21.8	*16.7*	4459
Negative	Active	12.4	10.1	*9.8*	**13.0**	2228
Negative	Passive	**28.3**	*19.9*	*17.8*	23.7	4428
Number		5346	4563	5173	4576	19658
Percentage		27.2	23.2	26.3	23.2	

N = number of observations.

Bold italic figures: Relative frequencies significantly ($p < 0.001$; one-tailed) lower than expected if emotions were independent of social situations.

Bold figures: Relative frequencies significantly higher than expected if emotions were independent of social situations (adapted from Brandstätter, 1991, p. 182).

others (family members, relatives, friends, acquaintances, authority figures, or strangers), at leisure or at work, and at home or outside the home. It gives reliable information on the person's motive structure as well as on the setting's reward potential.

The person's motive structure is defined as the *intra-individual* relative frequencies of motive actualization (as indicators of motive importance). The reward potential of the settings is represented by the *collective* relative frequencies of motive satisfaction in the whole sample of participants (as indicators of the probability that a specific motive will be satisfied when actualized in a specific situation). Differences in correspondence between the *individual motive importance* profile and the *situational motive satisfaction* profile should allow to predict intra-individual variation of happiness across situations and intra-situational variation of happiness across persons. Happiness is measured by a person's relative frequency of feeling good in the specific type of situations.

Brandstätter (1994a) differentiated 16 settings by combining four classes of social situations (alone, family members only, relatives or friends, acquaintances or strangers) with leisure or work and home vs. outside-of-the-home.

The 188 participants, whose TSD data were collected in 7 studies, were classified with respect to their pattern of four 16PF second-order factor scores: Norm orientation, Emotional Stability, Independence, and Extraversion (Schneewind, Schröder, & Cattell, 1983). A median split in each dimension separately performed for female and male participants resulted in $2 \times 2 \times 2 \times 2 = 16$ categories, each category comprising highly similar personality structures and together representing all combinations of the most important personality dimensions.

Calculation of the motivational P-E fit. For explaining the steps undertaken in testing the hypothesis on motivational P-E correspondence we look at Table 2.2. Matrix A contains the motive actualization ratios (relative frequencies of motive actualization across situations) for each person or type of persons, respectively, whereas matrix B visualizes the motive satisfaction profiles (relative frequencies of motive satisfaction under the condition of motive actualization across persons) for each category of situations.

By correlating each motive actualization profile of persons (each column of matrix A) with each motive satisfaction profile of situations (each column of matrix B) we arrive at matrix C with elements indicating the motivational P-E-fit (motPEF) for each type of person and each type of situation. Matrix D has as elements the happiness scores (relative frequencies of feeling good) for the types of persons in the classes of situations. Correlating each row of matrix C with the corresponding row of matrix D, and each column of matrix C with the corresponding column of matrix D results in vectors containing the correlations between motivational P-E fit and well-being across situations (r_s) and across persons (r_p) (Table 2.2).

All three studies, by which the motivational PEF model was tested, support the hypothesis (Table 2.3). The subjective well-being of persons across various behavior settings of their daily life depends to a certain degree on the correspondence between the motive actualization profile of the person and the general motive satisfaction profile of the behavior setting. Looking in a different direction, we can compare a single person's variation of mood across different settings with his or her variation of PEF across the settings. Here, we get also quite substantial correlations. Whether the intra-setting or the intra-person correlations are higher depends mainly on the variance of the PEF measure and of the mood ratio.

Table 2.2 Data Processing for Testing the PEF Hypothesis (Fictitious Data)

	(A) Person profile Motive actualization				(B) Setting profile Motive satisfaction		
	P1	P2	P3	P4	S1	S2	S3
Activity	.21	.15	.18	.26	.56	.42	.68
Achievement	.17	.15	.09	.14	.64	.76	.64
Physical comfort	.18	.20	.21	.16	.62	.62	.49
Affiliation	.19	.16	.21	.21	.50	.74	.69
Power	.16	.24	.21	.14	.57	.56	.50
Higher motives	.10	.10	.10	.09	.68	.61	.59

	(C) PEF			(D) Mood ratios			
	S1	S2	S3	S1	S2	S3	r_S
P1	.71	.28	−.11	.67	.85	.64	.10
P2	−.18	.19	−.21	.63	.41	.62	−.99
P3	.09	.32	.07	.77	.75	.69	.30
P4	.77	.15	−.06	.88	.62	.60	.98
r_P				.54	.69	.69	

P1, P2, P3, P4 are four different persons.
S1, S2, S3 are three different situations.
r_P = correlation between person-environment fit index and mood ratios across persons.
r_S = correlation between person-environment fit index and mood ratios across situations.

Table 2.3 Correlations between Motivational P-E Fit and
Well-Being across Persons

Study	N of cases	r
Brandstätter (1989)	188	.22
Brandstätter (1994a)	68	.32
Brandstätter and Gaubatz (1997)	30	.36

Italic figures represent medians of correlations calculated separately for
each of a number of settings.

If we correlate each entry in the PEF matrix with the corresponding entry in
the P-E matrix of subjective well-being, forgetting for a moment statistical objec-
tions against the violation of model assumptions (which are actually irrelevant
in a descriptive context), we get an overall measure of the relationship between
PEF and well-being. In one of the studies for which this analysis has been performed (Brandstätter, 1994a), the correlation turned out to be $r(238) = .40$. Controlling for personality differences reduced the correlation between PEF and
mood only marginally (from $r = .40$ to $r = .38$). Therefore, we can be quite sure,
that PEF influences mood on its own.

I tested the motivational person-environment-fit model with individual motive
profiles of all 341 persons who had participated in 11 different TSD-studies.[2] The
prediction was that the motivational P-E correspondence would have a greater
influence on mood in work situations outside the home than in leisure situations
and in housework, because salaried work was supposed to be characterized by
less freedom and reduced control over the environment. Figure 2.1 shows quite
convincingly that the data are in agreement with the predictions.

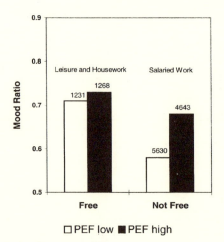

Figure 2.1. Mood as a function of motivational person-environment correspondence during leisure and housework (Free) and salaried work (Not Free). Mood
ratio is the relative frequency of positive mood. The numbers above the columns
represent N of observations.

Table 2.4 Correlations between Mood and Personality Depending on the Situation (N = 16 Personality Types Derived as Patterns of Median Split Conscientiousness, Emotional Stability, Independence, and Extraversion)

		Emotional stability	Extraversion
Alone	Leisure	*0.52*	0.16
	Work	0.41	−0.10
Family	Leisure	0.06	*0.46*
	Work	−0.05	−0.10
Relatives & friends	Leisure	*0.55*	*0.43*
	Work	0.37	0.13
Acquaintances & strangers	Leisure	0.19	*0.48*
	Work	0.16	*0.49*

ES Emotional Stability (−1 low, +1 high).
EX Extraversion (−1 low, +1 high).
Italic coefficients are significant ($p < 0.05$; one-tailed). Adjusted from Brandstätter (1994a).

Personality characteristics have an additional influence on mood, but only in certain situations. From Table 2.4 we can learn that emotional stability does not have an influence when participants are together with family members, but it contributes to well-being when a person is alone or with relatives or friends. Extraversion is particularly important in leisure with family and relatives/friends as well as in leisure and work with acquaintances/strangers.

In another study I have shown that extraverts (more so than introverts) feel better during leisure than during work when they are outside their homes (Brandstätter, 1994b). This can be explained by the fact that extraverts have stronger social motives and higher social skills, which become more salient during leisure than during work (Figure 2.2).

Example 3: The TSD Mirrors the Closeness of the Relationship between Married Couples

Retrospective diaries—records taken at the end of each day—have sometimes been used for exploring clients' experience during partner therapy, and they have also been used for analyzing close relationships between pairs of friends and siblings (Auhagen, 1987, 1991). The TSD was used for the first time with mostly unmarried couples of students by Kirchler in 1985–1986 (Kirchler, 1988). In addition to the standard questions, the participants had to answer the following questions whenever the partners were together in the moment of observation:

- How is the mood of the partner at the moment?
- Why does my partner feel as indicated?
- How much do I love my partner at the moment?
- How much does my partner love me at the moment?

Kirchler expected and found that happy couples—marital happiness was measured by a questionnaire by Olson & Porter (1983)—spent more of their time

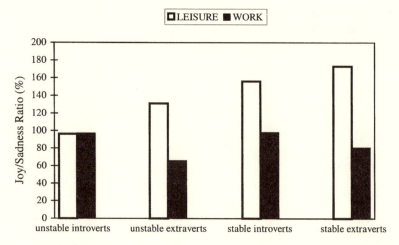

Figure 2.2. Joy/sadness ratio depending on personality structure and behavior set-ting. 120 means that the frequency of joy is 120% of the frequency of sadness. Each ratio is based on at least 1,000 observations.

together than less happy couples (44% vs. 34% of the time). This is about seven hours a day for happy and about five hours a day for less happy couples. In particular, the happy couples shared more recreation time. On average, the sub-jective well-being of happy couples was better, self-disclosure more frequent, per-ception of the partner's needs (motives) more accurate, and conflict (attributing one's negative feelings to the partner) less frequent than was the case for unhappy couples. Unexpectedly, the men's well-being depended more on the women's presence than did the women's on the men's presence.

Here, I will report on some aspects of a second TSD partner study with 34 middle-class married couples. First, I briefly mention some of the already pub-lished results (Brandstätter & Wagner, 1994), then add a few new findings.

1. In the transition from work (in the afternoon) to leisure time (in the evening), the mood of husbands with non-employed wives, but not the mood of husbands with employed wives, improves remarkably.
2. Couples with part- or full-time employed women have on the average lower levels of subjective well-being.
3. The influence of the wife's afternoon mood on the husband's evening mood is greater in couples with working women.
4. The influence of the husband's afternoon mood on the wife's evening mood is negligibly low in both types of couples.

On the basis of additional data analyses, the authors chose the work overload of women from a number of alternative explanations as the most plausible cause for these differences. Working women with double responsibilities (employed work and home work) are still mostly left alone by their husbands. With increas-ing hours of employed work, not only the women's mood during working hours deteriorates but also the mood during housework and during recreation spent at home or out of the home (see Figure 2.3). The effect sizes are quite remarkable,

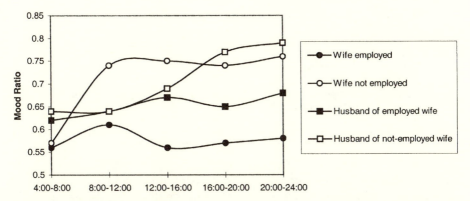

Figure 2.3. Mood ratio (relative frequency of positive mood) of husbands and wives as a function of the wife's employment status and time of the day (Adapted from Brandstätter & Wagner, 1994, p.138).

but the outcome of the study will not please those who are convinced that women cannot really be happy without a paid job. The sample is rather small—the TSD-technique is not viable with large sample sizes—and the results contradict prevalent ideas. Therefore, a replication of the study would be quite important.

Eysenck (1972) suggests that marital harmony is difficult to attain if husband and wife differ very much on the dimension of introversion-extraversion. In our study, extraversion turned out to be relevant for mutual affection, but not quite in the way as one would expect according to Eysenck. If both partners are extraverts, the mutual love (affection averaged across husband and wife) is more than a standard deviation lower than if both partners are introverts (Table 2.5). The partners' configuration of extraversion influences the husband's and wife's affection for the partner in the same way. The correlation of husband's affection with the wife's affection is $r(34) = .55$.

Is it that extraverts feel restrained by marriage, that they look around for alternative partners and new stimulation? This would be both the cause and the effect of lowered mutual attraction. One may be reminded of questionnaire studies reported by Eysenck (1972, chapter 2). The sexual attitudes and behavior patterns of extraverts seem indeed to be less favorable to a harmonious and stable marital relationship. Only Eysenck's conclusion that the discrepancy between

Table 2.5 Affection for the Partner Dependent on the Husband's and Wife's Extraversion

Extraversion of		Husband			Wife			Couple		
Husband	Wife	A.M.	S.D.	N	A.M.	S.D.	N	A.M.	S.D.	N
low	low	6.00	.79	6	6.08	.80	6	6.04	.77	6
low	high	5.98	.42	11	5.98	.82	11	5.98	.48	11
high	low	5.72	.51	10	5.81	.45	10	5.77	.41	10
high	high	5.18	.93	6	4.77	.88	6	4.98	.75	6

Table 2.6 Determinants of the Wife's Affection for Her
Husband

Variable	b	t	p
Husband's affection	.72	5.16	.000
Wife's emotional stability	.36	2.77	.010
Husband's independence	−.32	−2.34	.026
Multiple R	.72		
Adjusted R square	.47		

husband and wife on the introversion-extraversion dimension and not extraversion per se would imply a higher risk for marital conflicts may be wrong.

For each person one can calculate

- how closely the participant's mood covaries with the partner's mood
- how accurately the participant perceives the partner's mood.
- how closely the participant's affection for the partner is related to own or partner's mood

Establishing these covariations is only the very first step; much more is needed to clarify the functional relationship behind the statistical covariations.

If we find, for example, as we did, that the participants' momentary mood states are positively correlated with their partner's affection for them, we have to ask how such correlations come about. Is one's mood more the cause or the effect of the partner's affection? Calculating transition probabilities or lagged time series correlations can clarify the causal direction. Situational, personal, and relational characteristics, too, can moderate the dependence of one's mood on the partner's affection. There are many possibilities for testing reasonable hypotheses. It turned out that the correspondences (correlations) between the wife's affection for her husband and

- the husband's mood
- the husband's perception of his wife's mood
- the husband's affection for his wife

are high if the husband is emotionally stable and independent, but low if the husband is emotionally unstable and dependent.

In addition, one may ask which other variables are related to the wives' affection for their husbands (Table 2.6), and the husbands' affection for their wives (Table 2.7). Remember that affection is measured not by a questionnaire, but by multiple diary records for the moments of observation.

Whereas the husband's independence (dominance) is positively correlated with his affection for his wife, it is rather detrimental to her affection. Therefore, partialling out the husband's dominance increases the reciprocity of mutual affection from $r = .55$ to $r = .61$. Why the wife's emotional stability is beneficial to her affection for her husband, but detrimental to the husband's affection for his wife is rather difficult to explain. It could be that the men in our sample feel more comfortable if their wives are not too self-confident, which gives the men a chance to protect and comfort them when they are worried.

Table 2.7 Determinants of the Husband's Affection for the Wife

Variable	b	t	p
Wife's affection	.67	5.16	.000
Husband's independence	.47	3.27	.003
Wife's emotional stability	−.29	−2.27	.031
Multiple R	.75		
Adjusted R square	.51		

The wife's affection can be predicted from her emotional stability, the husband's affection, and his dominance (the latter with negative weight).

Complementarity and not similarity exists also in the dimension QIV (emotionality vs. rationality).[3] Mutual affection is lower if both partners are rational or if both are emotional.

Whereas the PEF analyses (reported under Example 2) involved hypotheses testing, the analyses of married couples' TSD-data had more of an exploratory character. Thus, it is by no means clear whether the pattern of effects of the partners' extraversion and some other findings will be replicable in further studies. The results may seem plausible, but plausibility alone is not a good guide in accumulating scientific knowledge. Would it be, for example, less plausible if we had found that similarity and not complementarity on the dimension emotionality vs. rationality fosters mutual acceptance? Anyway, I am curious whether these patterns can also be found in future TSD studies with married couples. If so, a more thorough analysis of how these personality patterns differ in other characteristics (e.g., motives, attributions, activities, and topics of conversation) should help in finding an improved theoretical explanation of the emotional experience in close relationships.

Example 4: Organizational Climate Mirrored in the TSD

Five TSD studies were run with fairly representative samples of participants from different organizations: a military unit (Kirchler, 1984), a charity organization (Auinger, 1987), a prison (Kette, 1991), a field of studies (socio-economics) at a German university (Brandstätter, 1981), and a field of studies (commercial studies) at an Austrian university (Ramoser, 1995). The collective motive profiles show big differences in the frequencies of motive actualization (Figure 2.4), as well as in the frequencies of motive satisfaction in cases where a motive has been actualized (Figure 2.5). The relative frequencies shown in Figure 2.4 represent the mean frequencies per person of frustration or satisfaction of the various motives, divided by the mean frequencies per person of observations. The relative frequencies of Figure 2.5 are calculated as mean frequencies per person of frustration or satisfaction of the various motives, divided by the mean frequencies per person of motive actualization (irrespective of frustration or satisfaction). The prison is the only setting in which affiliation was connected with high conditional probabilities of frustration (probabilities of frustration under the condition of actualization) (Figure 2.5). The power motive was about equally often actualized in

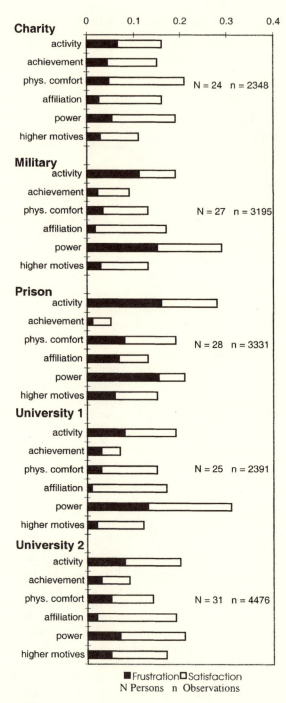

Figure 2.4. Relative frequencies of frustration and satisfaction of motives in five organizations.

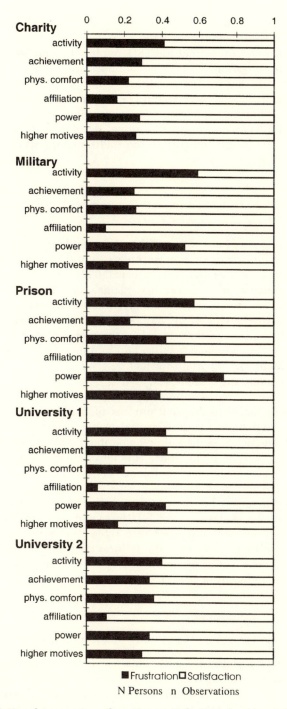

Figure 2.5. Relative frequencies of motive satisfaction (motive satisfaction ratio) under the condition of motive actualization.

the charity organization and in the prison (Figure 2.4), but in the prison it was much more often frustrated, if actualized.

On the whole, one can see that the TSD, applied to representative samples of members of an organization, gives valuable information about the members' typical motive structure and the organization's reward potential and emotional climate (cf. Brandstätter, 1992, July). It could be used in personnel selection in order to provide a better fit between person and organization, and it could be conceived of as a diagnostic technique in organizational development. As yet, we do not know how the TSD would compare to the traditional questionnaires in organizational assessment.

Example 5: Attribution of Emotional Experience during the First Six Months at a New Workplace

The first days, weeks, and possibly months are particularly important for a person in the process of adjusting to a new workplace, and the adjustment of the workplace to the person. Brandstätter and Gaubatz (1997) studied this process with 30 newcomers, all office workers, to various organizations. The participants kept the time-sampling diary through the first 10 days of the first, second, third, and sixth months of employment. One of the authors' predictions focused on the participants' causal attributions of their mood in the moment of observation. Coping with the new tasks, proving one's skills, and finding social acceptance was supposed to be particularly important for feeling good or bad in the early stages of organizational membership. Therefore, it was expected that the frequencies of (internal) attributions of mood to one's own abilities and of (external) attributions to the colleagues relative to the total number of attributions in the observation period would be highest during the first 10 days in the new workplace and would continuously decrease across the following periods. Table 2.8 shows that the data are in agreement with the predictions. This means that colleagues who support the newcomers' task-specific self-confidence are particularly helpful during the first weeks.

Remarkable differences between men and women appeared in the time sequence of relative frequencies by which failures and successes in pursuing goals were internally attributed (not presented in Table 2.8). At the beginning, women blamed themselves much more often for failures than did men. Only in the sixth month did women reach clear predominance of internal success attributions over internal failure attributions, a state that was characteristic of men right from the beginning.

Example 6: The Emotional Vocabulary of Women and Men

As the reader may remember, the participants in TSD studies always qualify their momentary mood states with a few self-generated adjectives in addition to characterizing the global mood categorization as negative, indifferent, and positive. This results, to my knowledge for the first time, in a large collection of emotion words that were actually used in everyday life situations and not compiled from dictionaries. Brandstätter, Grossman, and Filipp (1992) reanalyzed the data of two

Table 2.8 Frequencies and Mood Ratios of (Internal) Attributions of Motive Satisfaction in Work Situations to Own Abilities and (External) Attributions to Colleagues across Four Periods

Attributions	Period 1	Period 2	Period 3	Period 4
Abilities				
Frequencies	112 (17%)	120 (16%)	116 (15%)	81 (11%)
Mood ratio	0.68	0.79	0.66	0.64
Colleagues				
Frequencies	152 (23%)	135 (18%)	111 (15%)	90 (12%)
Mood ratio	0.70	0.65	0.72	0.84
Other sources				
Frequencies	410 (60%)	505 (66%)	535 (70%)	576 (77%)
Mood ratio	0.71	0.75	0.69	0.75
Total				
Frequencies	674 (100%)	760 (100%)	762 (100%)	747 (100%)
Mood ratio	0.70	0.74	0.69	0.75

The total number of attributions of all 4 periods (2943) is higher than the total number of observations (2118), because on the average 1.4 attributions were made at each time point of observation.

Percentages (in parentheses) are based on the total frequencies of observations within a period.

Mood ratio of attributions represents the relative frequency of positive mood under the specific attribution condition (from Brandstätter & Gaubatz, 1997).

studies with couples (Brandstätter & Wagner, 1994; Kirchler, 1988). The question under investigation was how men and women describe their emotional experiences in everyday life situations with adjectives in their own language. The researchers predicted and found that women used a richer vocabulary for emotions (a greater variety of words with a lower concentration on the most popular words) than men in situations where the spouse was present (Figure 2.6). The partner situation was chosen for this comparison in order to make sure that gender differences in the frequency distribution of emotion words were not caused by gender-specific situations. Another possible explanation—that women are more cooperative and invest greater effort in generating adjectives—could be excluded, too.

Merits and Shortcomings of Time Sampling Techniques

As one can see from the examples presented in this chapter, the TSD-technique generates very rich data sets on the emotional experience of people in everyday life situations, which allows us to test a great variety of hypotheses about environmental and personal conditions of subjective well-being. The technique lends itself to the idiographic approach in studying individuals as well as to the nomothetic approach in studying the regularities of emotional experience of people

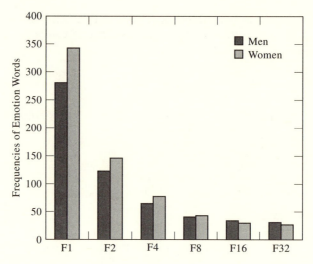

Figure 2.6. Frequencies of emotion words used by men and women once (F1), 2 or 3 times (F2), 4 to 7 times (F4), 8 to 15 times (F8), 16 to 31 times (F16), 31 times and more (F32).

in general or of categories of people who have a specific personality structure or a specific environment in common. The technique is particularly useful in analyzing the mutual influence of mood in couples, families, or small working groups. Sticking to the basic design in a longer series of studies has the advantage that a large data set can be used both for generating and testing hypotheses.

The main advantages of time sampling techniques in studying everyday emotional experience can be summarized as:

• Immediacy of the reports
• Representativeness of sampled situations
• Idiographic accuracy
• Exploratory potential

Immediacy of the reports. Answering the traditional questions about well-being and satisfaction with work, leisure, marriage, and so on demands from the participants rather difficult categorizations and résumés of their emotional experience in ill-defined situations and time periods. In addition, people often are tempted to answer in a socially desirable way. The complete privacy of the TSD and the focus of self-observation on the current moment can be expected to improve the validity of the reports.

Representativeness of sampled situations. Random time sampling is the only realistic way to generate a representative description of everyday life situations. The frequencies by which the situations appear in the diary are proportional to their actual frequencies and duration, if the monitoring of the random signals is efficient and if the participants perceive themselves as research partners who are responsible for generating high data quality.

Idiographic accuracy. The great number of observations per person—in our TSD studies usually four oberservations per day over four weeks—allows detailed idiographic analyses of how an individual interacts with his/her environment before the data are aggregated for more or less homogeneous collectives of persons.

Exploratory potential. Even if the TSD in its standard form is used for testing specific hypotheses, the data set provided by it is so rich that there are ample opportunities for looking after regularities in the data that originally were not thought of or to see whether additional statistical analyses support post hoc interpretations of unexpected results.

Of course, the TSD technique has also its shortcomings and flaws. These are mainly:

• High demands on time, money, and effort
• Changes of the observed experience by the observation technique
• Limited awareness of internal states
• Fragmentation of the continuous flow of experience
• Restriction to self-reports of emotions

High demands on time, money, and effort. The single TSD records usually do not take more than one minute, but the weekly coding of the diary entries needs about two hours each. In addition, the time necessary for instructing the participants and for weekly meetings of groups of participants and/or for repeated telephone contacts with individual participants for answering additional questionnaires at the beginning and at the end of the data collection, together with an interview, amounts to 20 to 25 hours per participant. This time investment deserves adequate financial compensation. The researchers, too, need more time and effort for the processing of the data than they would have to invest in traditional surveys or experiments.

Changes of the observed experience by the observation technique. Observing oneself again and again, keeping track of the time schedule (if no sophisticated and still quite expensive electronic equipment can be used; cf. Pawlik & Buse, 1982; Totterdell & Folkard, 1992), and coding the diary entries result in an atypical self-awareness. As yet, the impact on the TSD reports of this high level of self-consciousness is not well studied. Wicklund (1975) gives some evidence that self-focused attention ("objective self-awareness") augments the effects of a perceived discrepancy between what a person wants and what he or she gets. In the case of a negative discrepancy, which in his view is what occurs most of the time, the negative affect as well as discrepancy-reducing activities (Karoly, 1993) are intensified by self-focused attention. If the perceived discrepancy happens to be positive, the positive affect is intensified. Wilson, Dunn, Kraft, and Liske (1989) question the usefulness of asking people why they feel as they do, if one does not want to undermine the predictability of behavior from attitudes rooted mainly in affect and not in factual information and reasoning. This would mean that the TSD question—"Why do you feel this way?"—could diminish the influence of the affect on subsequent behavior.

Limited awareness of internal states. Referring to research on dissonance and attribution theory, Wilson, Hull, and Johnson (1981) argue that measures on "internal states," that is, on cognitive, emotional and motivational processes, postulated as intervening variables between the experimental manipulation (for example, in forced compliance studies) and overt behavior, would usually have a rather low "accessibility," and therefore low validity (in terms of correlation with behavioral measures), which would not be true if participants' attention were focused on their internal states by having them indicate reasons for their actions. This supports the idea that self-focused attention improves the validity of self-reports only if one does not follow the alternative (behavioristic) interpretation of Wilson et al. (1981), which says that people, instead of having direct access to their internal states, infer internal states from their behavior according to their cognitive schemata.

Fragmentation of the continuous flow of experience. Time-sampling gives a series of "still photographs" cut from the continuous flow of experience. The specific process of goal setting, action planning, and action regulation is not easily reconstructed from these time samples of experience. As a complement, interviews and narratives of how people perceive and interpret their present life situations, their pasts and their futures, are indispensable for a deeper understanding of their world-views and self-actualization (cf. Thomae, 1988).

Restriction to self-reports of emotions. Emotions are processes in which a number of conceptually and phenomenologically distinguishable components are intertwined. The TSD focuses on the subjective experience, which may be conceived of as the central component of an emotion, and takes additionally into account the events that elicit the emotions. The facial expression of emotions, as well as the concurrent physiological processes, are, however, outside the reach of the TSD-technique. New electronic measuring and data recording devices may be used more frequently in the future in order to overcome the neglect of physiological processes (Pawlik & Buse, 1982). Collecting information about a person's mood from relatives, friends, or acquaintances in addition to the TSD self-reports should help to widen the horizon of observation (Brandstätter & Wagner, 1994; Kirchler, 1988; Sandvik, Diener, & Seidlitz, 1993).

Conclusions

The Time Sampling Diary (TSD) provides representative samples of people's emotions in everyday life situations. Emotions are conceived of as a person's most "central" and most characteristic responses to failures and successes as he or she pursues motive satisfaction in continuously changing situations (behavior settings) qualified by certain activities under specific circumstances (time, place, persons present, freedom of choice). Thus, it gives a rather direct insight into a person's *real-time* experience of satisfaction and discomfort, which could be considered a validity criterion for any other global or specific life satisfaction or utility measure (cf. Kahneman, Wakker, & Sarin, 1997). Whether maximizing not the short term, but the life-time balance of happiness can and should be the ultimate personal and societal goal is less a psychological than a philosophical and religious question to which many different and controversial answers have been given throughout the cultural history of mankind, and will be given in the future. At least, let us hope that not too many people follow the principle and have the power to follow the principle of maximizing their personal life-time balance of happiness at the expense of the life-time balance of happiness of others in their neighborhood and around the world. Subjective well-being is an important criterion for evaluating one's life, but it may nevertheless not be the ultimate criterion. We can never escape the critical question behind the pursuit of happiness—whether the motives we want to satisfy and the goals we are striving for are the right ones.

Appendix A
The Time Sampling Diary (TSD) of Experience in Everyday Life Situations

Instructions for Keeping the Diary

What Is the Goal of the Study?   Psychologists still do not know much, certainly not enough, about the experiences and activities of ————[4] in their everyday lives during work and leisure, about events and circumstances that make them happy or unhappy. This study aims at improving our psychological understanding of the situation of ———— in order to find out how the professional and private lives of this important group of people could be improved. Time sampling, the method that will be explained in more detail later, is now quite frequently and successfully used to explore what people experience and do in their ordinary lives. It provides more concrete and more valid information on a person's interaction with her or his environment than any other technique.

What Will Be Done?   The study runs for 30 days and is expected to give a thorough picture of your personal experience, from the time you wake up to the time you fall asleep. You will take notes in a kind of diary about four times a day on how you feel at the moment, why you feel this way, where you are, what you are doing, who else is present, and how free you are to stay in or to leave the situation.

   IMPORTANT: Please be aware not to change your activities in order to accommodate keeping the diary. The data are valuable only if you organize your day as usual.

   The data are strictly confidential. Nobody can identify the source of the data, because you sign the questionnaires and the diary protocols with a code that is known only to you.

When Do You Make the Entries in Your Diary?   You will be provided with a wristwatch on which you can set the alarm to alert you to the need to record data according to your time schedule. Each person has a different random time schedule, which is not known to anybody else. When the alarm goes off, you complete the diary report immediately. In some exceptional situations you may go through the diary questions mentally, memorize the answers, and make the notes as soon as possible. In the diary you should record the alarm time (planned time), the time of observation (usually identical with the planned time), and the time you write down the observations (usually identical with planned and observed time). For each day you need six sheets of paper, which you number 1.1, 1.2, ... 1.6 for the first day, 2.1, 2.2, ... 2.6 for the second day, and so on. Should you once miss a scheduled time, perhaps because you forgot to set the next alarm, or because you didn't hear the alarm, you can take the diary notes just for the moment when you realize that you have missed a scheduled time. If a scheduled diary entry falls in your sleeping time, mark the respective page with *S* (sleeping) the next morning.

How Do You Answer the Diary Questions?   Each diary page refers to the same seven questions:

1. *How is my mood at the moment?* Here you have to indicate whether immediately before the alarm went off your feelings were just noticeably below or above the point of indifference. The question is definitely not whether the circumstances are such that you actually should feel bad or good. What counts is how you really feel. If you feel just noticeably bad (or clearly bad), you put down a minus sign (−), if you feel just noticeably well (or clearly well), you write a plus sign (+). In some rare situations, if you really can't tell whether your mood is negative or positive, you write zero (0).

2. *How can I describe my momentary mood by (up to three) adjectives?* Imagine you have to describe the weather of a summer day. You might say, it is sunny, humid, and windy. The common language provides many different adjectives by which one can describe emotions and mood states. Please try to characterize your mood in its specific quality as precisely as possible. Adjectives like good or bad are too general to be informative.

3. *Why do I feel as I have indicated?* Here you write down your subjective explanations of your feelings, for example: who (another person or yourself) or what (something around you or some characteristics of your personality) is the cause of your emotion. Is it something that you remember from the past, or that you are experiencing just now, or that you expect for the future? Which of your more general motives or more specific goals you are presently pursuing are affected.

4. *Where am I?* Indicate the place precisely so that you can remember the situation later when you code your diary!

5. *What am I doing?* Characterize the private or social activities in concrete terms! Indicate what you are doing and with whom!

6. *Who else is present?* Persons who are particularly relevant to you in the present situation should be recorded by their names, others by generic terms (e.g., colleagues, strangers).

7. *Do I feel free in the present situation?* If you could just leave the present situation or choose a different activity without negative consequences (being blamed by significant others or feeling personally guilty), you are free. Otherwise, your freedom is restricted by social norms and obligations you cannot escape without breaking rules. The question here is not

whether you would like to do something different, but whether you would have the external or internal freedom to do something different. **Note: Whenever you have difficulties with the diary, use the next group meeting to discuss the problem or call number xxx for assistance!**

Can You Confide All Your Experiences, Even Very Intimate Ones, to Your Diary?   Yes, you can and you should. Please be completely open in your diary. Otherwise, the data will not be very useful. Take precautions that nobody has access to your diary. You will not be asked to hand over your original diary entries to the researcher. What you deliver to the researcher for further analysis is just your anonymous codings of the diary entries. You will personally code your diary entries according to rules that are presented in the next paragraph.

Instructions for Coding the Diary Entries

The Time Sampling Diary is completely private. Since you were sure that nobody will have access to it, you have written down your very personal experience, no matter how intimate it might have been. You will not hand over your diary to any other person. Therefore, you personally have to code the diary entries before the data can be processed. This not only assures you of the unconditional privacy and anonymity of the data, but is also the best way to a classification of the diary records that best fits your personal perspective.

It is very important that you code the diary carefully. Otherwise, all the efforts you have put into observing your personal experience and writing down your observations will be fruitless.

Each coding sheet has 42 free rows and 25 columns (see Appendix C). Each row (line) corresponds to one time point of observations. Since each day has six random times of observations, a single coding sheet provides space for the 42 observations during seven days. You need four sheets for the whole observation period of 28 days. Please use a separate sheet for the trial period of two days! On the top of each page enter your code, the date of coding, and the number of the week.

Now we go through each column in order to clarify its meaning.

Column	Label	Explanation
3	*Nuob*	There are six lines for each day, one for each random time of observation. 11 means first day, first observation.
4	*M*	Month (01 January, 02 February, etc.).
5	*D*	Day of observation. If the first day were October 26, you would enter 10 in column 4 and 26 in column 5.
6	*Tpla*	Time planned; for example, 0906 means 6 minutes past 9 in the morning, and 2023 means 23 minutes past 8 in the evening.
7	*Tobs*	Time actually observed
8	*Trec*	Time recorded
9	*Mood*	Mood (Question 1 in the diary: How is my mood at the moment?): -1 (rather bad), 00 (indifferent), $+1$ (rather good).

10	*Adjc*	You look at your adjectives (Question 2 in the diary: How can I describe my momentary mood by adjectives?) and choose *one* from the Adjective List that comes closest to the meaning of your combination of adjectives.
11, 12	*t1, t2*	Time (1 = past, 2 = present, 3 = future) of the event (remembered, experienced just now, expected) that is influencing your mood.
13–15	*S1–S3*	Source 1 to Source 3. This is the place for causal attributions of your mood states. You ask yourself what or who is at the origin (the cause) of your mood or emotion (emotion in the sense of a transitory shift of your mood elicited by an observed event or by a thought that comes to your mind (e.g. remembering a past event or anticipating a future one). The causes can be external (e.g., another person, a TV program, the weather) or internal (your abilities or efforts, your appearance, some-other personality characteristics). You can enter up to three different sources (causes). The most important one should be entered on first place. Use *S1* if there is only one source.
16–17	*M1–M3*	Motive 1 to Motive 3. Select up to three motives from the list of motives. You enter an odd number, if a motive has been frustrated, and an even number, if a motive has been satisfied. The most important motive should be put in first place. Should you enter only one motive, please, use the first motive column!
19	*Pla*	Place
20, 21	*A1, A2*	Activities. The code number of the primary activity is put in first place.
22–24	*P1–P3*	Persons present. The person (or category of persons) with the highest relevance in the present situation is put in first place. If you use only one person column, please, use *P1*!
25	*Fri*	Write down the perceived degree of internal freedom (1 to 4), i.e., the freedom from inner obligations or self-imposed duties.
26	*Fre*	Write down the perceived degree of external freedom (1 to 4), i.e., the freedom from social pressure (social norms, social expectations).
27	*Adjectives*	Adjectives (literally transferred) as you have written them down in the diary.

Appendix B

Frustration and Satisfaction of Motives

	I feel rather bad at this moment because . . .	Motive Classes		I feel rather good at this moment because . . .
01	what I have achieved in my work is not good enough	Ach	02	I experience success in my work
03	my surroundings are monotonous and boring	Act	04	there are varied and novel experiences
05	I can not be active	Act	06	I can enjoy being active (irrespective of the outcome)
07	I am physically uncomfortable (hungry, thirsty, tired, sick)	Phy	08	I am physically comfortable (enjoying meals and drinks; feeling vigorous and healthy)
09	I am lonely and/or have difficulties in making contacts	Aff	10	I am enjoying the company of people I like
11	I can not retaliate an unjust treatment	Pow	12	I am able to retaliate for a bad treatment
13	my sexual desires are not fulfilled	Aff	14	I am sexually satisfied
15	I don't feel respected as much as I desire	Pow	16	others show appreciation and respect for me
17	I suffer from low self-esteem	Pow	18	I experience self-respect (irrespective of social approval)
19	I feel constrained and dependent	Pow	20	I am free and independent; there is nobody giving me orders
21	I can not assert myself	Pow	22	I can assert myself
23	I miss being loved	Aff	24	I love somebody and feel loved
25	the others do not listen to me	Pow	26	I have influence on others
27	there is nobody I could care for	Aff	28	I can care for others and be helpful to them
29	there is disorder and/or dirt around me	High	30	there is order and cleanliness around me
31	I have difficulties in understanding	High	32	I am making progress in understanding
33	I have to reproach myself	High	34	I acted conscientiously and with a sense of duty
35	my religious faith is shaky	High	36	I feel secure in my religious faith
37	my environment is ugly and unappealing	High	38	I enjoy beautiful things (nature, arts, music)

Classes of motives

Act	Activity/Sentience	Phy	Physical comfort	Pow	Power
Ach	Achievement	Aff	Affiliation	High	Higher Motives

Appendix C

Coding Schema

1	2	3	4	5	6	7	8	9	10	11	12	13	14	15	16	17	18	19	20	21	22	23	24	25	26	27
Nusu	Code	Nuob	M	D	Tpla	Tobs	Trec	Mood	adjc	t1	t2	S1	S2	S3	M1	M2	M3	Pla	A1	A2	P1	P2	P3	Fri	Fre	Adjt
		11																								
		12																								
		13																								
		14																								
		15																								
		16																								
		21																								
		22																								
		etc.																								
		etc.																								
		75																								
		76																								

1 Nusu — Serial number participant
2 Code — Code of participant
3 Nuob — Serial number of random point of time*
4 M — Month
5 D — Day
6 Tpla — Time planned
7 Tobs — Time observed
8 Trec — Time recorded

9 Mood — Mood
10 Adjc — Adjective category
11 t1, t2 — Time perspective
13 S1, S2, S3 — Sources
16 M1, M2, M3 — Motives
19 Pla — Place
20 A1, A2 — Activities
22 P1, P2, P3 — Persons

25 Fri — Freedom (internal)
26 Fre — Freedom (external)
27 Adjt — Adjective transcript

* Three-digit serial number (e.g., 275, which means the 5th random time point of the 27th day.

As e-mail attachment the SPSS 9.0 syntax of commands for analyzing TSD-data and a trial data set can be requested from the author at *h.brandstaetter@jk.uni-linz.ac.at.*

Notes

1. Under the assumptions of the classical test theory, the reliability r_{nn} of a test consisting of n components is $r_{nn} = nr_{tt}/(1 + [n - 1]r_{tt})$ where r_{tt} is the reliability of the component which is assumed to be equal for all components.

2. The studies were run by the author and his associates at the University of Augsburg (Germany) and at the University of Linz (Austria): two samples of students (social and economic sciences), faculty of a university unit, housewives, soldiers, unemployed, members of a charity organization, two samples of cohabitating or married couples, two samples of office workers at a new workplace. My associates, whose cooperation I appreciate very much, were (in alphabetical order) Franz Auinger, Erich Barthel, Peter Drescher, Gernot Filipp, Vera Fünfgelt, Martin Frühwirth, Sandra Gaubatz, Erich Kirchler, Hans Ott, Claudia Ramoser, Wolfgang Wagner. For a list of publications on time sampling studies of emotional experience contact the author: Johannes-Kepler-University, Social and Economic Psychology Unit, A-4040 Linz, Austria; e-mail <h.brandstaetter@jk.uni-linz.ac.at>.

3. Tough-mindedness would be an alternative label of this dimension.

4. Refer to the specific kind of subjects under study.

References

Auhagen, A. E. (1987). A new approach for the study of personal relationships: The double diary method. *German Journal of Psychology, 11*, 3–7.

Auhagen, A. E. (1991). *Freundschaft im Alltag. Eine Untersuchung mit dem Doppeltagebuch* [Friendship in everyday life. A study with the partner diary]. Bern: Huber.

Auinger, F. (1987). Subjektives Wohlbefinden als Klimabarometer in Organisationen [Subjective well-being as a measure of organizational climate]. Unpublished master's thesis, University of Linz, Austria.

Berscheid, E. (1994). Interpersonal relationships. *Annual Review of Psychology, 45*, 79–129.

Brandstätter, H. (1977). Wohlbefinden und Unbehagen, Entwurf eines Verfahrens zur Messung situationsabhängiger Stimmungen [Subjective well-being and uneasiness. Design of a technique for measuring situation dependent mood]. In W. H. Tack (Ed.), *Bericht über den 30. Kongreß der DGfPs in Regensburg 1976.* Göttingen: Hogrefe.

Brandstätter, H. (1981). Time sampling of subjective well-being. In H. Hartmann, W. Molt, & H. Stringer, (Eds.) *Advances in Economic Psychology* (pp. 63–76). Heidelberg: Meyn.

Brandstätter, H. (1983). Emotional responses to other persons in everyday life situations. *Journal of Personality and Social Psychology, 45*, 871–883.

Brandstätter, H. (1988). Sechzehn Persönlichkeits-Adjektivskalen (16 PA) als Forschungsinstrument anstelle des 16 PF [Sixteen Personality Adjective Scales (16 PA) as a substitute for the 16 PF in research settings]. *Zeitschrift für Experimentelle und Angewandte Psychologie, 35*, 370–391.

Brandstätter, H. (1989, May). *Motivational person-environment-fit and satisfaction in leisure and work settings.* Paper presented at the conference on "The individual and organizational side of selection and performance evaluation and appraisal." University of Stuttgart-Hohenheim.

Brandstätter, H. (1991). Emotions in everyday life situations. In F. Strack, M. Argyle, & N. Schwarz (Eds.), *The social psychology of well-being* (pp. 173–192). London: Pergamon.

Brandstätter, H. (1992, July). *Measuring emotional climate.* Paper presented at the Twenty-fifth International Congress of Psychology, Brussels.

Brandstätter, H. (1994a). Well-being and motivational person-environment fit. A time sampling study of emotions. *European Journal of Personality, 8*, 75–93.

Brandstätter, H. (1994b). Pleasure of leisure—pleasure of work. Personality makes the difference. *Personality and Individual Differences, 16*, 931–946.

Brandstätter, H., & Gaubatz, S. (1997). Befindenstagebuch am neuen Arbeitsplatz in differentialpsychologischer Sicht [Time-sampling diary at the new workplace. An individual difference perspective]. *Zeitschrift für Arbeits- und Organisationspsychologie, 41*, 18–29.

Brandstätter, H., Grossman, M., & Filipp, G. (1992). Gefühle im Alltag—berichtet von Frauen und Männern [Emotions in everyday life—reported by women and men]. *Zeitschrift für Sozialpsychologie, 23*, 64–76.

Brandstätter, H., & Wagner, W. (1994). Erwerbstätigkeit der Frau und Alltagsbefinden von Ehepartnern im Zeitverlauf [Employment status of the wife and marital partner's well-being in the course of time]. *Zeitschrift für Sozialpsychologie, 25*, 126–146.

Cantor, N. (1994). Life task problem solving: Situational affordances and personal needs. *Personality and Social Psychology Bulletin, 20*, 235–243.

Csikszentmihalyi, M., & Larson, R. (1987). Validity and reliability of the experience-sampling method. *Journal of Nervous and Mental Diseases, 175*, 526–536.

Csikszentmihalyi, M., Larson, R., & Prescott, S. (1977). The ecology of adolescent activity and experience. *Journal of Youth and Adolescence, 6*, 281–294.

Diener, E. (1984). Subjective well-being. *Psychological Bulletin, 95*, 542–575.

Diener, E., Larsen, R. J., & Emmons, R. A. (1984). Person x situation interactions: Choice of situations and congruence response models. *Journal of Personality and Social Psychology, 47*, 580–592.

Diener, E., Suh, E. M., Lucas, R. E., & Smith, H. L. (1999). Subjective well-being: Three decades of progress. *Psychological Bulletin, 125*, 276–302.

Dörner, D. (1985). Verhalten, Denken und Emotionen [Behavior, thinking, and emotions]. In L. H. Eckensberger & E. D. Lantermann (Eds.), *Emotion und Reflexivität* (p. 157–181). München: Urban & Schwarzenberg.

Eckes, T., & Six, B. (1984). Prototypenforschung: Ein integrativer Ansatz zur Analyse der alltagssprachlichen Kategorisierung von Objekten, Personen und Situationen [Research on prototypes: An integrative approach to analyzing lay categorizations of persons, objects, and situations]. *Zeitschrift für Sozialpsychologie, 15*, 2–17.

Emmons, R. A. (1986). Personal strivings: An approach to personality and subjective well-being. *Journal of Personality and Social Psychology, 51*, 1058–1086.

Emmons, R. A. (1996). Striving and feeling. Personal goals and subjective well-being. In P. M. Gollwitzer & J. A. Bargh (Eds.), *The psychology of action. Linking cognition and motivation to behavior* (pp. 313–337). New York: Guilford Press.

Forgas, J. P. (1992). Affect in social judgments and decisions: A multiprocess model. In M. P. Zanna (Ed.). *Advances in experimental social psychology* (Vol. 25, pp. 227–275). *San Diego: Academic Press.*

Frijda, N. H. (1986). *The emotions.* Cambridge: Cambridge University Press.

Heckhausen, H. (1991). *Motivation and action.* Berlin: Springer.

Hormuth, S. E. (1986). The time sampling of experience in situ. *Journal of Personality, 54*, 262–293.

Kahneman, D., Wakker, P. P., & Sarin, R. (1997). Back to Bentham? Explorations of experienced utility. *Quarterly Journal of Economics* (pp. 375–405), 1997.

Karoly, P. (1993). Mechanisms of self-regulation: A systems view. *Annual Review of Psychology, 44*, 23–52.

Kette, G. (1991). *Haft. Eine sozialpsychologische Analyse* [Imprisonment. A social-psychological analysis]. Göttingen: Hogrefe.

Kirchler, E. (1984). Befinden von Wehrpflichtigen in Abhängigkeit von personellen und situativen Gegebenheiten [Subjective well-being of recruits as function of personal and situational characteristics]. *Psychologie und Praxis. Zeitschrift für Arbeits- und Organizationspsychologie, 28*, 16–25.

Kirchler, E. (1998). Marital happiness and interaction in everyday surroundings: A time-sample diary approach for couples. *Journal of Social and Personal Relationships, 5*, 375–382.

Klinger, E. (1977). *Meaning and void: Inner experience and the incentives in people's lives*. Minneapolis: University of Minnesota Press.

Klinger, E. (1996). Emotional influences on cognitive processing, with implications for theories of both. In P. M. Gollwitzer & J. A Bargh (Eds.), *The psychology of action. Linking cognition and motivation to behavior* (pp. 168–189). New York: Guilford Press.

Lersch, Ph. (1970). *Aufbau der Person* [Structure of the person] (11th ed.). München: Barth [1st ed. 1938. Aufbau des Charakters. Leipzig: Barth].

Oatley, K., & Jenkins, J. M. (1996). *Understanding emotions*. Cambridge, MA: Blackwell.

Olson, D. H., & Porter, J. (1983). Family adaptability and cohesion evaluation scales. In E. E. Filsinger (Ed.), *Marriage and family assessment. A sourcebook of family therapy*. Beverly Hills: Sage.

Pawlik, K., & Buse, L. (1982). Rechnergestützte Verhaltensregistrierung im Feld: Beschreibung und erste psychometrische Überprüfung einer neuen Erhebungsmethode [Computer supported registering of field data. Description and first psychometric evaluation of a new data collection technique]. *Zeitschrift für Differentielle und Diagnostische Psychologie, 3*, 101–118.

Ramoser, C. (1995). *Wohlbefinden Studierender in Abhängigkeit von Fähigkeiten, Interesse und Persönlichkeit* [Subjective well-being of university students as a function of abilities, interests, and personality]. Unpublished master's thesis, University of Vienna, Austria.

Russell, J. A. (1980). A circumplex model of affect. *Journal of Personality and Social Psychology, 39*, 1161–1178.

Russell, J. A., & Carroll, J. M. (1999). On the bipolarity of positive and negative affect. *Psychological Bulletin, 125*, 3–30.

Sandvik, E., Diener, E., & Seidlitz, L. (1993). Subjective well-being: The convergence and stability of self-report measures. *Journal of Personality, 61*, 317–342.

Scherer, K. (1990). Theorien und aktuelle Probleme der Emotionspsychologie [Theories and current problems of a psychology of emotions]. In K. Scherer (Ed.), *Psychologie der Emotion*. Enzypklopädie der Psychologie, (Vol. CIV 3, p. 1–38). Göttingen: Hogrefe.

Schneewind, K. A., Schröder, G., & Cattell, R. B. (1983). *Der 16-Persönlichkeits-Faktoren-Test-16PF* [The 16 Personality Factors Test—16PF]. Bern: Huber.

Schwartz, S. H. (1992). Universals in the context and structure of values: Theoretical advances and empirical tests in 20 countries. *Advances in Experimental Social Psychology, 25*, 1–65.

Tennen, H., Suls, J., & Affleck, G. (1991). Personality and daily experience: The promise and the challenge. *Journal of Personality, 59*, 331–337.

Thomae, H. (1988). *Das Individuum und seine Welt* [The individual and his world] (2nd ed.). Göttingen: Hogrefe.

Totterdell, P., & Folkard, S. (1992). In situ repeated measures of affect and cognitive performance facilitated by use of a hand-held computer. *Behavior Research Methods, Instruments, & Computers, 24*, 545–553.

Vetter, A. (1966) *Personale Anthropologie* [Personal Anthropology]. Freiburg: Alber.

Wheeler, L., & Reis, H. T. (1991). Self-recording of everyday life events: origins, types, and uses. *Journal of Personality, 59*, 339–354.

Wicklund, R. A. (1975). Objective self-awareness. Advances in Experimental Social Psychology, *8*, 233–275. New York: Academic Press.

Wilson, T. D., Dunn, D. S., Kraft, D., & Liske, D. J. (1989). Introspection, attitude change, and attitude-behavior consistency: The disruptive effects of explaining why we feel the way we do. *Advances in Experimental Social Psychology, 22,* 287–343.

Wilson, T. D., Hull, J. G., & Johnson, J. (1981). Awareness and self-perception: Verbal reports on internal states. *Journal of Personality and Social Psychology, 40,* 53–71.

PART II

TEMPERAMENT AND EMOTIONS

Focus on Congruence

3

Temperament, Type A, and Motives

A Time Sampling Study

Andrzej Eliasz

Temperament and Type A in a Theoretical Perspective

Temperament as a Co-determinant of Stamina

Reactivity, which plays a crucial role in regulating stimulation, is one of the most important dimensions of temperament (Strelau, 1983, 1988, 1998). Strelau coined the term "reactivity" to replace the well-known Pavlovian term: "strength of excitation" (or "strength of nervous system"). This dimension includes such characteristics as sensitivity to weak stimuli and endurance against strong stimuli. The more reactive individuals are, the more sensitive they are to weak stimuli and the less resistant to strong ones. It means that "high-reactives" show high sensitivity and low endurance. In contrast to high-reactives, "low-reactives" are supposed to be low in sensitivity and high in endurance.[1]

Reactivity codetermines the need for stimulation: A low need for stimulation is typical of high-reactives, whereas a high need for stimulation characterizes low-reactives. In this way, reactivity shapes the capacity of individuals in coping with strongly stimulating conditions. Low-reactives can easily handle intense stimulation that is unbearable for high-reactives. However, high-reactives feel and perform better than low-reactives under weakly stimulating conditions. Hence, reactivity is a very important element of a system of stimulation control (Eliasz, 1981, 1985, 1990; Strelau, 1983, 1994, 1998).

Type A—An Intensive Life under Risk of Coronary Heart Disease

Type A, conceived as an element of personality structure,[2] reveals itself in strongly stimulating behavior, rooted in a perpetual desire to achieve ambitious goals, to work hard even up to one's limits. This is often done under time pressure and is coupled with the inability to relax. Type A individuals are characterized as persons who try to achieve the most in the shortest possible time. Friedman and Rosenman (1959), who developed the notion of a Type A behavior pattern in the 1950s, pointed out that it is an important risk factor for coronary heart disease (CHD). They describe Type A persons as those who are prone to compete with others and who have a strong desire to be appreciated and promoted to higher and higher professional positions. According to Rosenman, Swan, and Carmelli (1988), Type A individuals are also in habitual conflict with others. Type A, as defined in theoretical terms, commonly implies ambitiousness, competitive spirit, impatience, experience of time pressure, and high job involvement.

With respect to Type A as a CHD risk factor, the data are inconclusive so far, as Eliasz and Wrześniewski (1991) and Eliasz and Cofta (1992) have shown (see also Amelang, 1997; Booth-Kewley & Friedman, 1987; Jenkins & Lee, 1989; Myrtek, 1995).

Most authors suggest that CHD risk is associated with only one element of the Type A pattern, that is, with hostility (cf. Williams & Barefoot, 1988; Williams, Barefoot & Shekelle, 1985). Spence, Helmreich and Pred (1987) distinguished two factors in Jenkin's Activity Survey (JAS). One is related to achievement strivings and the other to impatience, irritability, and anger. Health measures correlated only with the Impatience-Irritability Scale. A very low correlation between the two factors suggests that they are actually independent of each other. Nevertheless, a strong need for achievement can go together with irritability and anger, if the person's ambitions are not accompanied by the capacities needed for reaching the ambitious goals.

Incongruence of Type A and Reactivity in a Developmental Perspective

The characteristics of Type A, as outlined in the preceding section, give grounds to assume that individuals with this type of personality structure typically have a preference for stimulating behavior. Thus, pathogenic consequences of Type A can be better understood by taking into account the role of reactivity in the development of Type A and the role of Type A in stimulation control. Type A should be treated as a factor encumbering stimulation control in individuals with a low need for stimulation, that is, high-reactives. Fulfilling the need for achievement, the vital element of Type A, can be impeded by a low need for stimulation. What we know about the development of Type A supports this point of view.

Eliasz and Wrześniewski (1988) showed that the sources of both the need for achievement and Type A are different in high- as compared to low-reactive boys aged 14–15 years. They found that the prerequisite for the development of the need for achievement and Type A were ambitious educational goals assigned by the parents to their sons. However, parents' influence depends on their upbringing styles and the reactivity of their offspring. Low-reactive individuals develop a high need for achievement and, many of them, also Type A behavior, if the parents do not exert pressure on their sons to achieve the ambitious goals they have set for them (see Table 3.1). Thus, in the case of low-reactives, these goals are

Table 3.1 Need for Achievement and Type A Depending on Social Pressure in High- and Low-Reactive Individuals (Constant = Ambitious Educational Goals Assigned by Parents to Their Sons)

Reactivity	Lack of pressure	Pressure
Low reactivity (Lr)	High nAch	Low nAch
	Type A	Type B
High reactivity (Hr)	Low nAch	High nAch
	Type B	Type A

just a trigger for achievement motivation. When parents put pressure on low-reactive sons to attain ambitious goals, the outcomes are the opposite of what the parents expect, because, then, their low-reactive children show reactance. Their need for achievement remains very low, and they are characterized as Type B individuals. Since low-reactives in general are not as susceptible to social influences as high-reactives (Eliasz, 1981, 1987; Strelau, 1983; Strelau & Eliasz, 1994), Type B low-reactives are satisfied with their accomplishments in life (Cofta, 1992), even if their environment has stressed achievement as a social value.

On the other hand, high-reactives develop a strong need for achievement and Type A characteristics only when put under pressure by their parents. This does not happen if goals are set without putting pressure on the children to attain them. High-reactives tend to develop both a very low need for achievement and Type B characteristics, if their parents content themselves with setting goals without exerting pressure. However, susceptibility to social stimuli affects a person's social awareness of the system of social values and social expectations concerning individual accomplishments. That is why Type B high-reactives, despite their low need for achievement, are not satisfied with their accomplishments (Cofta, 1992).

Type B is not just the opposite of Type A. How Type B persons interact with their environment depends in a very specific way on their level of reactivity. This is, however, a special issue to be explored in a separate study.

The data of Eliasz and Wrześniewski (1988) suggest that there is an internal inconsistency between the capacities of high-reactive individuals and Type A. Hence, pressure is necessary for children to assimilate their parents' goals. Mere goal assignment is sufficient for low-reactives, however, because there is congruence between their high need for stimulation and the high stimulation normally connected with behavior typical of Type A individuals. Striving for an ambitious goal is conducive to fulfilling the high need for stimulation typical of low-reactives. The fulfillment of the need for stimulation can be a major reinforcing factor.

To summarize, a strong need for achievement and Type A behavior develop in high-reactives if their parents apply external reinforcements, because there is an incongruence between high reactivity and Type A. High-reactives cannot oppose social pressure, even when it forces them to behave contrary to their temperament. They easily submit to social pressure in order to avoid direct punishment (Eliasz, 1987, 1995). This, however, may have negative consequences later in life.

According to Lazarus (Lazarus, 1993; Lazarus & Folkman, 1987), individuals' secondary appraisal of their coping resources is very important, perhaps even more important than the occurrence of stressful events (Bugental & Lewis, 1998; Chang, 1998). If this is the case, then high-reactives' negative appraisals of themselves, concerning, for example, their low endurance and their inability to concentrate on work for a long time, will enhance their stress. This is especially dangerous for the high-reactives among Type A persons, since Type A individuals are not able to accept their limits and to reduce their aspirations (Försterling, 1986). In contrast, internal reinforcements associated with fulfilling the need for stimulation are sufficient for the development of a high need for achievement and Type A in low-reactives. Low-reactives' secondary positive appraisal of their endurance resources can at least partially reduce their stress.

Emotional and Motivational Implications of Misfit between Type A and Reactivity

Eliasz and Wrześniewski (1991) and Eliasz and Cofta (1992) suggest that reactivity determines whether the highly competitive achievement orientation of Type A persons leads not only to high performance, but also to psycho-somatic health problems and loss of well-being. High-reactive Type A individuals can be easily overstimulated because their need for stimulation is rather low. They have relatively limited capacities for coping with the high stimulation connected with typical Type A behavior. The internal incongruence between temperament and personality is for them a source of permanent overload and tension.

In coping with this kind of stress, unrealistic goals and a dysfunctional use of means to achieve these goals can arise and aggravate the situation. M. Eysenck (1993) speaks of the deformation of cognitive processes through anxiety, which, in turn, increases anxiety (cf. also Lazarus, Kanner, & Folkman, 1980, for the interdependence of cognitive appraisal and emotion).

As to the relationship between Type A and reactivity, one can suppose that the high-reactive Type A individuals amplify the attributes of Type A. This means, for example, that time pressure commonly felt by Type A individuals is particularly pronounced in Type A high-reactives. Such an augmented intensity of Type A behavior can aggravate the difficulties faced by high-reactives. We will see that the intensification of Type A characteristics by reactivity becomes visible also in the high frequency of actualization of motives characteristic of Type A individuals.

Hypotheses

A Look at Type A, Low and High in Reactivity, in Terms of Intensity Motives

In characterizing Type A, specific motives are of particular significance. A strong need for achievement is in the core of Type A. It is displayed in a variety of *task motives*. These motives, together with *motives of control*,[3] which enhance the fulfillment of task motives, are the very attributes of Type A individuals (Glass, 1977; cf. also Byrne & Byrne, 1991; Miller, Lack, & Asroff, 1985; Perez-Garcia & Sanjuan, 1996a, 1996b). The fulfillment of task motives can be enhanced by strengthening one's control over the environment, thus possibly satisfying one's need for achievement. Therefore, motives of control are conceived of here as instrumental for task motives. Having insufficient control and difficulties in achieving goals causes irritation in Type A individuals and makes them susceptible to criticism by others (Glass, 1977). Type A's self-esteem seems to depend heavily on other people's opinion (Price, 1982), and, according to Frost and Wilson (1983), Type A individuals are inwardly insecure, although outwardly confident and self-assertive. This may be particularly true for high-reactive Type A persons, who are susceptible to social influences.

A negative secondary reappraisal of one's endurance against strong stimuli, such as working hard for a long time and competing with others, may enhance stress and, thereby, feeling of insecurity.[4] Type A individuals do not accept that they may be unable to attain their high aspirations (Försterling, 1986). If they nevertheless stay unsuccessful, a negative reappraisal of their situation leads to increased uncertainty about their self-value. Thus, *motives evoked by uncertainty about one's self-value* have to be considered, too, in clarifying the Type A motive structure. The uncertainty about self-value, resulting from difficulties in satisfying task motives or, according to Glass (1977), from insufficient control over one's environment, increases the importance (operationalized as the ipsative relative frequency of actualization) of the motives of control and of the motives induced by uncertainty about self-value.

Ineffective coping with difficulties, often as a consequence of high reactivity, can cause a person to become self-focused, which means a concentration on both one's "self" and one's body's state. Such self-concentration, however, does not help the individual to meet his or her goals but causes additional problems. Task-focused individuals, facing less difficulty in meeting their goals (probably, low-reactives), are supposed to pay less attention to issues that interfere with their task realization.

As mentioned earlier, Type A is treated as a risk factor for coronary heart disease (CHD) and other illnesses (cf. Wrześniewski, 1993). Persons at risk for coronary heart disease have a better chance in preventing a heart attack if they are attentive to certain body stimuli that function as signals of danger while still relatively weak. Therefore, one has to consider, in addition to motives related to task, control, and self-value, *motives that concern the state of one's body* and that are aimed at physical comfort and well-being.

There are reasons to believe that high-reactives magnify stimuli coming from their body, whereas low-reactives suppress such stimuli (cf. Eliasz, 1987, 1995), a tendency that can be enhanced or weakened by a person's style of coping with stress. Problem-focused coping can divert a person's attention from the body's stimuli. In contrast, emotion focused coping can induce concentration on such stimuli.

Motives concerning self-value (protecting self-value) and state of one's body (avoiding physical discomfort) are typical *self-centered (ipsocentric)* motives, (Jarymowicz, 1991; Reykowski, 1992), which tend to interfere with Type A persons' striving for high achievement.

On the basis of these thoughts about the combined effects of Type A and reactivity on motivation, we arrive at the first hypothesis:

Hypothesis One: Motives of control, motives induced by the uncertainty about self-value and motives concerning the state of one's body are more frequently actualized in high-reactive Type A (HrA) than in low-reactive Type A (LrA) individuals.

HrA > LrA

There is no ground for a hypothesis claiming differences between low- and high-reactive Type A participants in the manifestation of task motives.

Situational Stimulants and Cross-situational Consistency of Type A Behavior

Friedman and Rosenman (1959) pointed out that Type A persons are especially excited by situations that require haste, severe competition (in particular with other Type A individuals), and similarly arousing activities. We may assume that the functioning characteristic of Type A is actualized foremost during *work* and in *the presence of others*, in particular in the presence of other Type A individuals.

Houston (1988) refers to another situational stimulant of Type A behavior in reporting the biggest differences between Type A and Type B in dealing with moderately difficult tasks. A similar preference of achievement-oriented people for tasks of average difficulty, reported for the first time by McClelland, Atkinson, Clark, and Lowell (1953), underlines the achievement motive as a characteristic of the Type A personality. Very much like Type A, individuals with a high need for achievement (a) choose an average level of risk, which means that they prefer goals or tasks with an average level of difficulty; (b) put great effort into accomplishing the tasks or achieving the goals; (c) demonstrate great persistence in task solving or in their efforts to achieve goals.

Friedman and Rosenman (1959) conceived of Type A as a behavior pattern, because they assumed that personality evinces a cross-situational consistency. Although, among others, Mischel (1990, 1998) warns against an overstatement of cross-situational consistency, there is certainly *some* consistency in the behavior of Type A persons, in particular of high-reactive Type A persons, who tend to behave as if they were under stress even in neutral situations (for the effects of stress on stimulus generalization see Brebner, 1991). Type A individuals can even feel tempted to compete with small children. They feel time pressure not only at their workplace but also at home or elsewhere. Such generalization or cross-situational consistency means that different, though superficially similar, situations provoke the same kind of behavior.

I assume that high-reactives face more difficulties in fulfilling Type A needs than low-reactives. What is more, the secondary negative reappraisal of their temperamentally shaped capacities intensifies their stress. Emotions associated with stress can cause a generalization of motives characteristic of Type A individuals. Thus, the second hypothesis states:

Hypothesis Two: The actualization frequencies of motives characteristic of Type A are more consistent across situations in high-reactive Type A (HrA) than in low-reactive Type A (LrA) participants.

HrA > LrA

Method

The Time Sampling Diary (Brandstätter, 1983, 1989, 1994) was used to assess the frequencies with which Type A participants who are low and high in reactivity (mean split) refer to four classes of motives (task, control, self-value, and physical comfort).

The seven questions of the TSD.   Participants had to answer seven questions whenever the random signal for self-observation is given (see chapter 2 in this volume). One of them, *"Why do I feel as I have indicated?"* (question 3), makes it possible to assess the attributions made by participants and, indirectly, the motives affected by their experience. The questions *"Where am I?"* (question 4) and *"Who else is present?"* (question 6) give grounds for categorizing situation types.

The situations considered in this study.   In studying Type A behavior, two differences are of special importance to the researcher. One is the distinction between work and leisure, and the other is the distinction between being alone and being with others. The focus of the present research is, however, the difference between work performed in the office ("work-in") and work performed at home ("work-out").[5] This situational factor is taken into account on the grounds of prior empirical evidence that control over one's environment is a crucial element for Type A individuals. It is assumed here that such control can more easily be realized outside, rather than in, the workplace. In order to keep the two contrasting situations comparable in other respects, both situations imply work and the presence of others.

The motives.   In recording the motives involved in their emotional experience, the participants could choose up to three different motives from a list. Experts ascribed these motives to four categories distinguished beforehand by the present author on theoretical grounds. The categories and the subsumed motives are as follows:

1. *Task motives*
   I managed to do my work well.
   I know what I am expected to do in my work.
2. *Motives of control*
   I can influence others.
   I am successful in defending my standpoint against others.
   I have enough time to do everything that I would like to do or am expected to do.
   I understand things better than ever before.

My surroundings are clean and tidy.
3. *Motives induced by uncertainty about self-value*
   I evaluate myself irrespective of others' opinion.
   I have not noticed vicious remarks about myself.
   I am respected.
   Nobody acts superior to me.
   I can take revenge for the harm done to me.
4. *Motives concerning the meeting of biological needs and the state of one's body*
   I don't feel any physical discomfort.
   I am satiated, rested, and comfortable, and I don't feel any pain.

These statements refer to motive satisfaction. The participants could refer to the same categories of motives in reporting a negative mood (motive frustration). A motive counted as actualized if the participants referred to that motive, irrespective of satisfaction or frustration.

Up to three different motives could be indicated as satisfied or frustrated in each moment of observation. The following rule is adopted here: The category of motives counts as having been actualized when at least one motive from a given category of motives is mentioned in a moment of observation. The relative importance of a given category of motives for the particular group is reflected in the ratio of actualized motives within the group of participants to the total number of actualized motives of a given category by all groups of participants.

The measures of reactivity and Type A.   *Reactivity* (discussed earlier) was assessed by Pavlov's Temperament Inventory (previously named Strelau Temperament Inventory—Revised) developed by Strelau, Angleitner, Bantelman, and Ruch (1990). The coefficient Alpha reliability of the reactivity scale is .80 (Strelau, Zawadzki, & Angleitner, 1995).

Type A was assessed by the Jenkins Activity Survey (short form). The JAS is the most commonly used scale for assessing Type A. It comprises the following subscales: Speed and Impatience, Job Involvement, and Hard-Driving Competitiveness (Jenkins, Zyzanski, & Rosenman, 1979; Wrześniewski, Zyzanski, & Jenkins, 1980).

The sample.   Data were collected from 97 bank employees, ages 20–54 years (mean age 33.1, standard deviation 8.6 years). Participants were sampled from different departments; their education ranged from high school to master's degree. They kept the TSD over 40 days (10 days per month in three consecutive months and in a fourth month after a two-month break). Only data on motive actualization in specific types of situations of Type A individuals, low and high in reactivity, are presented.[6]

Results

Overview.   Generally, the analyses of variance revealed significant differences between neither Type A and Type B nor between high-and low-reactives in the

Table 3.2 Number of Participants per
Group

	Type	
Reactivity	B	A
high-reactives (Hr)	22	30
low-reactives (Lr)	22	23

frequencies of actualized motives when the data were aggregated across situations. Theoretically meaningful differences, however, come to the fore in specific situations.

The results presented in this section concern the reactivity-conditioned functioning of Type A individuals only in work situations in the presence of others.

In looking for significant inter-individual as well as cross-situational differences (i.e., inconsistencies), I have decided to use non-parametric statistics based on the chi-square distribution. The distribution of JAS (mean of JAS 2.57 with a range of −61.1 to +23.2) and of reactivity (mean 47 with a range of 27 to 76) were dichotomized and, crossed with low versus high reactivity and with Type B and Type A, results in four groups (Table 3.2).

The frequencies in Table 3.2 are unequal, and consequently there are differences concerning the frequencies of observations for Type A high-reactives and Type A low-reactives. Therefore, random samples of observations were taken to equalize the frequencies in all the cells. The observations were random, based on the tables of random numbers. As Table 3.3 shows, low-reactives and high-reactives contributed about equal frequencies of observations in "work-in" and "work-out" situations.

Figure 3.1 shows the differences in frequencies of motive actualization between low and high-reactive Type A participants within work in the office ("work-in") and work at home ("work-out"). With this figure at hand, one can focus on inter-individual differences within situations or on inter-situational differences (cross-situational inconsistencies) within classes of persons. Figure 3.2 is based on the same data, but presents the intra-individual (ipsative) *relative* frequencies of motive actualization for high and low-reactive participants in "work-in" and "work-out" situations.

Summing up, the outcomes presented here concern interindividual differences (Hr-Lr) and cross-situational consistency ("work-in"/"work-out") in Type A individuals in the presence of others. The results are summarized in Table 3.4.

Table 3.3 Frequencies of Random Sample Observations in High- and Low-Reactive Participants in Two Work Situations: "Work-in" and "Work-out"

Reactivity	Work-in	Work-out	Total
High	941 25.0%	965 25.6%	1906 50.6%
Low	928 24.6%	933 24.8%	1861 49.4%
Total	1869 49.6%	1898 50.4%	3767 100.0%

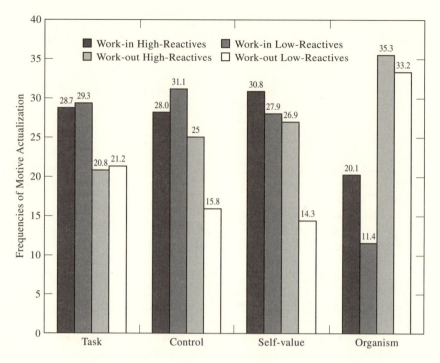

Figure 3.1. Motive actualization frequencies of low-reactive and high-reactive Type A participants during work in the office (work-in) and work at home (work-out).

No group differences in task motives.   Task motives are the core of Type A behavior, and the data show that in this respect there are no differences between Type A high-reactives and Type A low-reactives (Table 3.4, 2nd column). The frequencies of actualization of *task motives* are the same in both groups in the two situations, "work-in" and "work-out" (Table 3.4, 3rd column). Type A individuals have a strong desire to achieve more and more, especially in work situations. There are grounds to conclude that this desire is independent of reactivity.

Group differences in the other motives.   The actualization frequencies of the remaining three classes of motives (control, self-value, and state of organism) turned out to be higher in high-reactive than in low-reactive Type A participants, seemingly confirming hypothesis one (Table 3.4, 2nd column). However, the results need qualifications: For the control motives and the self-value motives, the predicted difference is found *only* in "work-out" situations (Table 3.4, 3rd column). For the state of organism motives, the difference is more pronounced in "work-in" than in "work-out" situations (see Figure 3.1, Figure 3.2, and Table 3.4, 3rd column).

Cross-situational consistency in actualization of motives.   The actualization of the four classes of motives depends heavily on situations (Table 3.4, 4th column). We

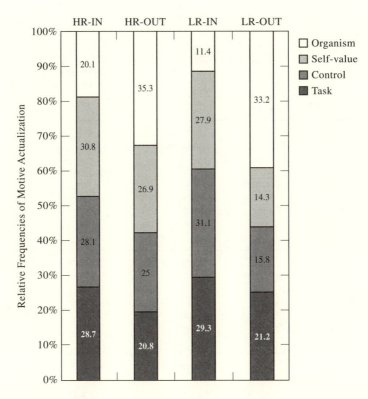

Figure 3.2. Intra-individual relative frequencies of motive actualization of low-reactive and high-reactive Type A participants during work in the office (work-in) and work at home (work-out).

see that Type A low-reactives actualize the three kinds of motives (task, control, and self-value) significantly less frequently in "work-out" than in "work-in" situations (Table 3.4, 5th column). In this respect, Type A low-reactives are cross-situationally inconsistent. Both groups of individuals (high and low-reactive participants) actualize motives relating to the state of one's body less frequently in "work-in" than in "work-out" (Table 3.4, 4th and 5th column), whereas motives related to task, control, and self-value are more often actualized in "work-out" than in "work-in" situations.

Discussion

In clarifying Type A behavior, complex interactions of reactivity, kinds of motives involved, and types of situations have to be taken into account. There are no differences between high- and low-reactive participants regarding *task motives*, which implies high achievement as a central goal of Type A people. Reactivity doesn't make a difference here, although high-reactive Type A participants might be overstimulated in competitive achievement situations and, therefore,

Table 3.4 Interindividual Differences and Cross-Situational Consistency in Actualization of Motives

Motives	Individual differences Hr/Lr		Cross-situational consistency work-in/work-out (WI/WO)	
	Main effects	Simple effects	Main effects	Simple effects
Task	Hr = Lr	WI: Hr = Lr	WI > WO $\chi^2 = 35.38$ $p < .0001$	Hr: WI > WO $\chi^2 = 17.54$ $p < .0001$
		WO: Hr = Lr		Lr: WI > WO $\chi^2 = 17.83$ $p < .0001$
Control	Hr > Lr $\chi^2 = 4.11$ $p < .05$	WI: Hr = Lr	WI > WO $\chi^2 = 36.24$ $p < .0001$	Hr: WI = WO
		WO: Hr > Lr $\chi^2 = 22.33$ $p < .0001$		Lr: WI > WO $\chi^2 = 53.46$ $p < .0001$
Self-value	Hr > Lr $\chi^2 = 7.48$ $p < .01$	WI: Hr = Lr	WI > WO $\chi^2 = 9.47$ $p < .001$	Hr: WI = WO
		WO: Hr > Lr $\chi^2 = 11.98$ $p < .001$		Lr: WI > WO $\chi^2 = 13.57$ $p < .001$
State of organism	Hr > Lr $\chi^2 = 8.47$ $p < .01$	WI: Hr > Lr $\chi^2 = 17.65$ $p < .0001$	WI < WO $\chi^2 = 101.12$ $p < .0001$	Hr: WI < WO $\chi^2 = 30.74$ $p < .0001$
		WO: Hr = Lr		Lr: WI < WO $\chi^2 = 78.79$ $p < .0001$

Hr = high-reactives; Lr = low-reactives; WI = work-in; WO = work-out

respond to these situations with less positive emotions. Relating frequencies of motive actualization to conditional motive satisfaction ratios (satisfaction under the condition of actualization) for different personality structures and classes of situations is beyond the scope of the present research.

Motivation reflects the misfit of Type A and high reactivity.   The theoretically postulated internal misfit between Type A and high reactivity is reflected in differences of frequencies as well as in cross-situational consistency of situation-specific motive actualization by high- and low-reactive Type A persons.

Motives of control support the fulfillment of task motives (Glass, 1977). Thus, it is only natural that motives of control are actualized on the same level as task motives by both high-and low-reactive Type A individuals in the "work-in" situation when other individuals are present. However, a "work-out" situation in the presence of others offers much easier control over events than a "work-in" situation. Accordingly, the "work-out" situation evokes motives of control among low-reactive Type A persons less often than the "work-in" setting. In other words, for low-reactive Type A persons, we find cross-situational inconsistency (less generalization) concerning the intensity of control motives (operationalized as frequency of their actualization). Conversely, there is cross-situational consistency in this respect among high-reactive Type A individuals. These high-reactive Type A persons, manifesting some kind of rigidity, demonstrate lower levels of flexibility in adjusting to differences among situations. This probably reflects difficulties originating in the overstimulation of high-reactives by the functioning characteristics of Type A.

Insufficient control and difficulties in achieving goals result in irritation and susceptibility to criticism from others. The self-esteem of Type A persons in general and of high-reactive Type A in particular depends on the opinion of others. Although appearing confident and self-assertive, they quite often feel insecure. The fact that high-reactive Type A persons demonstrate high sensitivity to and insufficient endurance against strong stimuli associated with social competition and hard work provides grounds for a negative reappraisal in stressful situations (cf. Lazarus & Folkman, 1987), which aggravates stress and causes uncertainty and doubts about one's worth.

This reasoning was behind our expectation that the *motives evoked by uncertainty about self-value* would be actualized more often by high-reactive Type A than by low-reactive Type A people (see the first hypothesis: HrA > LrA, regarding frequency of motive actualization). It turned out that this is true only in "work-out" situations, whereas in "work-in" situations both groups actualize these motives on the same, relatively high, level. It is fairly obvious that, generally, persons in a "work-out" situation should feel more confident about others' opinions than they do in "work-in" situations. Therefore, in "work-out" situations, Type A low-reactives would be expected to be clearly relaxed and not to show as serious a concern about their self-value as high-reactive Type A persons would. In this regard, the latter are also rigid and unable to adjust their functioning to the specificity of situations. By contrast, low-reactive Type A persons modulate their functioning according to the characteristics of a situation. This is in line with the second hypothesis relating to cross-situational consistency and inconsistency.

Motives concerning the state of one's body are supposed to be associated with an individual's susceptibility to and concentration on the stimuli coming from his or her body. The data show, however, that, in the "work-out" situation, both groups actualize these motives on the same very high level, although one would expect that high-reactive Type A persons are particularly sensitive to stimulation in both situations. Therefore, the actualization of these motives is the likely result of individuals paying attention to them. Some situations can divert attention from these stimuli. One can assume that a higher concentration on tasks (see the discussion of task motives) in the "work-in" than in the "work-out" setting would divert attention from body signals. This is particularly visible in Type A low-reactive individuals. It may be that these individuals suppress such stimuli in the "work-in" situation. This probably reflects their concentration on their tasks, which leaves them unable to attend to matters, that could interfere with their tasks and weaken their drive to attain their goals. Obviously, reactivity makes a difference in the more stressful "work-in" situations, where low-reactive Type A participants, absorbed by their work, pay less attention than high-reactive Type A participants to signals of physical comfort or discomfort.

Both groups, Type A persons low and high in reactivity, actualize motives related to the state of their bodies in "work-in" situations significantly less often than in "work-out" situations. However, the difference between both situations is less pronounced in Type A high-reactives than in low-reactives. This is in keeping with the second hypothesis, although some cross-situational inconsistency is found in both Type A subgroups. In "work-in" situations, high-reactive Type A persons have a significantly higher motive actualization frequency than do low-reactive Type A persons, thus giving support to the first hypothesis concerning interindividual differences.

Low-reactive and high-reactive Type A persons differ in their health risks.   If in fact, in "work-in" situations, low-reactive Type A individuals are so absorbed by their work that their attention is diverted from their bodies' stimuli, this might suggest that there is a health risk specific to this subgroup of Type A. It may be that only alarming signals in "work-in" situations can divert their attention from tasks and direct it to their own bodies. Thus, possibly, an unexpected heart attack not preceded by any advance warning signals might pose a particularly high risk to Type A low-reactives.

Conversely, the danger for high-reactive Type A persons is probably associated with their inability to adjust their behavior to the specific demands of the various situations. This means that they show characteristic Type A functioning in situations that do not demand it and in which such behavior may even be a hindrance. It is worth recalling here that high-reactives develop Type A behavior in spite of their low need for stimulation under social pressure. Thus, on the one hand, this rigidity reveals their overstimulation, but, on the other hand, it can further aggravate the overstimulation and cause a psycho-somatic overload.

Conclusions

Data aggregated across situations do not show differences in motive actualization between high- and low-reactive Type A persons. One has to take into account the specificity of situations and to pay attention to situations that especially provoke the actualization of motives characteristic of Type A individuals (e.g., "work-in" vs. "work-out" in the presence of others). Only then can one show that importance or intensity (actualization frequency), as well as cross-situational consistency of specific motives, varies with reactivity.

These findings have been obtained with a tool that allows an assessment of both cross-situational and inter-individual differences in people's experience of and response to various situations. The Time Sampling Diary enables us to look into the internal structure of processes and helps us to avoid a premature generalization based on aggregated observations.

In general, the present data support both the hypotheses about inter-individual and cross-situational differences in the actualization of motives, shedding some light on two different kinds of Type A characteristics. It is possible to clarify the aspect of people's functioning that depends on reactivity only by careful consideration of the correspondence (or lack of correspondence) between motivational propensities and situational demands. The Type A behavior pattern does not fit the capacities of high-reactive individuals, whereas there is internal congruence between Type A and the capacities of low-reactive individuals. This disparity between high-reactive and low-reactive individuals is associated with the profile of Type A's motives characteristics.

Task motives are the core of Type A, and the data show that, with respect to the intensity and cross-situational consistency of these motives, no differences between Type A high-reactives and Type A low-reactives are found.

The remaining motives, aiming at control, protection of self-value, and physical well-being, concern the style of fulfilling the task motives and are more frequently actualized in high than in low-reactive Type A individuals. Type A high-reactives, but not Type A low-reactives, are inclined to display a distinctive Type A functioning even in situations that do not call for competitive high achievement. As the study has shown, the crucial point is whether a person's temperament, in particular his or her reactivity, is congruent or incongruent with his or her Type A way of life.

Acknowledgments

I am very grateful to Hermann Brandstätter for his specific comments on my contribution. They helped me to avoid some mistakes and improve the clarity of my thoughts. I would also like to extent my gratitude to two anonymous reviewers for their helpful comments.

Notes

This study was supported by the National Committee for Scientific Research (Grant no. 1P106 012 06).

1. Reactivity conceived in this way was usually assessed by the Strelau Temperament Inventory and later on by the Strelau Temperament Inventory—Revised, developed by Strelau, Angleitner, Bantelman, and Ruch (1990). Strelau, Zawadzki, and Angleitner (1995) currently contend that the dimension of reactivity is heterogeneous. The empirical grounds for this point of view are rather insufficient so far (Eliasz, 1995). Moreover, Strelau renamed the dimension of reactivity, as assessed by STI-R, and proposed to call it "strength of excitation" or, interchangeably, "strength of nervous system." Consequently, the Strelau Temperament Inventory—Revised is now called

the Pavlovian Temperament Survey (Strelau, Zawadzki, and Angleitner, 1995). Thus, they have come back to original Pavlovian terminology whereby high reactivity (Hr) is equivalent to a weak nervous system, while low reactivity (Lr) is linked to a strong one. Since the data concerning the latest reformulation of reactivity are still inconclusive, I do not intend to drop the understanding of reactivity found in STI-R. This remains useful because the reasoning presented in this paper is rooted in studies that analyze the regulative role of reactivity, the dimension assessed by STI-R (now PTS).

2. Type A is very often treated as a pattern of behavior and is named *Type A behavior pattern* (TABP). However, there are solid grounds for conceiving of Type A, at least diagnosed by inventories, as a personality factor. Inventories diagnose stable-over-time manifestations of Type A at least in some classes of situations ("*I usually . . .*" or "*I generally* behave . . ."). In some items we can even guess the assumptions behind the cross-situational consistency of Type A behavior patterns. In personality theories, stability of behavior over time is a solid ground for considering a given behavior form as determined by an internal personality mechanism (cf. Kohnstamm, 1986).

3. Motives of control relate to both behavioral and cognitive control. The former concerns an influence on events, others, and things. The latter pertains to understanding and /or foreseeing events.

4. It concerns mainly those who have high sensitivity and low endurance, that is, it relates mainly to high-reactives.

5. "Work-out" means work (including professional assignments) performed at home.

6. The preliminary data presented before (Eliasz, 1995) concerns a smaller sample. What is more, the categories of the motives had been distinguished there by the author before the experts assessed them. The latter categorization is a bit different from the former.

References

Amelang, M. (1997). Using personality variables to predict cancer and heart disease. *European Journal of Personality, 11*, 319-342.

Booth-Kewley, S., & Friedman, H. S. (1987). Psychological predictors of heart disease: A quantitative review. *Psychological Bulletin, 101*, 343–362.

Brandstätter, H. (1983). Emotional responses to other persons in everyday life situations. *Journal of Personality and Social Psychology, 45*, 871–883.

Brandstätter, H. (1989). Motives in everyday life situations: An individual difference approach. In F. Halisch & J. H. L. van den Bercken (Eds.), *International perspectives on achievement and task motivation* (pp. 327–349). Amsterdam: Swets & Zeitlinger.

Brandstätter, H. (1994). Well-being and motivational person-environment fit. A time sampling study of emotions. *European Journal of Personality, 8*, 75–93.

Brebner, J. (1991). Personality and generalization as a source of stress. In C. D. Spielberger, I. G. Sarason, J. Strelau, & J. Brebner (Eds.), *Stress and anxiety* (Vol. 13, pp. 93–100). New York: Hemisphere.

Bugental, D. B., & Lewis, J. C. (1998). Interpersonal power repair in response to threats to control from dependent others. In M. Kofta, G. Weary, & G. Sędek (Eds.), *Personal control in action. Cognitive and motivational mechanisms* (pp. 341–362). New York: Plenum Press.

Byrne, D. G., & Byrne, A. E. (1991). Occupational stress, Type A behavior, and risk of coronary disease. In C. D. Spielberger, I. G. Sarason, J. Strelau, & J. Brebner (Eds.), *Stress and anxiety* (Vol. 13, pp. 233–247). New York: Hemisphere.

Chang, E. C. (1998). Dispositional optimism and primary and secondary appraisal of a stressor: Controlling for confounding influences and relations to coping and psychological and physical adjustment. *Journal of Personality and Social Psychology, 74*, 1109–1120.

Cofta, L. (1992). *Zapotrzebowanie na stymulację jako czynnik modyfikujący wpływ Wzoru Zachowania A na zdrowie i jakość życia* [Need for stimulation as a factor modifying the influence of Type A behavior pattern on health and quality of life]. Unpublished doctoral dissertation. Warsaw. Institute of Psychology, PAN.

Eliasz, A. (1981). *Temperament a system regulacji stymulacji* [Temperament and system of stimulation control]. Warsaw: PWN.

Eliasz, A. (1985). Transactional model of temperament. In J. Strelau (Ed.), *Temperamental bases of behavior: Warsaw studies on individual differences* (pp. 41–78). Lisse: Swets & Zeitlinger.

Eliasz, A. (1987). Temperament contingent cognitive orientation toward various aspects of reality. In J. Strelau & H. J. Eysenck (Eds.), *Personality dimensions and arousal* (pp. 197–213). New York: Plenum.

Eliasz, A. (1990). Broadening the concept of temperament: From disposition to hypothetical construct. *European Journal of Personality, 4*, 287–302.

Eliasz, A. (1995). Temperament a wartości i możliwosci osób o wzorze A [Values/ potentialities: Temperament/Type A]. In W. Łukaszewski (Ed.), *W kręgu teorii czynności* (pp. 178–207). Warsaw: IP PAN.

Eliasz, A., & Cofta, L. (1992). Temperament a skłonność do chorób [Temperament and proneness to diseases]. In J. Strelau, W. Ciarkowska, & E. Nęcka (Eds.), *Różnice indywidualne: możliwości i preferencje* (pp. 65–80). Wrocław: Ossolineum.

Eliasz, A., & Wrześniewski, K. (1988). *Ryzyko chorób psychosomatycznych: środowisko i temperament a wzór zachowania A* [The risk of psychosomatic diseases: environment and Temperament Type A pattern]. Wroclaw: Ossolineum.

Eliasz, A., & Wrześniewski, K. (1991). Two kinds of Type A behavior pattern. In C. D. Spielberger, I. G. Sarason, J. Strelau, & J. Brebner (Eds.), *Stress and anxiety* (Vol. 13, pp. 275–282). New York: Hemisphere.

Eysenck, M. W. (1993). Cognitive factors in generalized anxiety disorder. In M. Vartiainen (Ed.), *European views in psychology-keynote lectures. III European Congress of Psychology*. Helsinki: Cosmoprint.

Försterling, F. (1986). Attributional conceptions in clinical psychology. *American Psychologist, 41*, 275–285

Friedman, M., & Rosenman, R. H. (1959). Association of specific overt behavior pattern with blood and cardiovascular findings. *Journal of the American Medical Association, 169*, 1286–1296.

Frost, T. F., & Wilson, H. G. (1983). Effects of locus of control and A-B personality type on job satisfaction within the health care field. *Psychological Reports, 53*, 399–405.

Glass, D. C. (1977). *Behavior patterns, stress and coronary disease*. Hillsdale, NJ: Erlbaum.

Houston, B. K. (1988). Cardiovascular and neuroendocrine reactivity, global Type A, and components of Type A behavior. In B. K. Houston & C. R. Snyder (Eds.), *Type A behavior pattern. Research, theory, and intervention* (pp. 212–253). New York: Wiley.

Jarymowicz, M. (1991). Czy jesteśmy egoistami. W: M. Kofta i T. Szustrowa (red.), *Złudzenia które pozwalają żyć. Szkice z psychologii społecznej* [Illusions that help live] (pp. 103–140). Warsaw: PWN.

Jenkins, C. D., & Lee, D. J. (1989). Type A behavior pattern and coronary heart disease: A re-examination. *Quality of Life and Cardiovascular Care, 5*, 80–87.

Jenkins, C. D., Zyzansky, S. J., & Rosenman, R. H. (1979). *Jenkins Activity Survey. Manual*. New York: Psychological Corporation.

Kohnstamm, G. A. (Ed.). (1986). *Temperament discussed. Temperament and development in infancy and childhood.* Lisse: Swets & Zeitlinger.

Lazarus, R. S. (1993). Coping theory and research: Past, present, and future. *Psychosomatic Medicine, 55,* 234–247.

Lazarus, R. S., Kanner, A. D., & Folkman, S. (1980). Emotions: A cognitive phenomenological analysis. In R. Plutchik & H. Kellerman (Eds.), *Emotion: Theory, research, and experience. Vol. 1: Theories of emotion* (pp. 189–217). New York: Academic Press.

Lazarus, R. S., & Folkman, S. (1987). Transactional theory and research on emotions and coping. *European Journal of Personality, 1,* 141–170.

McClelland, D. C., Atkinson, J. W., Clark, R. A., & Lowell, E. L. (1953). *The achievement motive.* New York: Appleton-Century-Crofts.

Miller, S. M., Lack, E. R., & Asroff, S. (1985). Preference for control and the coronary-prone behavior pattern: "I'd rather do it myself." *Journal of Personality and Social Psychology, 49,* 492–499.

Mischel, W. (1990). Personality dispositions revisited and revised: A view after three decades. In L. A. Pervin (Ed.), *Handbook of personality: Theory and research* (pp. 111–134). New York. Guildford Press.

Mischel (1998, July). *Toward a unified cumulative science of personality.* Keynote address at Ninth European Conference on Personality, Guildford, Great Britain.

Myrtek, M. (1995). Type A behavior pattern, personality factors, disease, and psychological reactivity: A meta-analytic update. *Personality and Individual Differences, 18,* 491–502.

Perez-Garcia, A. M., & Sanjuan, P. (1996a). Type A behavior patterns (global and main components), attentional performance, cardiovascular reactivity, and causal attributions in the presence of different levels of interference. *Personality and Individual Differences, 20,* 81–93.

Perez-Garcia, A. M., & Sanjuan, P. (1996b, July). *Attributional style and Type A components.* Paper presented at the Eighth European Conference on Personality, Ghent, Belgium.

Price, V. A. (1982). *Type A behavior pattern: A model for research and practice.* New York: Academic Press.

Rosenman, R. H., Swan, G. E., & Carmelli, D. (1988). Definition, assessment, and evolution of the Type A behavior pattern. In B. K. Houston & C. R. Snyder (Eds.), *Type A behavior pattern: Research, theory, and intervention* (pp. 8–31). New York: Wiley.

Reykowski, J. (1992). *Procesy emocjonalne, motywacja, osobowść* [Emotional processes, motivation, personality]. Warsaw: PWN

Spence, J. T., Helmreich, R. L., & Pred, R. S. (1987). Impatience versus achievement strivings in the Type A pattern: Differential effects on students' health and academic achievement. *Journal of Applied Psychology, 72,* 522–528.

Strelau, J. (1983). *Temperament—personality—activity.* London: Academic Press.

Strelau, J. (1988). Temperament dimensions as codeterminants of resistance to stress. In M. P. Janisse (Ed.), *Individual differences, stress, and health psychology* (pp. 146–169). New York: Springer.

Strelau, J. (1994). The concepts of arousal and arousability as used in temperament studies. In J. E. Bates & T. D. Wachs (Eds.), *Temperament: Individual differences at the interface of biology and behavior* (pp. 117–141). Washington, DC: APA Books.

Strelau, J. (1998). *Temperament: A psychological perspective.* New York: Plenum Press.

Strelau, J., Angleitner, A., Bantelmann, J., & Ruch, W. (1990). The Strelau Temperament Inventory—Revised (STI-R): Theoretical considerations and scale development. *European Journal of Personality, 4,* 209–235.

Strelau, J., & Eliasz, A. (1994). Temperament risk factor and Type A behavior pattern.

In W. Carey & S. McDevitt (Eds.), *Prevention and early intervention: Individual differences as risk factors for the mental health of children* (pp. 42–49). New York: Bruner/Mazel.

Strelau, J., Zawadzki, B., & Angleitner, A. (1995). Kwestionariusz Temperamentu PTS: Próba psychologicznej interpretacji podstawowych cech układu nerwowego według Pawłowa [Pavlovian Temperament Survey (PTS): An effort of a psychological interpretation of Pavlov's basic properties of the nervous system]. *Studia Psychologiczne, 33,* 9–48.

Williams, R. B., Barefoot, J. C., & Shekelle, R. B. (1985). The health consequences of hostility. In M. A. Chesney & R. H. Rosenman (Eds.), *Anger and hostility in cardiovascular and behavioral disorders* (pp. 173–185). New York: Hemisphere.

Williams R. B., & Barefoot, J. C. (1988). Coronary prone behavior: The emerging role of the hostility complex. In B. K. Houston & C. R. Snyder (Eds.) *Type A behavior pattern: Research, theory, and intervention* (pp. 188–211). New York: Wiley.

Wrześniewski, K. (1993). *Styl życia a zdrowie: Wzór zachowania A* [Style of life and health: Type A pattern]. Warsaw Wyd IP PAN.

Wrześniewski, K., Zyzansky, S. J., & Jenkins, C. D. (1980). Polsko-amerkańskie badania nad wzorem zachowania stanowiąym czynnik ryzyka zawału serca [Polish-American studies on behavior pattern being a risk factor of heart infarction]. *Przegląd Psychologiczny, 23,* 35–46.

4

Self-Regulatory Abilities, Temperament, and Volition in Everyday Life Situations

Magdalena Marszał-Wiśniewska

The study addresses four basic questions:

1. Do temperamental properties (reactivity and mobility) differentiate the importance and efficiency of self-regulatory abilities in everyday life situations, as reported by participants?
2. Do volitional properties (action versus state orientation) differentiate the importance and efficiency of self-regulatory abilities in everyday life situations, as reported by participants?
3. Does the interaction between temperament and volition (temperament-volition coherence and incoherence) differentiate the importance and efficiency of self-regulatory abilities in everyday life situations, as reported by participants?
4. Do volitional and temperamental properties affect *the fit between* self-regulatory ability and situational demands?

The objects of analysis are the main self-regulatory abilities, as distinguished by Kuhl, that help protect and maintain an intention against the pressure from competing action tendencies. They are: (1) active attentional selectivity, (2) emotion control, (3) parsimony of information processing, (4) motivation control, and (5) environment control.

Kuhl's Action Control Theory: The Modern View of Volitional Control

We all know from everyday experience that the mere intention, for example, to stop smoking, is not sufficient for the enactment. To be initiated and enacted, even simple activities require control processes (action control, volitional control) that help shield a selected action tendency from the continuous pressure of alternative action tendencies. Kuhl's theory focuses on those action control processes that mediate the formation and enactment of intentions. It extends the conventional expectancy-value theory of motivation, to include the parameters of action control.

According to Kuhl's theory (1986), the efficiency of action control is possibly a function of two factors: the self-regulatory (volitional) abilities (strategies) of the individual and enactment difficulty, that is, the extent of self-regulatory ability needed to enact an intention (Kuhl, 1986). These self-regulatory abilities (strategies) help protect and maintain an intention against the pressure from competing action tendencies. Kuhl (1985) has described six such abilities (strategies):

1. *Active attentional selectivity* refers to the selective processing of external information supporting the current intention.
2. *Encoding control* refers to pre-attentional selection of perceptual input. It facilitates the protective function of volition by selectively encoding those features of a stimulus that are related to the current intention.
3. *Emotion control* refers to the strengthening of levels of emotions that facilitate the protection and maintenance of a difficult intention (or the weakening of the emotional states that might undermine the efficiency of the protective function of volition).
4. *Motivational control* aims at a change in the current hierarchy of tendency strengths. It refers to an increase in the evaluative strength of intention and the degree of initiative. Imagining positive and negative outcomes in an action is among the major strategies people employ to generate intention-strengthening emotions.
5. *Environment control* refers to the act of changing the environment. It develops from the more basic strategies dealing with emotion control or motivation control. Emotional and motivational states can be controlled by manipulating the environment. Making social commitments is one example. People who intend to stop smoking inform another person about their intention, in the hope of building up kind of some social pressure that may help them to maintain the intention.
6. *Parsimony of information processing* amounts to the act of optimizing the duration of the decision-making process. It relates to the definition of stop rules for information-processing. Theoretically, a person could go on forever, processing new information about various consequences of potential action alternatives, without even performing any of them. Efficient action control requires parsimony of information processing.

According to Kuhl's theory (1985), the difficulty of enactment of an intention depends on the mode of control that is currently activated. Two modes of control can be distinguished: action and state orientation. Action orientation is characterized by internal or external operations that promote the execution of a realistic, context-adequate intention (Kuhl, 1994). In the state-oriented mode, an individual ruminates cognitively about past, present, or future states. This activity does not increase his or her action readiness (Kuhl, 1994). In other words, an individual is action oriented, if his or her attention is focused on a fully developed action structure and he or she can perform the intended action. A high degree of action orientation facilitates the enactment of intentions. If the individual focuses his or her thoughts on the remaining elements, without being able to initiate the intended action, he or she is state-oriented. Because state orientation involves repetitive and dysfunctional focusing on some fixed aspects of the situation, it impedes the performance of an intention (Kuhl, 1986). Depending on which element to which the individual directs his or her attention, various forms of state orientation may develop. Kuhl distinguishes three different forms of state orientation: (1) failure related (disengagement vs. preoccupation), (2) decision related (initiative vs. hesitation) and (3) performance related (persistence vs. volatility). A personal disposition toward action or state orientation is postulated. Kuhl assumes that there are relatively stable differences between individuals in the extent to which they are action or state oriented (Kuhl, 1994). He has developed a questionnaire to assess individual differences in those volitional properties, that is, in state versus action orientation (Kuhl, 1985). Most of the research based on Kuhl's questionnaire, assessing individuals' disposition toward an action or a state orientation, demonstrates the efficiency-reducing effects of a state orientation (Kuhl, 1985, 1992). A global and stable disposition towards a state orientation is maladaptive to the extent that it impairs the flexible utilization of important supervisory control functions. For example, if one cannot escape ruminant thoughts, despite one's realization that they interfere with a subjectively important current task, the maladaptive effects of the state orientation are obvious (see also Scott & McIntosh, 1999).

Although, according to Kuhl's theory (1984, 1985, 1994), all self-regulatory abilities are less developed in state-oriented participants, their functional significance in relation to the state versus action orientation distinction is considered an open question. Functional significance of self-regulatory ability should be understood in terms of importance, that is, whether it is actualized (engaged) in carrying out the intention, and efficiency, that is, how it protects and maintains the intention. It should be emphasized that there still are no satisfactory data concerning the importance and efficiency of those abilities in action versus state oriented participants in various everyday life situations. However, the empirical material gathered so far (Kanfer, Dugdale, & McDonald, 1994; Kuhl & Beckmann, 1994; Marszał-Wiśniewska, 1992; Zalewska, 1992) warrants an assumption that importance and efficiency vary across everyday life situations depending on action vs. state orientation.

Person-environment fit theory (Brandstätter, 1994; Holland, 1985; Jahoda, 1961; Pervin, 1976) implies that, if people are to feel good and perform well, their motives (goals) and abilities (skills) must correspond to the gratifications and demands of their environment. Thus, we may assume that individual differences in action versus state orientation covary with the person-environment fit of motives and abilities. "Does action versus state orientation differentiate the fit between self-regulatory ability and the self-regulatory demands of the particular situation fit?" is one of the questions put in the present study.

Volition and Temperament: The Relations between Temperamental and Volitional Properties

Volition has been traditionally associated with temperament. Nowadays, the modern interactionism (Endler & Magnusson, 1976; Hettema, 1989) and new transactional models of temperament (Eliasz, 1990) do not merely justify, but encourage the investigation of these relations. The crucial question is how temperamental factors influence action control. The transactional model of temperament (Eliasz, 1985, 1990) contends that temperament is an element of a complex stimulation control system. Reactivity, as a basic dimension of temperament, determines a person's relatively stable and characteristic intensity (magnitude) of reactions, as well as the individual's need for stimulation (the higher the reactivity, the less the need for stimulation and vice versa). High reactive individuals, with a relatively low need for stimulation, prefer non-highly stimulating actions (Eliasz, 1981, 1990; Strelau, 1983). Mobility as a secondary temperamental dimension is revealed in temporal characteristics of reactions. It has been defined as an ability to react quickly and adequately to changing conditions. Empirical data (Strelau, 1983) showing that high reactive persons are characterized by rather low mobility and vice versa are not very surprising if we consider the fact that the novelty and changeability of situations are highly stimulative (Fiske & Maddi, 1961; Zuckerman, 1979) and that highly mobile persons manage these situations much better. We assume that high mobility entails a high need for stimulation (the higher the mobility, the greater the need for stimulation and vice versa). We can suppose, that high-reactive (or low-mobile) persons will more often choose behaviors that protect them against too intense a stimulation, such as, for example, procrastinating in decision-making, which is connected with so-called "fear of the irrevocable" (typical of the vacillating type of state orientation) or passive behaviors such as ruminating about failures while not changing the situation (typical for the ruminating type of state orientation).

This reasoning is supported by Gray's thesis (Gray, 1972, 1982) of the prevalence of high sensitivity to punishment (low tolerance) among anxious (i.e., introvert, neurotic) people, who in terms of temperament are high reactives.[1] Focusing on emotions elicited by expecting or experiencing punishment, however, is a characteristic of state orientation. In addition, Eliasz's thesis (1981) of the relatively low tolerance of high reactive individuals to information discrepancies, and their small range of optimal stimulation, suggests that high-reactive people will more quickly and strongly identify such information discrepancies and hence develop their state orientation. According to Kuhl's theory (Kuhl, 1985), if the incongruence between an individual's expectations and new information, or between a person's conflicting expectations exceeds a critical level, a state-oriented response should be expected, whereby the person focuses attention on the incongruence-producing information and the experienced cognitive-emotional state resulting from it. On the whole, theoretical considerations as well as empirical results (Marszał-Wiśniewska, 1992) show, that low reactivity (high need for stimulation) favors the development of an action orientation, whereas high reactivity (low need for stimulation) favors the development of a state orientation.

This pattern of internal "temperament-volition" coherence appears, when volitional properties (action vs. state orientation) develop according to the physiological mechanism of reactivity. As we know, however, volitional properties, like other personality properties, are determined also by the social environment. Thus, specific social influences can generate internal "temperament-volition" incoherence. By internal "incoherence" we mean a discrepancy between volitional and temperamental properties, that is, low reactivity or high mobility (high need for stimulation) and state orientation, or high reactivity or low mobility (low need for stimulation) and action orientation. The results of my previous studies show that the main differences in functioning are connected with these two groups ("coherent" and "incoherent") (Marszał-Wiśniewska, 1994, 1998). In that light, the problem of the relationship between self-regulatory abilities and temperament-volition interaction ("coherence" and "incoherence") seems to be important and worth testing.

Method

Participants

The participants were 97 bank employees (70 female and 27 male). Their ages ranged from 20 to 54 years, with a mean age of 33.1 years, and a standard deviation of 8.6 years. Participants were sampled from various departments and represented all kinds of positions in the bank, not including management.

Instruments

Temperament Inventory. Temperamental properties (reactivity and mobility) were measured with *Strelau's Temperament Inventory—Revised* (STI-R) (Strelau, Angleitner, Bantelmann, & Ruch, 1990). The inventory consists of 57 items and measures four temperament traits. Responding to the items, participants rate themselves on a four-point scale (I definitely don't agree, I don't quite agree, I quite agree, I definitely agree). Two scales of that inventory were used: the Strength of Excitation Scale and the Mobility Scale. The STI-R was scored for reactivity (reverse score on the Strength of Excitation Scale,[2] 19 items; score range 19–76) and mobility (Mobility Scale; 19 items; score range 19–76). Coefficient Alpha reliabilities are 0.80 for the first scale and 0.83 for the second scale (Strelau, Zawadzki, & Angleitner, 1995).

Action Control Scale. Volitional properties, that is, the level of action orientation, was measured with *Kuhl's Action Control Scale* (Kuhl, 1985). Three subclasses were taken into account: (1) AOP, which assesses performance-related action versus state orientation [i.e., persistence (focusing on the activity) versus volatility], (2) AOF, which assesses failure-related action versus state orientation [i.e., ruminating about failures (preoccupation) versus ignoring failures (disengagement] and (3) AOD, which assesses decision-related action versus state orientation [i.e., determinate (initiative) vs. vacillating decision making (hesitation)].

Time Sampling Diary. The importance and efficiency of self-regulatory abilities in everyday life situations, as reported by participants, were measured with *Brandstätter's Time Sampling Diary* (Brandstätter, 1994).

The participants had to make notes on their momentary experiences, roughly four times a day, over a period of 40 days. The random time samples (generated by a computer program) were different for each day and each person. There were seven questions to answer each time (see Brandstätter in this volume). The diary notes were coded by the participants themselves. Among the categories used to describe different aspects of situations, there were positive and negative ability attributions. The list of abilities, given to participants during the coding procedure, consisted of 26 statements, indicating the individual abilities as the causes of success and the abilities, the lack of which was the cause of failure (i.e., positive and negative ability attributions). For each page of their diaries corresponding to one point in time, participants had to mark at least one and no more than three abilities. Among these abilities were those referring to self-regulatory abilities (i.e., active attentional selectivity, emotion control, motivation control, environment control, and parsimony of information-processing).[3] Those statements were as follows:

I succeeded (I achieved what I wanted) because of:

- my ability to focus my attention on the most important information with respect to my goal (active attentional selectivity);
- my ability to activate positive feelings, not to get upset during the intended action (emotion control);
- my ability to protect myself against discouragement, by thinking about (a) profits or advantages resulting from execution of intention, or (b) negative effects if I give up (motivation control);
- my ability to make a decision relatively fast (parsimony of information-processing);
- my ability to get the support of other people (e.g., at home, at work) in the enactment of my own intention (environmental control).

I failed (I did not achieve what I wanted) because of:

- my paying too much attention to unimportant details (insufficient active attentional selectivity);
- my falling into a bad mood, experiencing negative feelings during the intended action (insufficient emotion control);
- my inability to protect myself against discouragement by thinking about (a) profits (advantages) resulting from execution of intention, or (b) negative effects if I give up (disability of motivation control);
- my procrastinating about decision making (lack of parsimony of information-processing);
- my inability to get the support of other people (e.g., at home, at work) in the enactment of my own intention (lack of environmental control).

Two indices of self-regularity abilities, as reported by participants, were taken into account: ability actualization and satisfaction ratio.

Ability actualization is the relative frequencies (percentages) of actualization, based on the total number of observations, that is, the frequencies with which each ability is actualized (marked by participant). Whenever a person relates his or her success or failure to a specific ability, we say that this ability has been actualized. Ability actualization is the index of the importance of each self-regulatory ability to a given person.

Satisfaction ratio (ability-related success) is the relative frequencies, based on the corresponding actualization frequencies, with which each ability is marked as a cause of success. Satisfaction ratio is the index of efficiency of each ability in the subjective opinion of a given person ["I succeeded (I achieved what I wanted) because of my ability to . . ."], I decided to use these terms (ability actualization and satisfaction ratio) in analogy to Brandstätter's motive actualization and motive satisfaction ratio.

Thus, the importance of self-regulatory ability in the subjective perception of examined persons was operationalized by the ability actualization ratio, while the efficiency of self-regulatory ability was operationalized by the ability satisfaction ratio.

General and situation-specific ability actualization and ability satisfaction ratio scores were computed. We took into account four classes of situations (work-home, leisure-home, work-out, leisure-out). "General" means that, by aggregating over the whole variety of situations in which the ability in question had been actualized, we need not bother about situation-specific individual differences in abilities.

The data collected with the Time Sampling Diary also provide a good opportunity for relating a person's ability structure to the demand structure of situations. The correlation between the individual ability profile and the situational demand is the measure of ability-demand fit, that is, a kind of person-environment fit (abiPEF).

Statistics

All computations were performed in four classes of situations and without reference to situations (general score) using 2 by 2 factorial design of ANOVA's with covariance control (action vs. state orientation x low vs. high reactivity, with mobility as covariate; and action vs. state orientation x low vs. high mobility, with reactivity as covariate). The criterion for dichotomization of groups of reactivity (low and high), mobility (low and high), and orientation (state versus action orientation) was ±0.3 standard deviation from the mean value, which corresponds roughly to one-third of the participants at the bottom end and one-third at the top end of the distribution. The unit of analysis is the person.

There are five dependent variables (abilities). Analyzing each ability separately is justified not only by the theoretical, but also by the empirical independence of those variables. The coefficients of correlation for the five ability actualization scores range from 0.01 to 0.25, and for the five satisfaction ratio scores, from 0.05 to 0.25, and all are insignificant.

Analyses of variance were performed separately for each class of situations. Actually, MANOVA would have been more appropriate because a person's way of responding in one class of situations is usually correlated with the way he or she tends to respond in other situations. However, since the SPSS-MANOVA excludes cases with missing values for any variable named on the MANOVA variable list, the sample of persons would have been too small and biased, favoring participants with activation and efficiency scores in each of the four classes of situations. Although ANOVA does not allow for testing the statistical significance of differences between situations in the effects of temperament and state versus action orientation on the actualization and efficiency of self-regulatory abilities, it shows how temperamental and volitional properties differentiate self-regulatory abilities in various kinds of situations.

Interdependence of both temperamental factors (the correlation between reactivity and mobility equals -0.55; $p < .001$; $N = 97$) determined the use of ANOVA with covariance control. The variance analysis results were adjusted for the linear relationships between the dependent variables and the covariates (reactivity or mobility as covariate respectively). The results, obtained from the analysis of variance in this way, demonstrate the clear influence of a single temperamental factor (reactivity and mobility, respectively), after excluding the influence of its covariate.

Results

Diary entries of five self-regulatory abilities on 40 days (four times a day) amounted to 5484 entries, which made up about 33% of all 26 abilities marked by participants (the total number of observations of abilities amounted to 16689). There were on average 56.5 diary entries of five self-regulatory abilities per person.

The results are presented in four subsections, corresponding to four research questions. The first presents the results concerning the effect that the temperamental and volitional properties have on the importance and efficiency of self-regulatory abilities in everyday life situations. The second deals with the effects of volitional characteristics. The third presents the results concerning the temperament-volition interaction effect on the importance and efficiency of self-regulatory abilities. Whenever the main effect turned out to be significant, there was no interaction effect involved that would have prevented the interpretation of the main effect.

Finally, the results concerning the temperament and volition effect on self-regulatory ability-demand fit are presented.

Self-Regulatory Abilities Related to Temperament

The significant differences between high- and low-reactive, and high- and low-mobile participants in mean values of (1) relative frequencies of ability actualization and (2) satisfaction ratios of abilities are shown in Table 4.1, which contains only those classes of situations, in which there are significant ($p < .05$) differences. Remember that the effects of reactivity are controlled for mobility and vice versa.

As shown in Table 4.1, low-reactive and, less frequently, high-mobile persons tend to have higher satisfaction (efficiency) ratios than high-reactive and low-mobile persons, respectively, particularly in leisure-home situations where all five self-regulatory abilities come up with effects significant at the 5%-level (two-tailed). Due tó missing data, the degrees of freedom of the error sum of squares vary between 11 and 59.[4] Because the direction of the difference had been predicted, a one-tailed test would have been justified, which would have given a

Table 4.1 Differences between High- (HR) and Low- (LR) Reactive Subjects and High- (HM) and Low- (LM) Mobile Subjects in Actualization and Satisfaction Ratios of Self-Regulatory Abilities

	Situations					
	General		Leisure-home		Leisure-out	
Abilities	1 Actualization	2 Satisfaction	3 Actualization	4 Satisfaction	5 Actualization	6 Satisfaction
1 Active attentional selectivity		**HM > LM** $M = 0.84$ $M = 0.69$ $SD = 0.17$ $SD = 0.17$ $F(1,59) = 6.24$; $p = .015$		**HM > LM** $M = 0.85$ $M = 0.64$ $SD = 0.30$ $SD = 0.33$ $F(1,40) = 8.13$; $p = .007$		
2 Emotion control	**LR > HR** $M = 4.69$ $M = 2.69$ $SD = 2.61$ $SD = 2.39$ $F(1,59) = 10.48$; $p = .002$			**LR > HR** $M = 0.94$ $M = 0.78$ $SD = 0.14$ $SD = 0.28$ $F(1,45) = 5.65$; $p = .022$		**HM > LM** $M = 0.93$ $M = 0.71$ $SD = 0.15$ $SD = 0.35$ $F(1,40) = 5.30$; $p = .027$
3 Parsimony of information-processing				**LR > HR** $M = 0.83$ $M = 0.41$ $SD = 0.35$ $SD = 0.46$ $F(1,11) = 10.23$; $p = .008$	**HM > LM** $M = 4.20$ $M = 1.21$ $SD = 6.09$ $SD = 2.63$ $F(1,56) = 6.55$; $p = .013$	

4 Motivation control		**LR > HR** $M = 0.86$ $M = 0.55$ $SD = 0.32$ $SD = 0.47$ $F(1,38) = 4.88$; $p = .033$
5 Environment control	**LR > HR** $M = 0.90$ $M = 0.76$ $SD = 0.22$ $SD = 0.25$ $F(1,59) = 7.08$; $p = .010$	**LR > HR** $M = 0.96$ $M = 0.75$ $SD = 0.12$ $SD = 0.31$ $F(1,26) = 7.80$; $p = .010$

Only significant ($p < .05$, two-tailed) differences are given in Table 4.1. After Scheffé adjustment for post hoc comparisons, the effects in the following cells are significant at the 5%-level (one-tailed): 21 (row 2, column 1), 52, 14, 34, and 54.

range of Type I error probabilities between .001 and .013. Of course, the true error probabilities are underestimated, because each effect was tested for four classes of situations, and reported in Table 4.1 only if $p < .05$ (two-tailed). Applying the Scheffé correction, post hoc comparisons (cf. Keppel, 1991, p. 172f.) yield five of the 10 effects reported in Table 4.1 as significant after adjustment of the alpha-level ($p < .05$, one-tailed), namely effects 21 (second row, first columns), 52, 14, 34, and 54.

Self-Regulatory Abilities Related to Action versus State Orientation

Significant differences between action- and state-oriented participants in mean values of ability actualization and satisfaction ratios are shown in Table 4.2.

Volitional properties differentiate chiefly satisfaction ratios of self-regulatory abilities, mostly in "work-out" situations. They do not affect self-regulatory abilities in "leisure-home" situations. Moreover, performance-related action versus state orientation (AOP) affects self-regulatory abilities only in "leisure-out" situations, whereas failure-related (AOF) and decision-related action versus state orientation (AOD) are particularly relevant in work situations (home and out).

In work situations, action-oriented persons (AOF and AOD) refer more often to self-regulatory abilities than state-oriented persons, and they also report more often efficient use of their abilities, that is, they attribute their momentary well-being to their efficient use of their self-regulatory abilities. In leisure-out situations, however, performance-related action-oriented persons (AOP) refer less often to their ability of environmental control and less often report the efficient use of motivation control than do performance-related state-oriented persons (SOP).

Temperament and Volition Interaction on Self-Regulatory Abilities

The analysis of the interaction between volitional and temperamental properties revealed that interaction of mobility (temperamental property) and decision-related action versus state orientation differentiates the actualization of motivation control in "work-out" situations ($F[1,59]; = 4.38.; p = .041$). This is illustrated in Figure 4.1.

According to Figure 4.1, the participants with internal "incoherence" between temperamental (mobility) and volitional properties revealed less actualization of motivation control in "work-out" situations than did the participants with "temperament-volition" coherence ($F[1,60] = 4.57, p = .037$). This means, that for the participants with "temperament-volition" coherence, motivation control in "work-out" situations is more important than for the participants with internal "incoherence". As mentioned before, "internal incoherence" means that there is a discrepancy between volitional and temperamental properties, that is, high mobility (high need of stimulation) and state orientation, or low mobility (low need of stimulation) and action orientation.

The actualization pattern of motivation control in "work-out" situations (presented in Figure 4.1) is the same for the interaction of mobility and failure-related action versus state orientation (another type of action vs. state orientation) ($F[1,57] = 11.12$; $p = .002$). This means that participants with internal "coherence" between temperamental (mobility) and volitional properties (AOD and AOF) perceived motivation control as a more important ability for "work-out" situations than did "incoherent" participants (no figure).

"Coherent" participants also have a higher satisfaction ratio of motivation control in "work-out" situations than do "incoherent" ones. This means that the self-reported efficiency of motivation control is higher in the case of "coherent" participants. The interaction of mobility and decision-related action versus state orientation (Mobility × AOD) ($F[1;39] = 4.59$; $p = .038$) (Figure 4.2), as well as the interaction of reactivity and decision-related action versus state orientation (Reactivity × AOD) ($F[1;42] = 7.24$; $p = .01$) (Figure 4.3) differentiates the satisfaction ratio of motivation control in "work-out" situations.

As shown in Figure 4.3, AOD differentiates satisfaction ratio mainly on a low level of reactivity. "Coherent" participants (low reactive and action oriented) more often than "incoherent" participants (low reactive and state oriented) marked motivation control as the cause of their success in "work-out" situations.

Moreover, the interaction of mobility and decision-related action versus state orientation (AOD) affects the satisfaction ratio of parsimony of information processing in "work-home" situations ($F[1;15] = 8.59$; $p = .01$). The pattern of satisfaction ratio of this ability is the same as the one presented in Figure 4.2. "Coherent" participants marked, more often than "incoherent" ones, parsimony of information processing in "work-home" situations as the cause of their success.

Temperament and Volition Effect on Ability-Demand Fit (abiPEF)

As a measure of ability-demand fit (abiPEF), the correlation (Pearson r with Fisher's norm transformation) (Góralski, 1976) between the individual self-regulatory ability profile and the situational demand profile was computed for each person. The individual ability profile was computed as the relative frequencies (based on the frequencies of actualization) with which a person marks each self-regulatory ability as a cause of success across situations. The situational demand profile was computed as the collective relative frequencies of actualization of abilities in the whole sample of participants in a specific situation (averages in specific situations across persons). This understanding of an ability-demand fit index follows Brandstätter's need-offer (motive-gratification) fit index (Brandstätter, 1994).

The situational demand structure, that is, the mean values[5] and standard deviations of relative frequencies of actualization of self-regulatory abilities in the entire sample of participants in a specific situation, are presented in Table 4.3.

As shown in Table 4.3, the list of abilities contains four general ones (conscientiousness, psychological endurance, having one's way, will power) that are included in the complete list of 26 abilities given to participants during the coding procedure in Brandstätter's TSD. They are, despite the different (more general) level of description, connected with self-regulatory abilities, and they facilitate the protection and maintenance of current intention. This is the reason for including them in the "ability-demand" analysis.

Table 4.2 Differences between Action- and State-Oriented Participants in Actualization and Satisfaction Ratios of Self-Regulatory Abilities

	General		Leisure-home		Work-home		Work-out	
Abilities	1 Actualization	2 Satisfaction	3 Actualization	4 Satisfaction	5 Actualization	6 Satisfaction	7 Actualization	8 Satisfaction
1 Active attentional selectivity					**AOF > SOF** $M = 10.65$ $M = 5.35$ $SD = 9.2$ $SD = 7.70$ $F(1,50) = 4.04;$ $p = .050$			**AOF > SOF** $M = 0.82$ $M = 0.62$ $SD = 0.21$ $SD = 0.30$ $F(1,47) = 7.71;$ $p = .008$ **AOD > SOD** $M = 0.85$ $M = 0.70$ $SD = 0.19$ $SD = 0.29$ $F(1,53) = 4.73;$ $p = .034$
2 Emotion control		**AOD > SOD** $M = 0.89$ $M = 0.72$ $SD = 0.20$ $SD = 0.35$ $F(1,57) = 4.57;$ $p = .037$						**AOF > SOF** $M = 0.81$ $M = 0.58$ $SD = 0.31$ $SD = 0.36$ $F(1,49) = 4.05;$ $p = .050$

3 Parsimony of information-processing	**AOD > SOD** $M = 0.78$ $M = 0.59$ $SD = 0.26$ $SD = 0.32$ $F(1,57) = 5.00$; $p = .029$			**AOF > SOF** $M = 2.41$ $M = 1.09$ $SD = 3.15$ $SD = 1.79$ $F(1,54) = 4.03$; $p = .050$	**AOD > SOD** $M = 0.84$ $M = 0.51$ $SD = 0.26$ $SD = 0.42$ $F(1,29) = 7.02$; $p = .013$
4 Motivation control	**AOD > SOD** $M = 5.71$ $M = 3.66$ $SD = 3.32$ $SD = 3.50$ $F(1,59) = 8.84$; $p = .004$	**AOP < SOP** $M = 0.50$ $M = 0.97$ $SD = 0.49$ $SD = 0.09$ $F(1,21) = 8.08$; $p = .010$	**AOF > SOF** $M = 0.81$ $M = 0.61$ $SD = 0.20$ $SD = 0.44$ $F(1,23) = 4.41$; $p = .047$	**AOF > SOF** $M = 0.85$ $M = 0.54$ $SD = 0.30$ $SD = 0.41$ $F(1,40) = 7.33$; $p = .010$	
5 Environment control	**AOP < SOP** $M = 2.58$ $M = 12.12$ $SD = 4.04$ $SD = 17.54$ $F(1,48) = 4.05$; $p = .050$	**AOP < SOP** $M = 0.59$ $M = 0.90$ $SD = 0.44$ $SD = 0.28$ $F(1,28) = 7.65$; $p = .010$		**AOF > SOF** $M = 0.85$ $M = 0.48$ $SD = 0.32$ $SD = 0.46$ $F(1,37) = 5.95$; $p = .020$	

Only significant ($p < .05$, two-tailed) differences are given in Table 4.2. After Scheffé adjustment for post hoc comparisons, the effects in the following cells are significant at the 5%-level (one-tailed): 41 (row 4, column 1), 44, 54, 18 (first entry), 38, and 48.

AOP—performance-related action-oriented participants
AOF—failure-related action-oriented participants
AOD—decision-related action-oriented participants
SOP—performance-related state-oriented participants
SOF—failure-related state-oriented participants
SOD—decision-related state-oriented participants

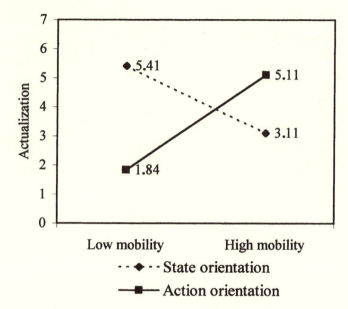

Figure 4.1. Actualization percentages of "motivation control" in "work-out" situations in relation to subjects' level of mobility and their decision-related action versus state orientation (AOD).

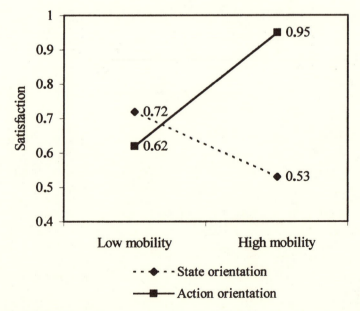

Figure 4.2 Satisfaction ratio of "motivation control" in "work-out" situations in relation to subjects' level of mobility and their decision-related action versus state orientation (AOD).

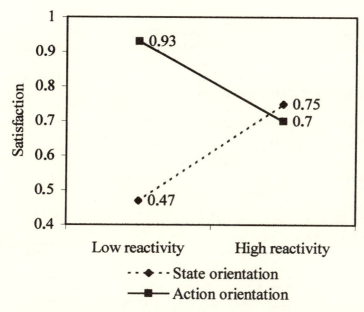

Figure 4.3. Satisfaction ratio of "motivation control" in "work-out" situations relation to subjects' level of reactivity and their decision-related action versus state
orientation (AOD).

Table 4.3 Situational Demand Structure for Self-Regulatory Abilities

Abilities	Situation			
	Leisure-home	Leisure-out	Work-home	Work-out
Conscientiousness	M = 5.93	M = 5.42	M = 8.37	M = 7.62
	SD = 8.18	SD = 8.74	SD = 14.13	SD = 8.71
Psychological endurance	M = 5.52	M = 3.77	M = 4.26	M = 4.38
	SD = 8.89	SD = 5.65	SD = 6.46	SD = 8.71
Having one's way	M = 2.45	M = 3.75	M = 3.14	M = 2.69
	SD = 6.93	SD = 6.63	SD = 15.98	SD = 3.11
Will power	M = 6.78	M = 3.97	M = 5.86	M = 3.11
	SD = 9.86	SD = 6.80	SD = 12.31	SD = 3.95
Active attentional selec-tivity	M = 7.34	M = 9.03	M = 7.90	M = 15.55
	SD = 10.41	SD = 10.06	SD = 10.94	SD = 11.04
Emotion control	M = 10.30	M = 10.56	M = 10.42	M = 9.87
	SD = 10.46	SD = 10.99	SD = 14.66	SD = 7.64
Parsimony of information processing	M = 1.64	M = 2.21	M = 2.00	M = 1.73
	SD = 3.61	SD = 4.42	SD = 3.84	SD = 2.75
Motivation control	M = 5.87	M = 5.06	M = 5.58	M = 4.11
	SD = 9.28	SD = 9.77	SD = 15.13	SD = 4.63
Environment control	M = 3.61	M = 6.68	M = 5.24	M = 4.01
	SD = 5.85	SD = 12.46	SD = 11.39	SD = 5.97

Since the present report concentrates on ability-demand fit, we do not go into a detailed analysis of the situational demand structure. However, we can see that active attentional selectivity has the highest relative frequency of actualization in work-out situations, and emotion control in all other situations.

A 2 (action vs. state-orientation) by 2 (low vs. high reactivity or low vs. high mobility) ANOVA with covariance control of mobility and reactivity, respectively, revealed that only volitional property, that is, failure-related action versus state orientation (AOF), affects the ability-demand fit in all classes of situations:

- In "leisure-home" situations ($F[1;59] = 4.18$; $p = .045$) M (mean value of Pearson r with Fisher's norm transformation) for action-oriented participants (AOF) = 0.45; M for state-oriented participants (SOF) = 0.26)
- In "leisure-out" situations ($F[1;59] = 6.27$; $p = .015$) M(AOF) = 0.59; M(SOF) = 0.31
- In "work-home" situations ($F[1;59] = 5.11$; $p = .028$) M(AOF) = 0.56; M(SOF) = 0.38
- In "work-out" situations ($F[1;59] = 5.25$; $p = .026$) M(AOF) = 0.58; M(SOF) = 0.33

The correlation between the individual self-regulatory ability profile and the situational demand profile is higher among action-oriented participants than among state-oriented participants in all classes of situations.

Discussion

The analysis of the main effects of temperament and volition revealed that temperamental and volitional properties differentiate the importance and efficiency of self-regulatory abilities in different kinds of situations. Temperamental properties mostly affect the satisfaction, caused by self-regulatory abilities, and mostly in "leisure-home" situations. They do not differentiate the satisfaction derived from self-regulatory abilities in work situations (either at home, or out). Referring frequently to an ability as the perceived cause of success (self-reported measure of efficiency) can be conceived of as an indirect indication of a high individual efficiency in that ability. Therefore, we can conclude that temperament affects the efficiency of self-regulatory abilities mainly in situations that are under the control of the individual, with self-initiated activities and with relatively few social pressures (demands).

The low-reactive persons more often refer to emotion control, that is, the importance of emotion control as a self-regulatory ability is generally (across situations) higher for low-reactive persons than for high-reactive ones. They also more frequently attribute their success in "leisure-home" situations to emotion control, parsimony of information processing, motivation control, and environment control than do high-reactive persons. This means that the self-reported efficiency of those abilities in "leisure-home" situations is higher for low-reactive persons than for high-reactive ones. These results (mainly those concerning emotion control and parsimony of information processing) are consistent with empirical evidence concerning the differences between high- and low-reactive persons (low reactives are less impulsive, more effective in stress situations, and more resistant emotionally) (Strelau, 1983). They are also less neurotic (Strelau, 1983). Neu-roticism is connected with excessive procrastination during decision-making (anxiety is characterized by a degenerated intention, which may result in insuf-ficient parsimony of information-processing, i.e., the process of generating new information regarding various action alternatives may be dilatory) (Kuhl, 1984).

Highly mobile participants more frequently relate their success to active atten-tional selectivity than do low-mobile ones. According to the arousal model, per-formance depends on the amount of stimulation provided by the task (Eysenck, 1967). Thus, participants with a greater need for stimulation (extraverts, low reac-tives, high mobiles—there is a correlation between these variables) perform better (demonstrate better attentional selectivity) in more demanding tasks (Matthews, 1985). On the other hand, high-mobile persons more frequently attribute their success to active attentional selectivity in "leisure-home" situations, that is, in situations with relatively low social pressure and distractions. This result is con-sistent with my previous findings obtained in an experimental study (Marszał-Wiśniewska, 1998). Experimental data reveal that mobility in relation to a task condition (distraction) affects the efficiency of attention selectivity. Only low-mobile persons were stimulated by the increase in task difficulty. High-mobile persons demonstrated a shorter reaction time (the measure of efficiency) than did low-mobile ones, especially in the no-distraction condition, which can be per-ceived as somewhat similar to "leisure-home" situations.

Unlike temperament, volitional properties affect self-regulatory abilities in "work-out" situations and not in "leisure-home" situations. Action versus state orientation, as well as temperament, affects primarily the self-reported efficiency of self-regulatory abilities (satisfaction ratios). As expected, according to Kuhl's theory, the action-oriented individuals, more often than the state-oriented ones, attribute their success to their self-regulatory abilities, especially in "work-out" situations. In these situations, the decision-related action-oriented participants, more often than the state-oriented participants, attributed their success to parsi-mony of information-processing and active attentional selectivity, whereas the failure-related action-oriented participants attributed it to emotion, motivation, and environment control, and also to active attentional selectivity. These findings indicate a similar, but not identical pattern of association with both types of ac-tion orientation with respect to the self-reported measures of self-regulatory abil-ities. Evidence for functional differences between the failure and decision com-ponents of action orientation with respect to self-regulation was also obtained by other authors (Kuhl & Beckmann, 1994). The pattern of relation between the performance-related action orientation and the self-regulatory abilities differs from the one obtained for the failure and decision components. The performance-related action orientation affects self-regulatory abilities only in "leisure-out" sit-uations. In these situations, the importance and efficiency of environment control is lower for performance-related action-oriented participants than for state-oriented ones. We do not have enough information to explain this result. How-ever, we may suppose that the actualization pattern of environment control for state-oriented participants is probably connected with their focusing on the goal, rather than on the action itself.

The analysis of interaction of volitional and temperamental properties re-vealed that motivation control as a self-regulatory ability is more important in "work-out" situations for the participants with internal "coherence" between temperamental and volitional properties than for the participants with internal "incoherence." The efficiency of motivation control in the same situations is also higher for "coherent" participants. This result confirms my thesis about the efficiency-reducing effects of a discrepancy between volitional and temperamental properties, and is consistent with my previous findings (Marszał-Wiśniewska, 1998). Motivation control is one of the most complex self-regulatory abilities (it may involve selective attentional process and is especially important whenever the current intention is supported by a weak action tendency, which may very frequently occur during work-related, routine activities).

In accordance with theoretical consideration, action-oriented participants are characterized by better ability-demand fit than state-oriented ones. However, this result refers only to failure-related action-oriented participants, and is similar in all classes of situations. Failure-related state orientation, having the highest positive correlation with level of anxiety of all state-orientation types (Kuhl, 1984), seems to be more strongly connected with the ability-demand misfit than the other types of state orientation.

The results presented form a coherent picture and are in line with the theoretical reasoning integrating the construct of temperament with the construct of action versus state-orientation in analyzing self-regulatory processes in a variety of everyday life situations. Nevertheless, the study, as a first attempt at using time-sampling diary data for exploring action-control activities in relation to temperament and action versus state orientation, was designed mainly for exploring a field rather than for testing very specific hypotheses. This justifies the research strategy of performing multiple comparisons and reporting only significant contrasts, without adjusting the alpha-level for multiple comparisons. Further research is needed to verify and strengthen the conclusions drawn from the presented study.

Conclusions

The following conclusions may be drawn from this study:

1. The results indicate, that temperamental and volitional properties affect the efficiency of self-regulatory abilities in different kinds of situations. Temperamental properties affect that efficiency mostly in "leisure-home" situations, whereas volitional properties affect primarily "work-out" situations.

2. The study confirms the thesis about the efficiency-reducing effects of discrepancy between volitional and temperamental properties. The participants with internal "coherence" between temperamental and volitional properties more often actualize their "motivational control" ability, and more frequently relate their success to that ability in work situations. The importance and efficiency of motivation control in work situations is higher for "coherent" participants than for "incoherent" ones.

3. The findings concerning the relation between action versus state orientation and self-regulatory abilities, as reported by subjects, are consistent

with Kuhl's Action Control Theory (Kuhl, 1985, 1994). Moreover, they may indicate, that failure-related state orientation is more strongly connected with the ability-demand misfit than the other types of state orientation.

Notes

This study was supported by the National Committee for Scientific Research (Grant no. 1P106 012 06).

1. There is a similarity between the physiological mechanism of introversion/extraversion and the physiological mechanism of reactivity as a basic temperament dimension (Strelau, 1983).
2. In most studies, the assessment of reactivity is indirect, that is, based on the Pavlovian strength of excitation. Reactivity is the opposite of the strength of excitation: The higher the strength of excitation, the lower the reactivity (Strelau, 1983).
3. I omitted "encoding control" as an ability connected with "active attentional selectivity" and difficult to assess with self-report measures.
4. Considerable differences in the degrees of freedom for particular satisfaction ratios result from the different number of persons who actualized particular self-regulatory abilities.
5. Mean values for each self-regulatory ability in a specific situation were calculated as the sum of relative frequencies of actualization (based on the frequencies of actualization of all abilities) of each person divided by the number of persons.

References

Brandstätter, H. (1994). Well-being and motivational person-environment fit. A time sampling study of emotions. *European Journal of Personality, 8,* 75–93.

Eliasz, A. (1981). *Temperament a system regulacji stymulacji* [Temperament and system of stimulation control]. Warsaw: PWN.

Eliasz, A. (1985). Transactional model of temperament. In J. Strelau (Ed.), *Temperamental bases of behavior: Studies on individual differences* (pp. 41–78). Lisse: Swets & Zetlinger.

Eliasz, A. (1990). Broadening the concept of temperament: From disposition to hypothetical construct. *European Journal of Personality, 4,* 287–302.

Endler, N. S., & Magnusson, D. (1976). *Interactional psychology and personality.* Washington, DC: Hemisphere.

Eysenck, H. J. (1967). *The biological basis of personality.* Springfield, IL: Thomas.

Fiske, D. W., & Maddi, S. R. (1961). *Functions of varied experience.* Homewood: Dorey.

Góralski, A. (1976). *Metody opisu i wnioskowania statystycznego w psychologii* [Methods of statistical description and inference in psychology]. Warsaw: PWN.

Gray, J. A. (1972). The psychophysiological nature of introversion-extraversion: A modification of Eysencky's theory. In V. D. Nebylitsyn & J. A. Gray (Eds.), *Biological basis of individual behavior* (pp. 182–205). London: Academic Press.

Gray, J. A. (1982). *The neuropsychology of anxiety.* New York: Oxford University Press.

Hettema, P. J. (1989). *Personality and environment. Assessment of human adaptation.* Chichester: Wiley.

Holland, J. L. (1985). *Making vocational choices* (2nd ed.) Englewood Cliffs, NJ: Prentice Hall.

Jahoda, M. (1961). A social-psychological approach to the study of culture. *Human Relations, 14,* 23–30.

Kanfer, R., Dugdale, B., & McDonald, B. (1994). Empirical findings on the action control scale in the context of complex skill acquisition. In J. Kuhl & J. Beckmann (Eds.) , *Volition and Personality. Action versus state orientation* (pp. 61–77). Göttingen: Hogrefe.

Keppel, G. (1991). *Design and analysis. A researcher's handbook* (3rd ed.). Englewood Cliffs, NJ: Prentice Hall.

Kuhl, J. (1984). Volitional aspects of achievement motivation and learned helplessness: Toward a comprehensive theory of action control. In B. A. Maher (Ed.), *Progress in experimental personality research* (pp. 99–171). New York: Academic Press.

Kuhl, J. (1985). Volitional mediators of cognition-behavior consistency: Self-regulatory processes and action versus state orientation. In J. Kuhl & J. Beckmann (Eds.), *Action control: From cognition to behavior* (pp. 101–128). Berlin: Springer.

Kuhl, J. (1986). Motivation and information-processing: A new look at decision making, dynamic change, and action control. In R. M. Sorrentino & E. T. Higgins (Eds.), *The handbook of motivation and cognition: Foundations of social behavior* (pp. 404–434). New York: Guilford Press.

Kuhl, J. (1992). A theory of self-regulation: Action versus state orientation, self-discrimination, and some applications. *Applied Psychology, 41*, 95–173.

Kuhl, J. (1994). A theory of action and state orientations. In J. Kuhl & J. Beckmann (Eds.), *Volition and Personality. Action versus state orientation* (pp. 9–46). Göttingen: Hogrefe.

Kuhl, J., & Beckmann, J. (Eds.). (1994). *Volition and personality. Action versus state orientation.* Göttingen: Hogrefe.

Marszał-Wiśniewska, M. (1992). Temperament a kontrola wolicjonalna u młodzieży [Temperament and volitional control among young people.] In A. Eliasz & M. Marszał-Wiśniewska (Eds.), *Temperament a rozwój młodzieży* (pp. 53–74). Warsaw: Institute of Psychology, Polish Academy of Sciences.

Marszał-Wiśniewska, M. (1994). Temperament, action versus state orientation and Type A Behavior in group of managers. *Polish Psychological Bulletin, 25*, 25–31.

Marszał-Wiśniewska, M. (1998). Temperamental and volitional determinants. *Personality Psychology in Europe, 6*, 132–137.

Matthews, G. (1985). The effects of extraversion and arousal on intelligence test performance. *British Journal of Psychology, 76*, 479–493.

Pervin, L. A. (1976). Performance and satisfaction as a function of individual-environment fit. In N. S. Endler & D. Magnusson (Eds.), *Interactional psychology and personality* (pp. 71–89). New York: Wiley.

Scott, V. B., & McIntosh, W. D. (1999). The development of a trait measure of ruminative thought. *Personality and Individual Differences, 26*, 1045–1056.

Strelau, J. (1983). *Temperament—personality—activity.* London: Academic Press.

Strelau, J., Angleitner, A., Bantelmann, J., & Ruch, W. (1990). The Strelau Temperament Inventory—Revised (STI-R): Theoretical considerations and scale development and scale development. *European Journal of Personality, 4*, 209–235.

Strelau, J., Zawadzki, B., & Angleitner, A. (1995). Kwestionariusz Temperamentu PTS: Próba psychologicznej interpretacji podstawowych cech układu nerwowego według Pawłowa [Pavlovian Temperament Survey (PTS): An effort of a psychological interpretation of Pavlov's basic properties of the nervous system]. *Studia Psychologiczne, 33*, 9–48.

Zalewska, A. (1992). Przejawy konformizmu w systemie wartości a siła woli u młodzieży o różnej reaktywności [Conformity in values system and will power in youth with different level of reactivity]. In A. Eliasz & M. Marszał-Wiśniewska (Eds.), *Temperament a rozwój młodzieży* (pp. 75–100). Warsaw: Institute of Psychology, Polish Academy of Sciences.

Zuckerman, M. (1979). *Sensation seeking: Beyond the optimal level of arousal.* Hillsdale, NJ: Lawrence Erlbaum.

5

Value-Motive Congruence and Reactivity as Determinants of Well-Being

Anna M. Zalewska & Hermann Brandstätter

Well-being is a notion that has been studied by a large number of disciplines. It has been defined in many terms and labeled with many names, including happiness, quality of life, and life satisfaction. Veenhoven (1991) presents a classification of current well-being concepts and underlines that, from an individual perspective, well-being should be measured only subjectively. Subjective well-being refers to the question of how much a person likes the life he or she leads. Appraisals of life can be considered in two aspects: an affective aspect (how well a person usually feels) and a cognitive aspect (how a person thinks about the fulfillment of her or his aspirations or needs). The first aspect usually is called happiness, the second life satisfaction. Happiness is considered an emotional state, whereas life satisfaction is related to a cognitive, judgmental process (Lewinsohn, Redner, & Seeley, 1991). Incongruent data about connections between these aspects of well-being are reported (Brandstätter, 1991; Veenhoven, 1991). Lewinsohn et al. (1991) point out that they may be conditioned by different factors—for example, age influences life satisfaction but not happiness. Well-being can be studied within certain domains (work, marriage, family) or with respect to life as a whole.

In this chapter only the affective aspect of subjective well-being (how well a person usually feels) is considered. Emotions are understood as the most immediate but complex responses of a person involved in the process of adaptation to the changes of internal states and external conditions. Two dimensions (frequency of positive and negative emotions and their intensity) of emotional responses to everyday life situations are included in one operational variable called "mood." The term "mood" is considered here as a continuum from very negative through indifferent to very positive emotions, regardless of their quality. The distinction between, for example, anger and fear, on the one

95

hand, or between happiness and triumph, on the other hand, is omitted. Thus, in this article "mood" is used as a synonym for the affective aspect of well-being in the moment of self-observation. A self-report on mood (in a broader sense) is supposed to mirror emotions elicited by remembered, presently experienced, or expected events of some personal relevance as well as the more basic hedonic tuning (mood in the narrow sense). As direct experience in a number of specific situations, mood is less open to defensive distortion and social desirability effects than is the cognitive appraisal of the quality of life (Brandstätter, 1991).

The present study aims at analyzing the interplay among a person's reactivity (in the sense of Strelau, 1983), the specific value-motive domain (achievement, affiliation, and power), and the situations (workplace or elsewhere) as they affect mood and motive satisfaction.

There are some theoretical premises and empirical data to suggest that well-being is connected with personality characteristics. Happy people tend to have an internal locus of control (Lewinsohn et al., 1991). Eysenck (1981) contends that high neuroticism increases sensitivity to punishment and failures, and facilitates negative emotions and worries. McCrae (1994) indicates a positive correlation between neuroticism and negative emotionality, as well as between extraversion and positive emotionality (see DeNeve & Cooper, 1998, for a recent metaanalysis). Significant connections of extraversion with positive emotions and with mood, moderated by types of situations, are also reported by Brandstätter (1991, 1994). We assume that how well-being is reflected in mood also depends on some other individual characteristics. One of these, considered later in this chapter, is the value-motive congruence, which, according to Rogers (1964), is an important factor in determining a person's well-being and health. Another factor is reactivity, a characteristic of a person's temperament, that is assumed to differentiate sensitivity to stimuli, a need for stimulation, and vulnerability to stress. Eliasz in his transactional model of temperament (1985, 1990, this volume) underlines the importance of consistency between temperament and personality dimensions for a person's functioning. According to this model, one can conclude that the impact of interactions between these two variables (value-motive congruence and reactivity) on well-being should also be considered. Extrapolating from the person-environment fit theory (Brandstätter, 1989, 1994, this volume), one can suppose that persons' well-being and effective performance depend on the interplay of individual properties and external conditions. It also means that the role of individual characteristics for well-being can be different in various situations.

In the present study, emotional responses are studied in two types of everyday life situations—at the workplace and out of it—with respect to reactivity and value-motive congruence as conditions of well-being. Of interest are interactions (a) between cognitive and affective evaluation (values and motives), showing disparity or congruence of the two systems, (b) between reactivity and value-motive congruence, and (c) between individual and environmental characteristics.

Hypotheses

Well-Being and Reactivity

According to Eliasz (1981, 1985, 1990) and Strelau (1983), reactivity is a basic dimension of temperament. It determines sensitivity to and ability to endure stimuli, intensity of reactions to stimuli, and a need for stimulation that is defined by an optimum or a range of stimulation that brings about a sense of well-being and high efficiency of action.[1]

Disturbances in stimulation control lead to discrepancy between the incoming and the desired stimulation. They can cause negative emotions and stress, a decrease of action efficiency, or an increase of psychosomatic costs, evident in physiological indicators and emotional tension (Klonowicz, 1974, 1987; Strelau, 1983, 1988, 1998) or in the form of somatic diseases (Eliasz & Wrześniewski, 1991) and somatic complaints (Zalewska, 1995, 1996a), especially when persons have to adapt themselves to excessive stimulation. We assume that the prolonged incidence of excessive stimulation leads to increased sensitivity (a passive form of stimulation control, according to Eliasz, 1981, 1985) and makes a person focus on his or her inner state, characterized mostly by a diminished sense of well-being.

Persons who are high-reactive (HR) need a lower degree of stimulation to feel good and to perform in their best manner than low-reactive (LR) persons. Thus, the former are more often in danger of being overstimulated than the latter, who are more often in danger of being understimulated, which is connected with smaller costs. This is especially true today, since everyday life situations in our times are often highly stimulating because of the rapid pace of life, the variability of situations, and the impact of the huge amounts of information with which we all are inundated. Moreover, high sensitivity to social stimuli and low resistance to social pressure (Eliasz, 1981, 1987; Strelau, 1983) provokes HR persons to undertake tasks or behavior that are in compliance with social demands in spite of their highly stimulating value (Eliasz, this volume; Eliasz & Wrześniewski, 1991). Furthermore, Eliasz (1981, 1985, 1990) claims that HR persons notice smaller deviations from the optimal level of stimulation and react more strongly to them than do LRs. As a result, they can suffer more than the LRs in situations with too high or too low stimulation. An experiment with sensory deprivation reported by Strelau (1983) confirms this assumption concerning the negative effects of suboptimal stimulation. Finally, findings from many studies tell us that HR persons are higher on neuroticism and anxiety, as well as more vulnerable to stress, than the LRs (Strelau, 1983, 1988, 1995, 1998).

These premises lead to the conclusion that HR persons more often than LRs have to act at non-optimal levels of stimulation and therefore experience stress more often. Data obtained from students on health complaints and two kinds of anxiety are congruent with this conclusion (Zalewska, 1995). Furthermore, there are good reasons to assume that the HRs are more prone to negative emotions and as a result experience worse moods in everyday life situations than LRs. Data from bank employees confirm that the LRs show better moods at a new workplace (Zalewska, 1997), as well as in general across various life situations (Zalewska, 1996a), than do HRs and those who have moderate (MR) reactivity.

Additionally, LR persons, in comparison to HRs and MRs, demonstrate more satisfaction associated with all categories of actualized motives but one (Higher Motives composed of religion, altruism, and aesthetics) (Zalewska, 1996b). Thus, we can expect that reactivity influences well-being in a similar way in various kinds of situations:

> *Hypothesis H1: Low-reactives (LRs) generally feel better than high-reactives (HRs).*

Well-Being and Value-Motive Congruence

Like Epstein (1989), Feather (1990), and Zalewska (1996b), we assume that values and motives fulfill the same functions—they make up the criteria of choices and preferences, assign valence and importance to objects and events, and organize experiences and actions. Thus, it seems reasonable to treat them together as a valuation system. However, in spite of Epstein's (1989) suggestion, we conceive of values and motives as different, not because of their subject—as Feather (1990) claims—but because of their formal characteristics, since all the values have common formal features (Schwartz & Bilsky, 1990). Values differ from motives in the modus of preference expression (evaluative opinions on a cognitive level vs. emotions and behavioral tendencies on an affective level), generality level, degree of consciousness, and verbalization. Values and motives differ with respect to the contribution of cognitive processes, the dependence on culture, and the type of measurement.

In our view, motives are preferences closely linked to affect and influenced by culture only to a minor degree. They are expressed primarily in emotional reactions in particular situations and need not be conscious. We can infer them from behavior, emotions, and thoughts associated with emotions. In contrast, values are preferences expressed in stable, general, conscious, and easy-to-verbalize beliefs, that are strongly influenced by culture. They may be investigated by direct verbal expressions.

Schwartz and Bilsky (1990) claim that there is a correspondence between the importance of values and the importance of motivation domains. We agree, however, with Epstein (1989), McClelland (1980), and Winter, John, Steward, Klohnen, and Duncan (1998), who contend that the outcomes of valuation processes can be different on both the cognitive and the affective levels, dependent on the kind of situation and type of person.

Generally, there are three sources of the values' importance: organism's needs, social impacts, and information processing (Reykowski, 1992). It is possible that incongruence between the importance of values and the importance of motives can occur as a result of long-term social impact and social desirability effects. A person's needs can be neglected or restrained by the culture in which the person lives. As a result, events and the objects connected with them may be important on the affective level (important motives), but at the same time be treated as unimportant on the cognitive level (value with low importance). In other words, a person can react strongly to something on an emotional level, even though she or he knows or thinks that it is not really important. Inversely, some socially desirable events or objects may become important for a person only on the cognitive level, even though the person does not react emotionally to them: the person knows or thinks that something is important, although she or he does not feel that it is. This is the other form of value-motive incongruence. Incongruence may also come from excessive satisfaction or deprivation of a person's needs. Like Maslow (1954), we assume that deprivation of motive satisfaction augments its importance, which is not necessarily reflected in changes of values. Sometimes, because of defensive mechanisms (especially rationalization), we can observe even the reverse effects. When a person is not effective in achieving goals or objects connected with important motives, she or he tends to understate their importance ("sour grapes") and at the same time accentuates the importance of obtainable goals and objects ("sweet lemons") on the cognitive level.

Additionally, we assume that value-motive congruence can be trans-situationally inconsistent, because the importance of motives can vary across different classes of situations. For example, achievement motives probably are more important at the workplace than outside of it, although the person can have relatively stable general beliefs about the importance of achievement values. It could also be that, for some people, achievement motives are very important only at the workplace, whereas for other persons these motives may be important in almost all situations. Thus, for a certain person values and motives may be congruent in one class of situations and incongruent in another one.

Incongruence between values and motives appears in two forms: values may be less important than the motives, or values may be more important than the motives. It is assumed that congruence allows us to predict behavior from declared values, but incongruence makes such a prediction difficult. Whether values or motives are the better predictors of behavior is, however, an open question. Congruence is supposed to facilitate a person's well-being and efficiency, whereas incongruence leads to inner conflicts and hesitations, making a person's goal striving difficult and causing negative mood (cf. Sheldon & Elliot, 1999; Wilson, 1967). Rogers (1964) points out the disturbing effects of inconsistency between valences on the cognitive and the affective levels. For example, it can block a person's development and cause disorders and diseases.

> *Hypothesis H2: Congruence of values and motives is accompanied by better mood than their incongruence.*

Interaction of Value-Motive Congruence and Reactivity

Since incongruence of values and motives is a source of higher internal stimulation, one should expect an interaction between reactivity and value-motive congruence.

> *Hypothesis H3: Value-motive congruence affects well-being of HRs more strongly than the well-being of LRs.*

Interaction of the Situation with Value-Motive Congruence and Reactivity

In this study, two types of situations are taken into account—situations at the workplace and situations outside it. "Work-in" situations are assumed to offer the individual less freedom and fewer possibilities for control as well as presenting stronger external control (being under supervision, experiencing work demands and evaluations), than are available in "work-out" situations.

It seems likely that in situations with restricted freedom and strong external control, in contrast to situations with more freedom and less external control, the impact of individual qualities on subjective well-being becomes less important and less visible (see Kiss, Dornai, & Brandstätter, this volume). The data concerning mood in general and mood at a new workplace (Zalewska, 1996a, 1997) are congruent with this suggestion, although other categories of motives have been used here and there. Probably, mood at work is strongly conditioned by external variables (work demands) or both instrumental (demands-abilities) and motivational person-environment fit. Brandstätter (this volume) presents data that accord with this suggestion in relation to the motivational person-environment fit.[2]

These premises allow us to expect:

> Hypothesis H4: Reactivity and value-motive congruence strongly influence well-being outside the workplace, whereas their impact on well-being at the workplace is rather light.

Method

Participants and Procedure

Sixty bank employees, 20 to 55 years of age, about two-thirds women, who had entered the company one to three months before, participated in the study, which extended over six months. Questionnaires were administered between the four periods of self-observation with the Time Sampling Diary (TSD).

Instruments and Indices

The Strelau Temperament Inventory-Revised (Strelau, Angleitner, Bantelman, & Ruch, 1990), now called the Pavlovian Temperament Survey, was used to assess reactivity. The higher the score on the "Excitation Scale," the lower the reactivity (for more details see Eliasz, in this volume).

The importance of values was assessed with the Orientation to Work Values Inventory by Seifert and Bergmann (1983), adapted from Super's (1970) Work Values Inventory. It comprises 16 specific values (the Orientation to Work Values Inventory contains one modified value—"leisure orientation" instead of "style of life"-and one additional value—"possibility of promotion"—that distinguish it from Super's inventory). Each value is described by three statements about work values, which the respondent must rate on a five-point scale from 5 (very important) to 1 (not important). For example, one of the three statements for Achievement is: "For me, in my professional job, the realization that I have done something very well is. . . ."

The Time Sampling Diary (TSD) by Brandstätter (1989, 1991, this volume) was used to diagnose emotional states, actualized motives, and their importance for a person in different types of everyday life situations. Participants answered seven questions:

1. Is my mood at the moment rather negative, indifferent or rather positive?
2. How can I describe my momentary mood state using one or two adjectives?
3. Why do I feel as I have indicated?
4. Where am I?
5. What am I doing?
6. Who else is present?
7. To what extent do I feel free to choose to stay in or leave my present activity?

Each person answered the questions at randomly selected moments (different for each day and person), on average four times per day for 10 days over three consecutive months and for 10 days in the sixth month of research (about 160 measurements per person).

Well-being at the workplace and outside of it has been estimated on the basis of answers to the first question coded from 1 (very negative) to 5 (very positive) and on the relative frequencies with which the motives have been rated as satisfied if actualized.

Regarding the third question of the TSD, the participants related each of the reported momentary mood states to up to three motives (out of a list of 26 motives) as satisfied or frustrated. The original list (see Brandstätter, this volume), which contained 19 motives, was complemented by seven additional motives in the Polish version. Importance of a given motive (or category of motives) has been estimated by the relative frequency of actualization of this motive (or category of motives) in the respective class of situations, whether satisfied or frustrated.

An attempt to match the value classification with the motive classification by running separate factor analyses of the two domains and coordinating their factor scores failed. Therefore, we chose an intuitive phenomenological approach combined with the use of internal consistency coefficients in matching broad categories of values with broad categories of motives, relying to some extent on nine expert judges who had suggested which categories of values belonged to which categories of motives (Table 5.1).

Only three classes of motives, comprising the most commonly used and most extensively studied categories of achievement, affiliation, and power (cf. Heckhausen, 1991), are considered in the following analyses in order to keep the number of variables at a manageable level. Because of the ipsative scoring of motive importance (for each person the importance scores, i.e., the relative frequencies of motive actualization, sum to 1.00), selecting these three categories, which comprise about 50% of all motive diary entries, means that the regression analyses to be reported later refer actually to four motive classes: achievement, affiliation, power, and "all others."

Results

Internal Consistency of Value Importance, Motive Importance, and Reactivity

Table 5.2 presents the coefficients of internal consistency (Cronbach's alpha) for the value and motive scales.

Table 5.1 Matching of Values and Motives

Domains	Values	Motives
Achievement	Intellectual stimulation (4)	Achievement (1)
	Achievement (6)	Experience (2)
	Variety of activities (14)	Activity (3)
		Understanding (16)
		New difficult tasks (25)
Affiliation	Altruism (1)	Affiliation (5)
	Relations with superiors (12)	Sex (7)
	Relations with colleagues (13)	Love (12)
		Nurturance (14)
Power	Autonomy (5)	Revenge (612)
	Prestige (7)	Prestige (8)
	Social influence (8)	Self-esteem (9)
		Assertiveness (11)
		Social influence (13)
		Unassailability (22)
		Superiority (23)

The numbers in parentheses in the second column represent the sequence in the list of values (Seifert & Bergmann, 1983). The motives in the third column are numbered according to the list used by the participants in coding their diary entries.

For the short version (24 items) of the reactivity scale of the Strelau Temperament Inventory (STI-RS), Strelau et al. (1990, p. 225) report a Cronbach alpha of .84 for a German sample. Strelau, Zawadzki, and Angleitner (1995, p. 29) report a Cronbach alpha of .80 for the Polish STI-RS with 19 items.

Stability (Retest Reliability) of Values and Motives Importance Scores

Seifert and Bergmann (1983, p. 165) report retest reliability coefficients between .74 and .88 (two-weeks time interval) and between .42 and .66 (two-and-a-half years interval) for the global value importance scales of the original English version of the work values inventory. The correlation (N = 60) of the motive importance scores of two types of situations (at the work place vs. elsewhere), representing a mixture of internal consistency and temporal stability, are .45, .36, and

Table 5.2 Internal Consistency (Cronbach's Alpha) of the Value and Motive Scales

Domains	Value	Motive
Achievement	Items 4, 6, 14	Items 1, 2, 3, 16, 25
	$a = .51$	$a = .63$
Affiliation	Items 1, 12, 13	Items 5, 7, 12, 14
	$a = .63$	$a = .24$
Power	Items 5, 7, 8	Items 6, 8, 9, 11, 13, 22, 23
	$a = .41$	$a = .64$

Table 5.3 Correlation Coefficients, Means, and Standard Deviations of
Importance Scores for Motive and Value Domains (Achievement, Affiliation,
and Power)

$N = 120$	1	2	3	4	5	6	M	SD
1 Achievement motive		−.33	.11	.02	−.14	.10	.25	.16
2 Affiliation motive			−.01	−.12	.05	.01	.12	.07
3 Power motive				−.05	.14	.02	.13	.09
4 Achievement value					.49	.54	4.09	.45
5 Affiliation value						.31	4.30	.44
6 Power value							3.64	.54

.59 for achievement, affiliation, and power, respectively. The test-retest correlations of motive importance scores of the four periods of observation, which were
one to five months apart, are on the average .50 (achievement), .41 (affiliation),
and .59 (power).

Correlation of Value Importance Scores with
Motive Importance Scores

The correlation coefficients for value and motive scores are close to zero. The
three motive importance scores are independent, too, whereas the value scores
are correlated (average correlation $r =.44$) (see Table 5.3).

Motive Actualization and Motive Satisfaction
Dependent on the Situation

As Table 5.4 shows, the achievement motive and the power motive are much less
often actualized outside the workplace than at work ($M = .15$ vs. $M = .35$ for the
achievement motive and $M =.10$ vs. $M = .16$ for the power motive). The opposite
is true for the affiliation motive ($M = .15$ vs. $M = .09$). If the achievement motive
and the power motive are actualized, they are also less often satisfied outside the
workplace than at work. Generally, under the condition of actualization, the affiliation motive is more often satisfied than the power motive.

Regression of Satisfaction on Situation, Reactivity,
Value, and Motive Importance

Multiple regression analysis seems to be the most appropriate model for testing
the main effects and interaction effects predicted by the hypotheses one to four.
There are three measures of value importance, three measures of motive importance, three product measures (normalized value importance scores multiplied
by normalized motive importance scores), representing the interaction between
value and motive importance, three higher-order product measures (reactivity
value importance motive importance, all components entered as normalized
scores), and reactivity, that is, 13 independent variables. Taking the interaction
with situation of these 13 variables into account gives altogether 26 independent
variables.

Table 5.4 Means and Standard Deviations of Motive
Actualization and Motive Satisfaction in Two Situations

	Outside workplace		At workplace	
	M	SD	M	SD
Actualization				
Achievement	.15	.07	.35	.15
Affiliation	.15	.06	.09	.07
Power	.10	.07	.16	.09
Satisfaction				
Achievement	.66	.23	.73	.21
Affiliation	.88	.18	.86	.22
Power	.59	.30	.65	.27

$N = 60$.

In all analyses, a person's motive satisfaction score, averaged across the three classes of motives (achievement, affiliation, and power), functions as dependent variable. One should be aware that motive satisfaction scores (relative frequencies of motive satisfaction under the condition of motive actualization) and motive actualization scores (motive importance scores, which are the relative frequencies of motive actualization, irrespective of motive frustration or satisfaction, based on the frequency with which a person referred to a motive of any kind in reporting his or her emotional experience) are technically independent. The correlation between the general mood score and the general motive satisfaction score is $r = 81$. "General" here refers to a person's average score across all his or her TSD-self-observations. Motive satisfaction scores are intuitively more appealing than mood scores because they represent the relative frequency with which a person's motives have been satisfied.

As Table 5.5 shows, 43% (adjusted) of the variance of motive satisfaction is explained by the stepwise (forward) selected set of independent variables ($N = 120$; two scores for each person). Reactivity has a strong influence on motive satisfaction: Low-reactives (high score) feel better than high-reactives (low score) ($\beta = .34$; $p = .000$). Thus, hypothesis 1 has been confirmed. The regression coefficient of affiliation value is negative ($\beta = -.28$; $p = .000$), whereas the regression coefficient of power value is positive ($\beta = .23$; $p = .003$). Since no hypotheses have been formulated with respect to the main effect of value importance scores, a post hoc explanation of this result is offered in the discussion section.

One of the three value by motive interactions (affiliation) has a positive and significant beta-coefficient ($\beta = .23$; $p = .003$). This means that mood (measured as motive satisfaction) tends to be positive when value and motive importance scores are congruent and negative when these scores are incongruent. Therefore, hypothesis 2 is confirmed for the affiliation value-motive domain only. However, as Table 5.6 (column 8) shows, there is a general tendency towards this type of interaction between value importance and motive importance.

Table 5.5 Motive Satisfaction as a Function of Situation and Normalized Scores of Reactivity, Motive Importance, Value Importance, and of Their Products (Interactions)

Predictor variable	b	β	t	p
Main effects				
1 Reactivity	0.066	0.34	4.77	0.000
2 Affiliation value	−0.055	−0.28	−3.78	0.000
3 Power value	0.044	0.23	3.08	0.003
Two-way interactions				
4 Affiliation value * Affiliation motive	0.044	0.23	3.07	0.003
5 Situation * Affiliation motive	0.035	0.14	1.94	0.055
Three-way interactions				
6 Reactivity * Achievement value * Achievement motive	0.050	0.19	3.44	0.010
7 Reactivity * Power value * Power motive	−0.079	−0.37	−5.18	0.000
8 Situation * Achievement value * Achievement motive	0.080	0.25	3.44	0.001
9 Constant	.735			

$R = 0.69\ R^2_{adj} = 0.43$
Stepwise regression with 26 independent variables and 120 observations (each of 60 participants in two situations).

The three-way interaction (reactivity by value by motive) for the achievement domain with a positive beta-coefficient ($\beta = .19$; $p = .010$) indicates that value-motive congruence is tied to motive satisfaction of low-reactives only. A strong three-way interaction (reactivity by value by motive with $\beta = −.37$; $p = .000$) is found for the power domain: For high-reactive persons (low score), value-motive-congruence is connected with good mood, but for low-reactive persons the opposite is true. This means that hypothesis 3 is confirmed only for the power domain. The two situations, workplace (situation = 1) and elsewhere (situation = 0) show about the same strong effects with respect to this three-way interaction (Table 5.6, column 7).

The three-way-interaction situation * achievement value * achievement motive in row 8 of Table 5.5 ($\beta = .25$; $p = .001$) means that the interaction achievement value * achievement motive is found only at the workplace. Obviously, hypothesis 4 is not supported by the data.

The means are calculated for patterns of normalized scores of situation (0, 1), reactivity (−1, 1), value importance (−1, 1), and motive importance (−1, 1). Value-motive congruence, operationalized as the product of normalized value and motive importance scores, and reactivity are not more important outside the workplace than in it.

The regression analysis was also performed with the mood score (from 1 = very negative to 5 = very positive) as the dependent variable. The proportions of

Table 5.6 Motive Satisfaction Predicted by Regression Analysis from Type of Situation (1 = Workplace, 0 = Elsewhere), Reactivity (−1 High, +1 Low), Value Importance, and Motive Importance

1 Situation	2 Reactivity	3 Value	4 Motive	5 Achievement	6 Affiliation	7 Power	8 Total
0	−1	−1	−1	0.62	0.77	0.70	0.70
0	−1	−1	1	0.72	0.68	0.55	0.65
0	−1	1	−1	0.72	0.57	0.63	0.64
0	−1	1	1	0.62	0.66	0.79	0.69
0	1	−1	−1	0.82	0.90	0.68	0.80
0	1	−1	1	0.75	0.81	0.84	0.80
0	1	1	−1	0.75	0.70	0.93	0.79
0	1	1	1	0.85	0.79	0.77	0.80
1	−1	−1	−1	0.70	0.73	0.70	0.71
1	−1	−1	1	0.64	0.71	0.55	0.63
1	−1	1	−1	0.64	0.54	0.63	0.60
1	−1	1	1	0.70	0.69	0.79	0.73
1	1	−1	−1	0.93	0.87	0.68	0.83
1	1	−1	1	0.67	0.85	0.84	0.79
1	1	1	−1	0.67	0.67	0.93	0.76
1	1	1	1	0.93	0.83	0.77	0.84

From the fifth to the eighth column there are motive satisfaction scores predicted by the regression equation (independent variables normalized) for combinations of situation, reactivity, value importance, and motive importance (−1 and +1 means 1 SD below and above the mean, respectively). The regression equation can be found in Table 5.5.

explained variance were somewhat lower (R^2_{adj} = 0.29 for the stepwise selected set of variables), but the sets of selected variables (those that contributed most to the prediction of mood) were about the same.

Table 5.6 gives an impression of the rather complex dependence of motive satisfaction on interactions of reactivity, value importance, and motive importance for two kinds of situations (1 = workplace, 0 = elsewhere). Column 8 of Table 5.6 tells us what the motive satisfaction score would be if all three value-motive domains had the same pattern of normalized predictor scores which, of course, rarely occurs. Nevertheless, it suggests that, on the average, value-motive congruence is more important for well-being with high-reactives than with low-reactives. This was predicted by hypothesis 3.

Discussion

Internal consistency of motive importance scores. The internal consistency coefficients of value and motive importance scores (Cronbach's alpha) presented in Table 5.2 seem to be rather low, indicating that the components of the broad categories of values and motives, albeit similar with respect to psychological meaning and statistical relationships, represent different facets of the construct. One should be aware that low internal consistency does not preclude medium or even high stability.

Correlation between value importance and motive importance. The lack of correlation between value importance and motive importance parallels a finding of McClelland (1980) that questionnaire measures (respondent measures) of motive strength have only a low correlation with TAT-measures (operant measures). McClelland's explanation is that they are rooted in different strata of the personality structure. The low coefficients of correlation between the three motive importance scores are in part a consequence of the ipsative scoring but also an indication of some kind of functional independence of the different motives. The correlation of the three value importance scores reveals that people have a tendency to find values generally more important or generally less important. From this correlation necessarily follows a weak positive correlation between the three product scores (value importance * motive importance).

Reactivity and motive satisfaction. The results fully confirm hypothesis H1, which states that LR persons show a better mood than the HR ones in both kinds of situations (see Figure 5.1). This is consistent with the data presented by Farthofer and Brandstätter (this volume) related to personality traits, if one assumes that low reactivity corresponds to a combination of high extraversion and low neuroticism (Strelau, 1983).

The influence of value importance on motive satisfaction. Although it is generally recommended that one not look at the main effects of an independent variable if it is involved in significant interaction effects, it may be worthwhile to ask why respondents who placed high importance on value affiliation reported lower satisfaction than those who rated this value as being of low importance (cf. table 5.6 and figure 5.1). People who stress the importance of altruism and good relations with superiors and colleagues (high importance of the value affiliation) tend to experience low motive satisfaction. This could mean that their desire for good social relationships is rooted in some deficits in social skills that make them vulnerable. Negative coefficients of correlation between the importance of affiliation value and the 16PF global factors of emotional stability and independence are compatible with this interpretation.

On the other hand, people who give priority to the power value (people to whom autonomy, social prestige, and influence on people, i.e., management, is important) tend to feel generally better. It may well be that the power value, at least as it is measured by the work value inventory, is rooted not in prior experience of social shortcomings but rather in the experience of strength.

Value-motive congruence. As with affiliation, value-motive congruence is positively correlated to motive satisfaction, irrespective of the level of reactivity and of the type of situation (cf. row 4 in Table 5.5 and column 6 in Table 5.5). Value-motive congruence in the achievement domain is also connected with higher motive satisfaction, except when high-reactive participants are not at the workplace. In the domain of power, this is true only for high-reactives. The effect on well-being of value-motive congruence varies with the value-motive domain, with reactivity, and with the type of situations.

A post hoc explanation of the pattern of results given in Table 5.5 and Figure 5.1 could be based on the following statements:

1. The actualization of motives depends both on motivational dispositions of the person and on the incentives of the circumstances.

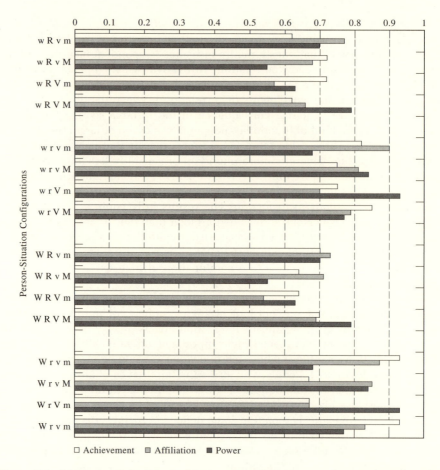

Figure 5.1. Motive satisfaction (achievement, affiliation, and power) as function of situation (w = not at work, W = at work), reactivity (r = low, R = high), values (v = low, V = high), and motives (m = low, M = high). Low and high in reactivity, values, and motives represent predictions based on scores 1 SD below and above the mean. A low score in reactivity means high reactivity (cf. Table 5.6).

2. The situation-specific incentives of the various kinds of motives differ with respect to the degree by which they cause arousal. Situations that provide incentives for the affiliation motive are highly arousing, whereas situations that provide incentives for the power motive are moderately arousing.

3. Congruence of value and motive importance is less arousing than incongruence of value and motive importance.

4. Persons differ in their degree of excitability (reactivity).

5. Feeling good is connected with an optimal level of arousal.

6. When the affiliation motive is involved, incongruence of value and motive importance causes overarousal, irrespective of the person's excitability (reactivity) and the type of situation.

7. When the power motive is involved, only high-reactives suffer from in-congruence, whereas low-reactives reach their optimal arousal level with value-motive incongruence.

The shortcoming of such an explanation is, of course, that the degree of arousal connected with the actualization of the different classes of motives has not been measured, but is theoretically postulated as an intervening variable. A possible approach to TSD arousal measures would be to have experts rate all adjectives used by the participants for describing their momentary mood states qualitatively with respect to valence and activation. The activation scores of the adjectives, averaged per person across the situations in which the specific class of motives has been actualized, would then be the arousal measure.

Even if one accepted the motivation specific arousal hypothesis in connection with the assumptions of the arousing effect of value-motive incongruence and of an arousal optimum depending on a person's excitability (reactivity) and the arousal intensity of external and internal stimulation, there remains the problem that the motive satisfaction pattern in the value-motive domain of achievement does not fit any optimum arousal explanation: When high-reactive participants are not at the workplace, value-motive incongruence is connected with higher motive satisfaction than value-motive congruence. The opposite is true in the other three situation by reactivity combinations (cf. column 5 in Table 5.6). Therefore, one can-not assume that achievement situations would be generally highly arousing and that value-motive incongruence, augmenting the arousal, would cause overarousal and lower satisfaction scores. If this were true, partic-ularly the high-reactives should feel better with value-motive congruence (pro-viding optimal arousal) than with value-motive incongruence (which in high-reactive persons should cause overarousal). As yet, there is no convincing explanation of the pattern of results in the achievement domain available.

Practical applications. One may ask what could help the high-reactives to feel better in both types of situation. Two kinds of intervention could be helpful: (1) dissemination of knowledge about susceptibility to stress, its consequences, and styles and strategies of coping with it as related to reactivity; and (2) training in avoiding extreme stress and coping with unavoidable stress. It seems important to learn to recognize both stress symptoms, and also states that imply optimal stimulation (when I feel good and perform well). It is equally important to learn about actions that lead to these states (What can I do in a given situation to feel better and act more effectively? How should I organize my job to work more efficiently?). Probably high-reactive persons also need some changes in their val-uation system, aiming at a better congruence between value and motive impor-tance, because value-motive incongruence tends to make them overaroused, lead-ing them to feel bad.

Perspectives for future research. This study was a first step in exploring the interplay among values, motives, and reactivity. The findings are promising but call for further research, which should especially look at the consistency of the results of the present study, in particular those results that were unpredicted. Also, the sustainability of their tentative post hoc explanations should be a subject of further research. How values and motives can be matched should be studied more systematically, from both a theoretical and an empirical perspective. The effects of value-motive congruence on subjective well-being should be studied also, with values and motives not considered in this report.

Notes

This study was supported by the National Committee for Scientific Research (Grant no. 1P106 012 06).

1. Since Strelau's reactivity measure derives from Pavlov's idea of strength of the nervous system (Strelau, 1988, p. 154), a high score on the reactivity scale, actually representing high tolerance of strong stimulation, means low reactivity. This is somehow unfortunate, because it makes talking about reactivity in terms of correlations and mean score differences susceptible to misunderstandings. However, a reversed scoring, though more convenient for the moment, would be at variance with the terminology established in the literature and would possibly add to the confusion.

2. That Kiss, Dornai, and Brandstätter (this volume) postulate a greater influence of personality characteristics (including value orientations) on mood in situations providing more freedom of action, whereas Brandstätter (this volume) reports a greater influence of motivational person-environment fit on mood in low-freedom situations, is no contradiction. The first hypothesis states a two-way (situational freedom by personality) interaction; the second hypothesis implies a three-way interaction (situational freedom by situational reward profile by individual motive importance profile). Moreover, the independent variables are different: global personality variables and value orientations in the first hypothesis versus individual motive profiles in the second hypothesis.

References

Brandstätter, H. (1989). Motives in everyday life situations. In F. Halisch & J. van den Bercken (Eds.), *International perspectives on achievement and task motivation* (pp. 327–349). Lisse: Swets & Zeitlinger.

Brandstätter, H. (1991). Emotions in everyday life situations: Time sampling of subjective experience. In F. Strack, M. Argyle, & N. Schwartz (Eds.), *Subjective well-being. An interdisciplinary perspective* (pp. 173–192). Oxford: Pergamon Press.

Brandstätter, H. (1994). Well-being and motivational person-environment fit. A time sampling study of emotions. *European Journal of Personality, 8,* 75–93.

DeNeve, K. M., & Cooper, H. (1998). The happy personality: A meta-analysis of 137 personality traits and subjective well-being. *Psychological Bulletin, 124,* 197–229.

Eliasz, A. (1981). *Temperament a system regulacji stymulacji* [Temperament and system of stimulation control]. Warsaw: PWN.

Eliasz, A. (1985). Transactional model of temperament. In J. Strelau (Ed.), *Temperamental bases of behavior. Warsaw studies on individual differences* (pp. 41–78). Lisse: Swets & Zeitlinger.

Eliasz, A. (1987). Temperament-contingent cognitive orientation towards various aspects of reality. In J. Strelau & H. J. Eysenck (Eds.), *Personality dimensions and arousal* (pp. 197–213). New York: Plenum Press.

Eliasz, A. (1990). Broadening the concept of temperament: From disposition to hypothetical construct. *European Journal of Personality, 4,* 287–302.

Eliasz, A., & Wrześniewski, K. (1991). Two kinds of type A behavior pattern. In C. D. Spielberger, I. G. Sarason, J. Strelau, & J.M.T. Brebner (Eds.), *Stress and anxiety* (Vol.13, pp. 275–282). New York: Hemisphere.

Epstein, S. (1989). Values from the perspective of cognitive-experiential self-theory. In N. Eisenberg, J. Reykowski, & E. Staub (Eds.), *Social and moral values* (pp. 11–32). Hillsdale: Lawrence Erlbaum.

Eysenck, H. J. (1981). *General features of the model.* In H. J. Eysenck (Ed.), *A model for personality* (pp. 1–37). Berlin: Springer.

Feather, N. T. (1990). Bridging the gap between values and actions: Recent applications of the expectancy-value model. In E. T. Higgins & R. M. Sorrentino (Eds.), *Handbook of motivation and cognition* (Vol. 2, pp. 151–192). New York: Guilford Press.

Heckhausen, H. (1991). *Motivation and action.* Berlin: Springer.

Klonowicz, T. (1974). Reactivity and fitness for the occupation of operator. *Polish Psychological Bulletin, 5,* 129–136.

Klonowicz, T. (1987). *Reactivity, experience & capacity.* Warsaw: University Press.

Lewinsohn, P., Redner, J., & Seeley, J. (1991). The relationship between life satisfaction and psychosocial variables: New perspectives. In F. Strack, M. Argyle, & N. Schwarz (Eds.), *Subjective well-being. An interdisciplinary perspective* (pp. 141–169). Oxford: Pergamon Press.

Maslow, A. H. (1954). *Motivation and personality.* New York: Harper & Row.

McClelland, D. C. (1980). Motive dispositions: The merits of operant and respondent measures. In L. Wheeler (Ed.), *Review of personality and social psychology* (Vol.1, pp. 10–41). Beverly Hills: Sage.

McCrae, R. R. (1994). New goals for trait psychology. *Psychological Inquiry, 5,* 148–153.

Reykowski, J. (1992). Emocje, motywacja, osobowość [Emotions, motivation, personality]. In T. Tomaszewski (Ed.), *Psychologia Ogólna* (Vol. 2, pp. 7–185). Warsaw: PWN.

Rogers, C. R. (1964). Toward a modern approach to values: The valuing process in the mature person. *Journal of Abnormal and Social Psychology, 68,* 2, 160–167.

Schwartz, S. H., & Bilsky, W. (1990). Toward a theory of the universal content and structure of values: Extensions and cross-cultural replications. *Journal of Personality and Social Psychology, 58,* 878–891.

Seifert, K.-H., & Bergmann, C. (1983). Deutschsprachige Adaptation des Work Values Inventory von Super [German adaptation of the Work Values Inventory of Super]. *Psychologie und Praxis. Zeitschrift für Arbeits-und Organisationspsychologie, 1,* 160–172.

Sheldon, K. M., & Elliot, A. J. (1999). Goal striving: The self-concordance model. *Journal of Personality and Social Psychology, 76,* 482–497.

Strelau, J. (1983). *Temperament—Personality—Activity.* London: Academic Press.

Strelau, J. (1983). Temperamental dimensions as co-determinants of resistance to stress. In M. P. Janisse (Ed.), *Individual differences, stress, and health psychology* (pp. 146–169). New York: Springer.

Strelau, J. (1995). Temperament and stress. In C. D. Spielberger & I. G. Sarason (Eds.), *Stress and emotions: Anxiety, anger and curiosity* (Vol. 15, pp. 215–254). Washington, DC: Hemisphere.

Strelau, J. (1998). *Temperament: A psychological perspective.* New York: Plenum Press.

Strelau, J., Angleitner, A., Bantelmann, J., & Ruch, W. (1990). The Strelau Temperament Inventory—Revised (STI-R): Theoretical considerations and scale development. *European Journal of Personality, 4,* 209–235.

Strelau, J., Zawadzki, B., & Angleitner, A. (1995). Kwestionariusz Temperamentu PTS: Próba psychologicznej injterpretacji podstawowych cech układu nerwowego według Pawłowa [Pavlovian Temperament Survey (PTS): An effort of a psychological interpretation of Pavlov's basic properties of the nervous system]. *Studia Psychologiczne, 33,* 9–48.

Super, D. E. (1970). *Work Values Inventory.* Boston: Houghton Mifflin.

Veenhoven, R. (1991). Questions on happiness: Classical topics, modern answers, blind spots. In F. Strack, M. Argyle, & N. Schwarz (Eds.). *Subjective well-being. An interdisciplinary perspective* (pp. 7–26). Oxford: Pergamon Press.

Wilson, W. (1967). Correlates of avowed happiness. *Psychological Bulletin, 67,* 294–306.

Winter, D. G., John, O. P., Stewart, A. J., Klohnen, E. V., & Duncan, L. E. (1998). Traits and motives: Toward an integration of two traditions in personality research. *Psychological Review, 105,* 230–250.

Zalewska, A. (1995). Two kinds of anxiety and somatic complaints according to reactivity. *Polish Psychological Bulletin, 26,* 319–329.

Zalewska, A. (1996a, July). Different aspects of health with regard to reactivity and cohesion in valuation system. Poster presented at the Eighth European Conference on Personality, University of Ghent, Belgium.

Zalewska, A. (1996b). System wartościowania pracujących w zależności od wieku i reaktywności [Workers' valuation system according to age and reactivity]. *Przegląd Psychologiczny, 39,* 211–226.

Zalewska, A. (1997). Adaptation to a new workplace according to reactivity and values-motives coherence at work. *International Journal of Occupational Safety and Ergonomics, 3,* 161–172.

6

Personal Resources and Organizational Well-Being

Tatiana Klonowicz

The purpose of this study was to evaluate the joint contribution that intelligence, reactivity, and mobility as determinants of personal resources make to the regulation of subjective well-being in a new organization. I have assumed that a new organizational environment forces newcomers to adapt themselves to it. The adaptive process enables an individual to achieve "congruence" or "fit" to the organizational requirements and variably engages his or her personal resources. Resources are viewed here as instrumental to achieving a person-organization fit: Individuals feel less distress if their personal resources enable them to manage the situation, that is, when they fit the requirements of a situation.

The "fit" or adaptational outcome has been assessed in a number of ways, usually involving various measures of performance and/or affect. The present study focuses on mood and health as adaptational outcomes related to well-being. Well-being is considered here as a function of fit between the personal resources and the organization.

The notion of personal resources (cf. Klonowicz, 1992) is introduced here in the hope of overcoming a major difficulty in this field of research. Although the relevance of personality variables for stress-related adaptational outcomes and, more specifically, subjective well-being has been widely recognized, research provides equivocal empirical evidence. A survey of the literature (e.g., Antonovsky, 1979; Cox & Ferguson, 1991; Diener, 1984; Edwards, 1988; Klonowicz, 1992; Kobasa, Maddi & Kahn, 1982; Lazarus & Folkman, 1984; Mullen & Suls, 1982; Parkes, 1991; Suh, Diener, & Fujita, 1996) reveals that previous research made use of a very broad range of personal variables, including, extraversion/introversion, neuroticism, emotionally, reactivity, locus of control, hardiness, Type A, sense of coherence, and private self-consciousness. In a recent study, DeNeve and Cooper (1998) listed 137 specific personality traits that were correlated with subjective well-being. Typically, these variables were investigated singly and there is a separate literature for each. Only some of these variables were well founded in theory. Some were conceptualized narrowly, whereas others were conceptualized broadly (i.e., the Big Five; cf. McCrae & Costa, 1991). All this makes the integration of literature extremely difficult.

A disappointment with this literature may have inspired a new body of research that relates mood and—more generally—well-being to yet another personal variable: a state/trait positive/negative affectivity, which is called upon to explain emotions and health regardless of the impact of external events (Burke, Brief, & George, 1993; Furr & Funder, 1998; Gross, Sutton, & Ketelaar, 1998; Larsen, 1987; Larsen & Diener, 1987; Parkes, 1990). However, this approach overlooks the substantial role of a person-environment interplay, and, moreover, it isolates the research on well-being from the mainstream of research on stress.

Organizational Demands and Personal Resources

To address such concerns I propose to organize personal variables into domains that correspond to broader concepts, that is, resources that make it possible to achieve and/or maintain a person-environment (P-E) fit. The main principle of this type of organization is the localization of various personal variables according to their roles in resource management. This proposition is depicted in Figure 6.1.

Resource theories (e.g., Kahneman, 1973; Kanfer & Ackerman, 1989; Navon, 1984; Sanders, 1983; Wickens, 1984) consider how a person copes with various

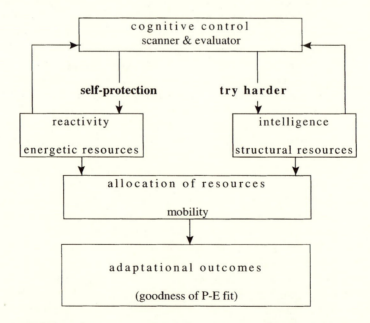

Figure 6.1. Relations between personal determinants of individual resources and adaptational outcomes.

demands. According to these theories, performance is a function of demands and the resources that a person can allocate to them. In the present chapter I adopt this general view and extend it by stressing the role of personal variables in determining resources and hence a P-E fit. The notion of P-E fit applies to a balance between environmental, for example, organizational, demands and the personal resources necessary to cope with these demands. In order to explain both individual and situational differences in P-E fit, the model distinguishes between two types of resources: energetic and structural. Individual and situational differences manifest themselves also in the allocation and cognitive control of resources.

Energetic resources. The notion of energetic resources is introduced to emphasize that individuals vary in the amount of activation they can trigger to meet environmental demands, particularly, task and social demands. Energetic resources are fine-tuned by the demands and aimed at improving or sustaining a person's performance and well-being. It is argued later in this chapter that individual differences in energetic resources depend on reactivity. Tasks on higher levels of complexity elicit a higher degree of activation and mobilize more energy. However, the notion of energetic resources alone cannot explain individual differences in task execution. The evidence in support of this view shows that only manipulations of difficulty—but not those of complexity—can be explained in terms of undifferentiated pool of resource models (cf. Ackerman, 1987; Stankov, 1989).

Structural resources. Another aspect of P-E fit relates to structural resources, that is, to individual differences in intelligence and competence used to establish responses to demands, ways of coping with demands, and their efficiency. Individual differences in structural resource volumes are of particular significance in complex, novel, and variable contexts; their role diminishes when responses to demands become automated. Although this point is not made in Figure 6.1, it is worth noting that energetic resources provide support for structural resources.

Resource allocation should be adequate to the tasks at hand. It hinges on environmental demands and individual differences. The latter explain why individuals differ in their ability to effectively pursue one or more activities at the same time and to pace activity sequences adequately to demands.

Cognitive control. Importantly, resources are also needed to support the adequate functioning of the more conscientiously regulated mechanism of cognitive control. The nature of the control mechanism is an interesting question in its own right, but it is not the prime concern in this study. To remain within the approach proposed by Brandstätter (this volume), it may be suggested that motives, values, and goals play the most important role here. The control system scans and evaluates events, decides whether resources should be enacted or saved, and rules affect that signals the occurrence of discrepancies between energy and ability demands, between actions, goals, and motives (cf. Carver & Scheier, 1990).

Only three personal variables are entered into the model in Figure 6.1: intelligence, reactivity, and mobility. They are considered important and relatively stable determinants of personal resources. A brief overview of findings pertinent to this conceptualization is given later in this chapter. Although other variables can also be incorporated as determinants of resource volumes and allocation, the present study is limited to the combined effect of intelligence, reactivity, and mobility on emotional and health outcomes as measures of P-E fit.

Temperament in the Perspective of Resource Theory

Reactivity and mobility are temperament traits pertinent to the process of stimulation control whereby the organism avoids the danger of overstimulation. My conceptualization of the regulatory roles of reactivity and mobility is based on arousal or activation theories (cf. Eliasz, 1981; Klonowicz, 1992; Strelau, 1983, 1998). Hebb (1961) defines arousal as a tonic level that extends from sleep to extreme emotional disorganization. He also proposes a framework for understanding the Yerkes-Dodson law that links performance and well-being to arousal. Both performance and well-being are at their heights at the optimal level of arousal. As noted above, energetic resources are directly related to arousal. Resource theories (e.g., Kahneman, 1973; Navon, 1984) hold that resources and arousal vary together in the low and medium range of arousal levels. Studies on temperament convince us that this general postulate needs revision. The inverted U-shaped curve is inadequate to explain systematic interindividual differences in behavior and must be supplemented by a postulate that there are stable differences in arousal between people. The Regulative Theory of Temperament (Strelau, 1983, 1998) explains this phenomenon by differences in stimulation regulation which relies on reactivity and mobility.

Reactivity

Reactivity has been defined as a trait that "determines a relatively stable intensity (magnitude) of reactions for a given individual . . . crucial for our understanding of reactivity is the fact that it co-determines the sensitivity (sensory and emotional) . . . and the organism's capacity to work" (Strelau, 1983, p. 177). The two extremes of the reactivity dimension are high reactivity (high sensitivity, low endurance) and low reactivity (low sensitivity, high endurance). The physiological mechanism of reactivity is directly responsible for stimulation processing: Its "program" either enhances (high reactivity) or dampens (low reactivity) the intensity of incoming stimuli.

This conceptualization received strong empirical support. The resting level of arousal, measured by EDA nonspecifics, pulmonary ventilation, and several other physiological and psychophysiological measures, is more elevated in 'high-reactives' than in 'low-reactives' (Klonowicz, 1987). High-reactives display more anticipatory arousal than low-reactives (Klonowicz, 1986). Experimental manipulations with either tasks or situations with different stimulation loads provide ample evidence to conclude that at moderate to elevated levels of stimulation persons low in reactivity perform better, at less cost, and are happier than those high in reactivity. The reverse has been demonstrated for low stimulation levels (for a review see Klonowicz, 1992; Strelau, 1983, 1998). The data also indicate that reactivity co-determines the individual propensity for settings of a given stimulation load, more or less stimulating recreational activities and even jobs (Eliasz, 1974, 1981). Finally, reactivity has been shown to be directly responsible for the mobilization and recovery of energetic resources as measured by cardiovascular activity (Klonowicz, 1992).

Although this evidence does not warrant the conclusion that the optimum levels of arousal in high- and low-reactives are not equivalent, it clearly points out the differences in the localization of the optimum along the stimulation dimension. Thus, reactivity determines when the energy is going to be mobilized and/or drained, that is, it determines a resource volume available under given conditions.

Signals that resources are insufficient, overtaxed, and/or dangerously depleted may enact the "self-protection feedback loop." An organism tends to seek protection from discrepancies between the optimum and the actual—either too low or too high—levels of arousal. It follows from the findings already cited that high-reactives require much lower levels of arousal in order to perform effectively and feel good. Low-reactives can and will accommodate much higher levels of arousal before their performance and well-being begin to suffer. This means that differences in reactivity govern individual sensitivity to deviations from the optimum and direct the regulation of energetic resources.

Mobility

Mobility has been defined as a "capacity of switching behavior in response to changing environment" (Strelau, 1983, p. 195–196), that is, as an adequate and timely response to changes in the environment. The role of mobility has been much less studied than the role of reactivity, and what little evidence exists is equivocal. However, my interest in mobility is caused not by the elusiveness of this trait but by the fact that mobility is closely related to reactivity. Strelau et al. (Strelau, Angleitner, Bantelmann, & Ruch, 1990; Strelau, Zawadzki, & Angleitner, 1995) report the median correlation coefficient between reactivity and mobility of −.54.[1] On these grounds it has been argued that mobility intervenes in the process of stimulation regulation whenever it is necessary to switch from one kind of activity to another and especially, whenever stimulation is novel and/or varied (Eliasz, 1981; Klonowicz, 1992; Strelau, 1983, 1998). Klonowicz has shown that cardiovascular activity as a measure of effort invested in a highly demanding task correlates significantly with reactivity but not with mobility. The higher the reactivity, the more effort is mobilized. The control of mobility accounts for additional 16–20% of total variance in cardiovascular activity. These data indicate that mobility functions as a mediating variable and, most probably, affects the allocation of capacity, that is, resource management. The model presented in Figure 6.1 reflects this specific role for mobility and tentatively generalizes it beyond the allocation of energetic resources.

Intelligence

Turning to structural resources, it should be noted that in spite of the claim that intelligence plays a key role in adaptation in general and in adaptation to a new environment in particular, very few investigations tackle this issue (e.g., Ree, Earles, & Teachout, 1994; Valliant, 1977). The reason for this is the fact that intelligence was found to be a good predictor of academic achievement but not of adaptation to real—life situations (Epstein, 1990; Sternberg & Wagner, 1986; see, however, Schmidt & Hunter, 1998). The model presented earlier (see Figure 6.1) addresses this issue in a different way. Intelligence is considered here as a determinant of a separate pool of structural resources or cognitive tools and the abilities to process information, manage problems and situations. Following Van Harrison (1978), it is suggested that person-organization fit may be described on the demand-ability dimension, which reflects the requirements of the organizational environment (and of the job itself) and the degree to which an individual can meet these demands (e.g., learn new procedures and tasks or, more generally, learn the ropes in a new organization). Also, Brandstätter (this volume) postulates that the quality of emotional experience, (e.g., mood ratio) depends on the fit between demands and abilities. Additional support for this view comes from findings reported by Hunter and Hunter (1984). On the basis of a meta-analysis of the research into various predictors of job performance, Hunter and Hunter conclude that "for entry-level jobs there is no predictor with validity equal to that of ability, which has a mean validity of .53" (p. 72). Unfortunately, contrary to the authors cited earlier, neither Brandstätter nor Hunter and Hunter considers the significance of the g factor (general intelligence) as measured by standard IQ tests, which may explain the difference of opinion between them and, for example, Epstein or Sternberg and Wagner. However, considering the previously cited literature together with the fact that whatever other abilities a test may measure, it always measures g, it seemed important to have this study embrace the significance of intelligence in adaptation. It is suggested that well-being occurs when organizational demands and individual structural resources are balanced or when additional, new requirements can be matched by the mobilization of more resources (see Figure 6.1, positive discrepancy reducing loop "try harder").

Hypothesis

The general hypothesis of the present study is that when both the energetic and structural resources available to an individual are sufficient, adaptation goes unhindered and is accompanied by a positive hedonic tone. When the demands exceed resources and/or last too long, resource-dependent coping options become limited, leaving an individual vulnerable to psychological distress. This study sets out to verify the hypothesis that the collated effects of reactivity, mobility, and intelligence are responsible for the goodness of person-organizational fit. More specifically, it is predicted that the combination of higher reactivity, lower intelligence, and lower mobility makes it more difficult to achieve a good person-organization fit than the combination of higher intelligence, higher mobility, and lower reactivity. If interperson differences in resources do play the postulated role, there should be substantial interpersonal differences in subjective well-being as evidenced by mood variability, mood ratio, and somatic health impairments.

The hypothesis focuses on individual characteristics as antecedents of reactions to a new and, hence, presumably difficult organizational environment. This study deals with individual characteristics that make a difference in the subjective level of stress or misfit between the person and the environment and does not deal with the environmental antecedents of stress. Thus, this study represents a macro-analytical approach and explores a total of broadly conceived occupational attributes subsumed under the superordinate notion of a new environment.

It is also worth noting that the investigation to be reported focuses on the interplay of intelligence, reactivity, and mobility and sets aside research on isolated effects of each of these three variables on the measures of well-being. In this line of argumentation, two types of resources are needed to explain individual differences in behavior, and three variables—intelligence, reactivity, and mobility—are crucial in determining both resource volumes and resource allocation. To further strengthen this point, I may add that in the light of the close functional ties between reactivity and mobility, any separate treatment of these two features seems undesirable, atheoretical, and counterproductive. In other words, the central issue here is how the temperament traits combine with each other and with intelligence in determining the dynamics of employees' well-being.

Method

To evaluate the combined contribution of these three personal variables to mood and somatic health, short-term longitudinal data were obtained in a natural work environment. The data were collected very soon after individuals had joined a new organization, that is, during the period that was potentially a key period for the shaping of future performance, regulation of well-being, and attitudes (cf. Louis, 1980).

Sample

The setting for the research was a bank. Sixty employees (18 male, 42 female) from various departments, ages 20–54 years (mean age 32.7; median 31.00), participated in the study. Education ranged from a high school or professional school diploma to a master's degree. All participants were newly employed in the bank, and for 13 participants this was their first job. Everybody participated in this study voluntarily.

Trait Measures

Temperament. Participants completed Strelau's Temperament Inventory (STI-R, short form; Strelau, Angleitner, Bantelmann, & Ruch, 1990; Strelau, Zawadzki, & Angleitner, 1995). The Inventory consists of 57 items and measures four temperament traits. In responding to the items, participants rate themselves on a four-point scale. The STI-R was scored for reactivity (a reversed score on the Strength of Excitation Scale; score range 1–76) and mobility (Mobility Scale; score range 1–76).[2]

Intelligence. Intelligence was assessed by means of Raven's Advanced Progressive Matrices (Polish Adaptation: Laboratorium Technik Diagnostycznych).

Emotional Responses

Emotional reactions were assessed by means of the Time Sampling Diary (TSD; Polish version developed by Marszał-Wiśniewska, 1993). Brandstätter (this volume) gives a detailed description of the method and coding procedures.[3]

The TSD contains seven questions. The present study focuses on answers to Question 1: "Is my mood at the moment very negative, rather negative, indifferent, rather positive, or very positive?" Question 4: "Where am I?" served as a criterion variable, delineating the setting.

Variability of mood. Two indices of emotional adaptation were computed: variability of mood and mood ratio. The estimate of variability of mood was the coefficient of variation of coded ratings of emotions. This index was obtained by dividing each participant's standard deviation for the responses by the participant's mean score for these responses, enabling us to control for the influence of response magnitude (Diekhof, 1992).[4] The mood ratio was computed as a ratio of positive mood ratings (scores 4 and 5) to the total mood ratings. Although the two measures correlate with each other ($r[58] = .48$, $p < .01$), they reflect different phenomena.

Variability of mood is a measure of fluctuations in emotional functioning and, hence, in well-being. The introduction of this measure is based on the assumption that newcomers in the organization respond emotionally to a wider range of external stimuli and that their reactions are also more differentiated with respect to the quality (positive or negative) of emotions. Switches in emotional responses engage resources. With time, the work environment loses its novelty, becomes more familiar, and, although sensitization to some stimuli cannot be excluded, employees' emotional reactions become, in general, less variable. Variability of mood is also controlled by personality, in particular, by extraversion and neuroticism (Eysenck & Eysenck, 1985; Hepburn & Eysenck, 1989; McConville & Cooper, 1992; Williams, 1990), which are closely related to reactivity and mobility (cf. Strelau, 1983, 1998). Thus, interindividual differences in mood variability reflect trait-specific differences in sensitivity to stimuli that originate within the organization and individual differences in adaptation to organizational demands.

Mood ratio. Mood ratio is a direct measure of hedonic tone. It is also one of the most widely used measures of emotional functioning (cf. Brandstätter, this volume). The significance of this measure stems from the research on the functional role of positive emotions in cognitive and social functioning (for recent reviews see Avia, 1997; Carver & Scheier, 1990; George & Brief, 1992).

Physical Health

Physical health symptoms were measured by the Somatic Symptoms Checklist (Cofta, 1992). The list consists of 16 physical health concerns (the 17th item is an open question) that are rated on 5-point Likert scales for frequency (scale running from "not at all," score 0, to "every day," score 4) and intensity (scale running from "not at all," score 0, to "very severe," score 4). Examples for the items are "back pains," and "palpitations." Both the frequency and the intensity scale are the sum of scores across the 16 items (means and standard deviations $M = 9.1$ and $SD = 7.0$ for frequency, $M = 17.1$ and $SD = 8.5$ for intensity).

Table 6.1 Mean Levels of Intelligence, Mobility, and Reactivity in Three Clusters of Subjects

Variable	Cluster I	Cluster II	Cluster III	$F\,(2,57)$
Intelligence	19.90	15.62	25.08	18.44
Mobility	60.65	47.31	51.54	54.33
Reactivity	51.05	39.62	48.58	18.60
Label	"eager"	"poor"	"bright"	
N	20	16	24	

Scores for reactivity are reversed: the lower the score, the higher the reactivity. All Fs significant at $p < .0001$.

Procedure

All participants completed questionnaires that contained measures of personal variables, emotional responses to everyday life situations, and physical health symptoms, as well as sociodemographic information. Personal variables and health symptoms were assessed once, whereas emotional responses were measured in the longitudinal design covering six months of employment. STI-R, Raven's Progressive Matrices, and the Somatic Symptoms Checklist were administered between Waves 3 and 4 of the study. The participants filled in the STI-R and the Somatic Symptoms Checklist at home, whereas Raven's Progressive Matrices were administered in the work setting. The earliest TSD started at the end of the first month of employment and the latest in the second month of employment. The first three waves covered three consecutive months of employment, and the final wave came three months later. The TSD questions were answered according to preset individual schedules (see Brandstätter, this volume). To protect anonymity, all techniques were coded by the participants themselves.

Results

To address the model of individual resources and P-E fit, it would seem most appropriate to submit the results to the multiple regression analysis. However, a significant correlation between reactivity and mobility ($r = -.42$, $df = 58$, $p < .01$) and between reactivity and intelligence ($r = .25$, $df = 58$, $p < .05$) excludes this procedure. Therefore, the first set of analyses was aimed at the identification of existing combinations of resources in the sample.

Clustering Persons According to Resources

The scores on STI-R and Advanced Progressive Matrices were submitted to proximities-between-subjects cluster analysis. The results are given in Table 6.1.

As the data in Table 6.1 show, the three identified clusters differ significantly with respect to three personal variables. The "eager" group combines low reactivity with high mobility and medium intelligence. In the "bright" group, moderate levels of the two temperament features—reactivity and mobility—are con-

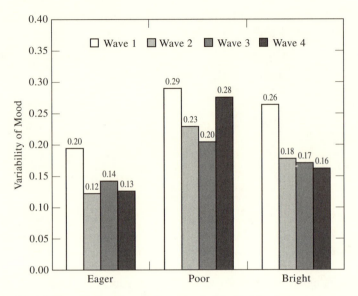

Figure 6.2. Variability of mood as a function of individual resources and time in the organization (wave of the study).

nected with high intelligence. In the "poor" group, reactivity is high, whereas mobility and intelligence are low.

Differences between Clusters in Emotions and Health

The second set of analyses involved between-clusters comparisons of the indices of P-E fit. The data on variability of mood, mood ratio, and somatic health are presented in Figures 6.2–6.4. However, to control for demographic variables (cf. Parkes, 1990), the data were converted into z-scores according to gender and age.[5] All subsequent computations were based on these converted scores. The converted data on emotional reactions, that is, variability of moods and mood ratio, were submitted to two separate repeated measures ANOVAs. Each ANOVA was a Cluster (3 clusters) by Wave (4 subsequent waves of assessment) design. The repeated measures ANOVA with factors Cluster (3 clusters) by Impairment (2 levels: frequency of somatic symptoms and intensity of somatic symptoms) was applied to the data on somatic health.

Variability of mood. The data with variability of mood as dependent variable are presented in Figure 6.2.

The repeated measures ANOVA yielded a significant main effect of Wave ($F[3,153] = 5.75$, $p < .001$) and a significant main effect of Cluster ($F[2,51] = 6.05$, $p < .01$). The mean score in Wave 1 is $M = .25$ and in Waves 2 through 4 $M = .18$. In general, variability of mood decreases with time. Thus, the aggregated data indicate that habituation occurs between the first two waves of the study. However, there are significant between-clusters differences in variability of mood. The "eager" ($M = .15$) display significantly less variability of mood than either

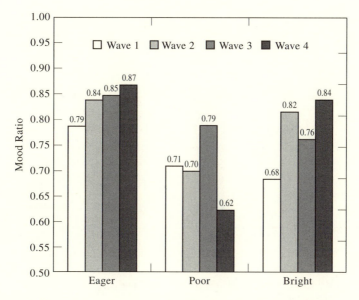

Figure 6.3. Mood ratio as a function of individual resources and time in The organization (wave of the study).

the "poor" (M = .25), F = 14.91, p < .001, or the "bright" (M = .19), F = 5.51, p < .02. Also, the "bright" show marginally less variability of mood than the "poor" (F = 3.11, p < .08).

Mood ratio. The data on mood ratio are presented in Figure 6.3.

The repeated measures ANOVA yielded a significant main effect of Cluster (F[2,47] = 3.22, p < .05) and a significant Cluster by Wave interaction effect (F [6,141] = 2.38, p < .05). Mood ratio is significantly more positive in the "eager" (M = .83) than in either the "poor" (M = .70) or the "bright" (M = .77), F = 6.71, p < .01.

As Figure 6.3 shows, a significant interaction effect reflects the occurrence of different, cluster-specific patterns of dynamics of mood ratio over time. A remarkably steady and highly positive mood ratio in the "eager" is contrasted with fluctuating levels of mood ratio in both the "poor" and the "bright." Contrast tests show:

- As compared with the "eager," the "poor" show marginally less positive mood ratio in Wave 2 (F = 3.41, p < .07) and significantly less positive mood ratio in Wave 4 of the study (F = 13.38, p < .001);
- The "eager" have a marginally more positive mood ration than the "bright" in Wave 1 and Wave 3 of the study (F > 3.34, p < 08);
- In Wave 4 mood ratio in the "poor" is significantly less positive than the "bright" (F = 8.45, p < .01).

Somatic health. The data on somatic health are presented in Figure 6.4.

As a test of hypothesis 4, the repeated measures ANOVA yielded a significant main effect of Cluster (F [2,57] = 3.54, p < .05). Somatic health impairments are

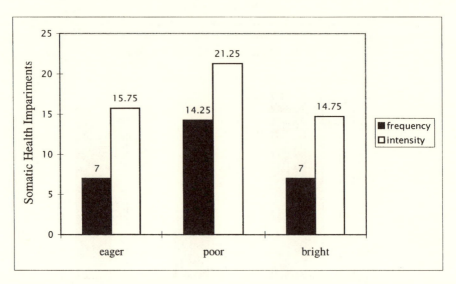

Figure 6.4. Individual resources (eager—poor—bright), frequency and intensity of somatic health impairments.

significantly greater in the "poor" as compared with both the "eager" ($F = 6.04$, $p < .05$) and the "bright" ($F = 5.08$, $p < .05$). The difference between the "eager" and the "bright" is not statistically significant. A more detailed analysis suggests that the differences are mainly a result of a significantly higher frequency of somatic symptoms in the "poor" as compared with both the "eager" ($F[1,57] = 7.23$, $p < .01$) and the "bright" ($F[1,57] = 5.94$, $p < .05$). Intensity of somatic symptoms is only marginally higher in the "poor" than in either of the two other groups ($F[1,57] < 2.52$, $p > .12$).

Discussion

The present study provided a test for the hypothesis on the impact of individual resources on person-organization fit by using short-term in situ assessments of emotions and data on somatic health impairments. The combined effect of individual resources, determined by intelligence, reactivity, and mobility, was examined in relation to predictions made about well-being. To empirically test the hypothesis, the data on variability of mood, mood ratio, and somatic health were compared across three clusters of participants. The "eager" group represented the combination of low reactivity, high mobility, and medium intelligence. The "bright" group showed the combination of moderate levels of temperamental variables with high intelligence. Finally, in the "poor" group, the level of all three individual resources was low.

In general, the data support the hypothesis that the combination of lower reactivity, higher mobility, and higher intelligence should result in a better person-organization fit than the combination of higher reactivity, lower mobility, and lower intelligence. The direct test for the hypothesis—the comparison of the "eager" with the "poor"—indicates that the former display less variability of mood, more positive hedonic tone, and less somatic health impairments.

The inclusion of the third cluster, the "bright," enables a better mapping of the combined effects of intelligence, reactivity, and mobility. Variability of mood was higher in the "bright" as compared with the "eager" but lower than in the "poor." This finding may indicate a linear relation between variability of mood and individual resources determined by reactivity and mobility. This outcome is consistent with the Regulative Theory of Temperament (Strelau, 1983, 1998), according to which reactivity determines the intensity of emotional reactions to stimuli, whereas mobility may be responsible for emotional shifts and emotional inertness. It seems that, at this level of the analysis, intelligence can be excluded from the regulation of mood variability. This position is consistent with the view that cognitive control and evaluation do not affect more basic, automatic reactions (cf. Hockey, 1986; Sanders, 1983).

The "bright" differed from the "eager" with respect to both the extent and the dynamics of hedonic tone. The overall hedonic tone was more positive in the "eager" than in the "bright." The "eager" achieved a highly positive mood ratio early and maintained a steady hedonic tone throughout the whole period covered by the study, whereas in both the "bright" and the "poor" the patterns of hedonic tone were less reliable. Together with the fact that the "bright" and the "poor" did not differ with respect to the overall hedonic tone, this outcome may indicate that the excess of resources beyond those actually required can be as disconcerting as a resource deficit. Analyses of the impact of organizational demands are now urgently needed to better understand the above reported results.

The data may add, albeit indirectly, to the literature on individual differences in variability of mood and hedonic tone. The key questions for the discussion of these issues are how much intrapersonal variability individuals display across time, situations, or both, and how to explain intrapersonal stability of mood variability and hedonic tone. There are three approaches to these issues in the literature. The situationalists (e.g., Mischel, 1990) claim that, for example, intrapersonal variability of mood reflects the effect of situations variability on mood. Other authors, like the present author, have taken a moderator variable approach by claiming that mood variability (as effects of varying situations on mood) and average mood level (mood ratio) depend on (are moderated by) some general personality traits (e.g., McConville & Cooper, 1992; Zuckerman, Bernieri, Koestner, & Rosenthal, 1989). The third approach postulates that intrapersonal variability of mood and average mood level are themselves stable aspects of personality (cf. Larsen, 1987). Although the present study uses a different methodology and does not address the problem of stability of mood variability or hedonic tone, the data suggest that both intrapersonal variability of mood as well as hedonic tone depend on the individual differences in personal resources.

It is also worth noting that Mancini and Bastianoni (this volume) raise the problem of mood variability as a function of fit between environment quality and motives. The present study differs from theirs in that it focuses on the person rather than on the environment and views the person-environment fit as a dynamic process. The combination of the two approaches should foster a better understanding of the impact of organizations on individuals.

Finally, a question may be asked about the practical significance of the data reported in this chapter. Recent research convinces that the issue of organizational well-being is, indeed, of primordial importance not just for individuals, who rightfully strive to achieve happiness, but also to organizations. The way people experience their work influences their intentions to quit or stay. Both a lack of and an excess of resources may lead to increased turnover. George (1991) and George and Brief (1992) have found that positive mood at work is a crucial factor in both extrarole as well as role-prescribed prosocial organizational behaviors, such as helping a colleague with a problem, protecting the organization, and providing a good customer service.

Conclusions

The purpose of this study was to evaluate the concerted role that the three determinants of personal resources—intelligence, reactivity, and mobility—play in the regulation of well-being. According to the general hypothesis, individuals feel better if their personal resources enable them to achieve a person-environment (P-E) fit. The proposed theoretical model organizes personal variables, that is, intelligence, reactivity, and mobility, into domains responsible for mobilization, allocation, and evaluation of resources and effort. The notion of energetic resources is introduced in order to emphasize that individuals vary in the amount of activation they have available for meeting various demands. Reactivity plays a crucial role in determining energetic resources. The notion of structural resources covers individual differences in intelligence, competency of responding to demands, and ways of coping with demands across the scale of efficiency. Mobility is regarded as a factor underlying the allocation of the two types of resources. Other variables can be entered into the model as determinants of resources volumes and/or the competency to use and allocate resources.

1. The study confirmed the prediction concerning the role of individual resources in adaptation to a new organization. A low resource supply and limited capacity of resource allocation (i.e., the combination of high reactivity with low intelligence and mobility) restrains and delays the achievement of person-organization fit.
2. The data on the dynamics of positive mood ratio, that is, the case of decreasing optimism in the "bright" (the combination of medium temperament with high intelligence) may indicate the disadvantage of having an excess of resources over and beyond what is necessary.
3. The findings contribute to the literature on positive mood as an important factor in both individual and organizational efficiency and development.

Notes

1. In most studies the assessment of reactivity is indirect, i.e., based on the Pavlovian strength of excitation. Reactivity is the opposite of the strength of excitation:

the higher the strength of excitation, the lower the reactivity (cf Strelau, 1983, 1988). This explains why a positive correlation between the strength of excitation and mobility becomes a negative one for reactivity and mobility.

2. More details on the assessment of temperament are given by Brandstätter and Eliasz as well as Eliasz (this volume).

3. In chapter 2 Brandstätter provides a comprehensive review of previous research with TSD. Therefore no references are made here to the earlier TSD studies and previous findings.

4. Despite the fact that Larsen (1987) advocates a spectral-analytic approach to the assessment of mood variability, the standard deviation remains the most widely used measure of emotional variability within the framework of psychology of individual differences (cf. Eysenck & Eysenck, 1985; Hepburn & Eysenck, 1989; McConville & Cooper, 1992; Williams, 1981, 1989). It is also worth noting that the method proposed by Diekhof (1992) answers Larsen's criticism that a standard deviation confounds the frequency of mood change with the extremity of change.

5. Ancillary analyses conducted on the unconverted data gave values of F greater than those reported below.

References

Ackerman, P. L. (1987). Individual differences in skill learning: An integration of psychometric and information processing perspectives. *Psychological Bulletin, 102,* 3–27.
Antonovsky, A. (1979). *Health, stress, and coping.* San Francisco: Jossey-Bass.
Avia, M. (1997). Personality and positive emotions. *European Journal of Personality, 11,* 33–56.
Burke, M. J., Brief, A. P., & George, J. M. (1993). The role of negative affectivity in understanding relations between self-reports of stressors and strains: A comment on the applied psychology literature. *Journal of Applied Psychology, 78,* 402–412.
Carver, C. S., & Scheier, M. F. (1990). Origins and functions of positive and negative affect: A control-process view. *Psychological Review, 97,* 19–35.
Cofta, L. (1992). *Zapotrzebowanie na stymulację jako czynnik modyfikujący wpływ Wzoru Zachowania A na zdrowie i jakość życia*[Need for stimulation as a factor modifying the influence of Type A behavior pattern on health and quality of life]. Unpublished doctoral dissertation. Warsaw: Institute of Psychology, PAN.
Cox, T., & Ferguson, E. (1991). Individual differences, stress, and coping. In C. L. Cooper & R. Payne (Eds.), *Personality and stress: Individual differences in the stress process* (pp. 7–30). Chichester: Wiley.
DeNeve, K. M., & Cooper, H. (1998). The happy personality: A meta-analysis of 137 personality traits and subjective well-being. *Psychological Bulletin, 124,* 197–229.
Diekhoff, G. (1922). *Statistics for the behavioral sciences: Univariate, bivariate, and multivariate.* Dubuque, IA: Brown.
Diener, E. (1984). Subjective well-being. *Psychological Bulletin, 95,* 542–575.
Edwards, J. R. (1988). The determinants and consequences of coping with stress. In C. L. Cooper & R. Payne (Eds.), *Causes, coping, and consequences of stress at work* (pp. 39–57). Chichester: Wiley.
Eliasz, A. (1974). Aktywność reaktywna i sprawcza a wybór sytuacji o rożnym stopniu stymulacji[Activity—reactive and operant—and the choice of situations with different stimulation loads]. In J. Strelau (Ed.), *Rola cech temperamentalnych w działaniu* (pp. 135–140). Wrocław: Ossolineum.
Eliasz, A. (1981). *Temperament a system regulacji stymulacji* [Temperament and system of stimulation control]. Warsaw: PWN.

Epstein, S. (1990). Cognitive-experiential self-theory. In L. A. Pervin (Ed.), *Handbook of personality: Theory and research* (pp. 165–192). New York: Guilford Press.

Eysenck, H. J., & Eysenck, M. W. (1985). *Personality and individual differences*. New York: Plenum.

Furr, R. M., & Funder, D. C. (1998). A multimodal analysis of personal negativity. *Journal of Personality and Social Psychology, 74*, 1580–1591.

George, J. M. (1991). State or trait: Effects of positive mood on prosocial behavior at work. *Journal of Applied Psychology, 76*, 299–307.

George, J. M., & Brief, A. P. (1992). Feeling good—doing good: A conceptual analysis of the mood at work-organizational spontaneity relationship. *Psychological Bulletin, 112*, 310–329.

Gross, J. J., Sutton, S. K., & Ketelaar, T. (1998). Relations between affect and personality: Support for the affect-level and affective-reactivity views. *Personality and Social Psychology Bulletin, 24*, 279–288.

Hebb, D. O. (1961). *Organization of behavior*. New York: Science Editions.

Hepburn, L., & Eysenck, M. W. (1989). Personality, average mood, and mood variability. *Personality and Individual Differences, 10*, 975–983.

Hockey, G. R. J. (1986). A state control theory of adaptation to stress and individual differences in stress management. In G. R. J. Hockey, A. W. K. Gaillard, & M. G. H. Coles (Eds.), *Energetics and human information processing* (pp. 285–298). Dordrecht: Nijhoff.

Hunter, J. E., & Hunter, R. F. (1984). Validity and utility of alternative predictors of performance. *Psychological Bulletin, 96*, 72–98.

Kahneman, D. (1973). *Attention and effort*. Englewood Cliffs, NJ: Prentice Hall.

Kanfer, R., & Ackerman, P. I. (1989). Motivational and skill abilities: An integrative/aptitude approach to skill acquisition. *Journal of Applied Psychology, 74*, 657–690.

Klonowicz, T. (1986). Reactivity, level of activation, and anticipation: A scary world. *Polish Psychological Bulletin, 17*, 15–26.

Klonowicz, T. (1987). Reactivity and the control of arousal. In J. Strelau & H. J. Eysenck (Eds.), *Personality dimensions and arousal* (pp. 183–196). New York: Plenum.

Klonowicz, T. (1992). *Stres w Weżay Babel* [Stress in the Tower of Babel]. Wrocław: Ossolineum.

Kobasa, S. C., Maddi, S. R., & Kahn, S. (1982). Hardiness and health: A prospective study. *Journal of Personality and Social Psychology, 42*, 168–177.

Larsen, R. J. (1987). The stability of mood variability: A spectral analytic approach to daily mood assessments. *Journal of Personality and Social Psychology, 61*, 80–84.

Larsen, R. J., & Diener, E. (1987). Affect intensity as an individual difference characteristic: A review. *Journal of Research in Personality, 21*, 139.

Lazarus, R. S., & Folkman, S. (1984). *Stress, appraisal, and coping*. New York: Springer.

Louis, M. (1980). Surprise and sense making: What newcomers experience in entering unfamiliar organizational settings. *Administrative Science Quarterly, 25*, 226–251.

Marszał-Wiśniewska, M. (1993). Dzienniczek Próbek Czasowych Hermanna Brandstättera[On Herman Brandstätter's 'Time Sampling Diary']. *Przegłiąd Psychologiczny, 36*, 481–490.

McConville, C., & Cooper, C. (1992). Mood variability and personality. *Personality and Individual Differences, 13*, 1213–1221.

McCrae, R. R., & Costa, P. T., Jr. (1991). Adding Liebe and Arbeit: The full Five-factor model and well-being. *Personality and Social Psychology Bulletin, 17*, 227–232.

Mischel, W. (1990). Personal dispositions revisited and revised: A view after three decades. In L. A. Pervin (Ed.), *Handbook of personality. Theory and research*. (pp. 334–372). New York: Guilford Press.

Mullen, B., & Suls, J. (1982). "Know thyself": Stressful life-changes and the ameliorative effect of private self-consciousness. *Journal of Experimental Social Psychology, 18*, 43–55.

Navon, D. (1984). Resources—a theoretical soup stone? *Psychological Review, 91*, 216–234.

Parkes, K. (1990). Coping, negative affectivity, and the work environment: Additive and interactive predictors of mental health. *Journal of Applied Psychology, 75*, 399–409.

Parkes, K. (1991). Locus of control as moderator: An explanation of additive vs. interactive findings in the demand-discretion model of work stress? *British Journal of Psychology, 82*, 291–312.

Ree, M. J., Earles, J. A., & Teachout, M. S. (1994). Predicting job performance: Not much more than g. *Journal of Applied Psychology, 79*, 518–524.

Sanders, A. F. (1983). Towards a model of stress and human performance. *Acta Psychologica, 53*, 61–97.

Schmidt, F. L., & Hunter, J. E. (1998). The validity and utility of selection methods in personnel psychology: Practical and theoretical implications of 85 years of research findings. *Psychological Bulletin, 124*, 262–274.

Stankov, L. (1989). Attentional resources and intelligence: A disappearing link. *Personality and Individual Differences, 10*, 957–968.

Sternberg, R. J., & Wagner, R. K. (1986). *Practical intelligence: Nature and origins of competence in the everyday world*. Cambridge: Cambridge University Press.

Strelau, J. (1983). *Temperament—Personality—Activity*. New York: Academic Press.

Strelau, J. (1998). *Temperament: A psychological perspective*. New York: Plenum Press.

Strelau, J., Angleitner, A., Bantelmann, J., & Ruch, W. (1990). The Strelau Temperament Inventory Revised (STI-R): Theoretical considerations and scale development. *European Journal of Personality, 4*, 209–235.

Strelau, J., Zawadzki, B., & Angleitner, A. (1995). Kwestionariusz temperamentu PTS: Próba psychologicznej interpretacji cech układu nerwowego według Pawłowa[Pavlovian Temperament Survey (PTS): An effort of a psychological interpretation of Pavlov's basic properties of the nervous system]. *Studia Psychologiczne, 33*, 9–48.

Suh, E., Diener, E., & Fujita, F. (1996). Events and subjective well-being: Only recent events matter. *Journal of Personality and Social Psychology, 70*, 1091–1102.

Valliant, G. (1977). *Adaptation to life*. Boston: Little, Brown.

Van Harrison, R. (1978). Person-environment fit and job stress. In C. L. Cooper & R. Payne (Eds.), *Stress at work* (pp. 175–208). Chichester: Wiley.

Wickens, C. D. (1984). Processing resources in attention. In R. Parasurman & D. R. Davies (Eds.), *Varieties of attention* (pp. 66–102). New York: Academic Press.

Williams, D. G. (1981). Personality and mood: state-trait relationships. *Personality and Individual Differences, 2*, 303–309.

Williams, D. G. (1989). Personality effects in current mood: Pervasive or reactive? *Personality and Individual Differences, 10*, 941–948.

Williams, D. G. (1990). Effects of psychotism, extraversion, and neuroticism in current mood: A statistical review of six studies. *Personality and Individual Differences, 11*, 615–630.

Zuckerman, M., Bernieri, F., Koestner, R., & Rosenthal, R. (1989). To predict some of the people some of the time: In search of moderators. *Journal of Personality and Social Psychology, 57*, 279–293.

PART III

EXPERIENCING WORK, FAMILY LIFE, AND UNEMPLOYMENT

7

Extraversion and Optimal Level of Arousal in High-Risk Work

Alois Farthofer *&* Hermann Brandstätter

In some professions, for example, surgery, transport, or the nuclear power industry (Bogner, 1994; Wickens, 1992; Wilpert & Qvale, 1993), the health and safety of people depends heavily on the quality of job performance. Accidents and dangerous incidents reveal the sensitivity of socio-technical systems to human errors, and these have stimulated a substantial amount of research on human factors in human-machine-systems, focusing mainly on information processing, which leads to either efficient or faulty performance in hazardous work systems (Carayon, 1994; Omodei & Wearing, 1995; Reason, 1990; Salvendy, 1997; Wickens, 1992, 1996; Wickens, Stokes, Barnett, & Hymann, 1993). Meister (as cited in Wickens, 1992, p. 3) defines the study of human factors as "the study of how humans accomplish work-related tasks in the context of human-machine system operation, and how behavioral and non-behavioral variables affect that accomplishment."

Because of its impact on information processing and decision making, which has been analyzed in a number of studies on affective states and cognitive processes, mood becomes an important variable (Isen & Geva, 1987; Isen & Patrick, 1983). The variability of mood as it accords with and results from person-environment interaction therefore is a matter not only of subjective well-being but also of safety.

Mood and Cognitive Performance

From our everyday life experience, we are familiar with the influence of mood on mental performance. If people are happy, they tend, for example, to spend money with less deliberation; if they are depressed, their decision making slows down. Research on the relationship between mood and information processing

(Mann, 1992, p. 223) indicates that "positive mood is associated with a simplifying style of information search in decision making—faster, more selective, less redundant." And, with regard to negative mood, Mann (1992, p. 223) points out that people who suffer from depression "are characterized by an inability to make decisions and a tendency to depend on others to decide for them." And further: "The effect of depression is to lead to a slowing down in decision making, a reluctance to make decisions, and marked tendencies to give greater weight to risks than to benefits, and to practice risk-avoidance in making choices." The influence of mood on information processing style has also been studied by Kuhl (1983), who postulates that emotions that signal fear, shame, guilt, or sadness promote sequential-analytical information processing, whereas positive emotions such as pleasure and interest favor intuitive-holistic information processing. Hesse and Spies (1993) argue that negative emotions call for "mood repair-strategies," whereas positive emotions lead to "mood maintenance strategies," resulting in more creative problem solving strategies. Bless and Fiedler (1995) and Bless (1997) also contend that emotions influence the style of information processing, and Melton (1995, p. 792) states that "findings imply a consistent tendency for positive mood subjects to put less time and effort into the task and are thus consistent with effort reduction accounts of mood-induced performance decrements." Thus, positive mood seems to cause shorter information-processing activities, which in consequence leads to faster decision making. However, if plenty of time is available for decisions, slower information processing may not cause problems. Hesse and Spies (1996), for example, report that participants in a negative mood profited from a more systematic approach when there was no time pressure. But serious problems may arise when an important decision has to be taken quickly.

The consequences of negative mood are summarized by Mann (1992), who concludes, that transient negative mood, stress, anxiety, and severe depression are associated with cautious and inefficient information processing, selective attention to risks at the expense of benefits, reluctance to choose, and in many cases, self defeating choices. Thus, the quality of mood affects the cognitive processes and consequently the safety aspects of performance in hazardous work systems.

More on the influence of affect on risk taking and decision making can be found in Dunegan, Duchon, and Barton (1992), Mano (1992, 1994), and Nygren, Isen, Taylor, and Dulin (1996). For a profound analysis of judgment under uncertainty from the perspective of cognitive psychology, the reader is referred to Kahnemann & Tversky (1982). Rusting (1998) elaborates on how personality traits and mood states interact in emotional information processing.

Mood in Person-Environment-Interaction

Although the term "mood" is traditionally defined as an unspecified feeling state (e.g., Clore, Schwarz, & Conway, 1994), it will be used in this study without making a distinction between transitory emotional responses to certain events and longer-lasting emotional tuning (mood in the narrow sense). It seems reasonable to conceive of emotions as transitory deflections from the prevailing, more slowly changing level of mood. The emotional responses to personally relevant events, relevant because they affect a person's success or failure in pursuing important goals, should be understood as combined (interactive) effects of personality traits, current mood, and event characteristics (cf. Rusting, 1998).

Affective states are the combined effects of personality and environment, more precisely, of the affective dispositions of the person and of the affective stimulation caused by remembered, perceived, or expected events in a person's environment. Brandstätter (1994a, 1994b) analyzed mood variation within and between different situations, comparing especially work and leisure. He found that the discrepancy between leisure and work, at the expense of work, was highest for stable extraverts and lowest for unstable introverts. This discrepancy could be explained by the extraverts' higher need for stimulation. If work doesn't provide sufficient stimulation, extraverts will feel more pleasure in out-of-work activities. This assumption is confirmed by the fact that extraverts feel best in situations providing high stimulation during both work and leisure (Brandstätter, 1994a). The theoretical explanation of these findings refers to Eysenck and Eysenck (1985), who assume that extraverts need more stimulation to reach an optimal level of arousal than do introverts. If the work itself is highly arousing, perhaps because people perceive and experience danger and risks, one would expect extraverts to feel better about it than introverts.

In its look at the combined effects of situational and personal characteristics on mood, which in turn may influence the cognitive functioning and performance in dangerous human-machine systems, the present study is concerned with the combined effects of the need for arousal, which is dependent on introversion/extraversion, and the level of environmental stimulation, which is dependent on the risk level of the situation. More specifically, it analyzes how the variation of risk across situations and variation in introversion/extraversion among people induces variations of mood in steel workers.

Hypotheses

In accordance with the individual difference concept of optimal arousal (Eysenck & Eysenck, 1985, p. 197) and the positive relationship between extraversion and subjective well-being reported in the literature (Larsen & Ketelaar, 1991; McFatter, 1994; Meyer & Shack, 1989), it is assumed that:

1. Extraverts have a higher need for stimulation.
2. High-risk work activities provide high stimulation.
3. Extraverts feel better than introverts, more so during work than during leisure activities (hypothesis 1), and more so during high-risk work activities than during low-risk activities (hypothesis 2).

Statements 1 and 2 are the theoretical premises from which the two hypotheses are derived. Behind hypothesis 1 is the idea that people have more freedom in leisure time than during work to choose situations that provide the preferred level of stimulation. This should lead to a narrowing of the gap between extraverts and introverts in subjective well-being, whereas, in highly arousing work situations with little freedom of choice, extraverts are expected to be better off than introverts.

Re-analyzing the TSD-data of several studies, Brandstätter (1994a) found that extraverts felt better than introverts only in leisure situations. This seems to contradict hypothesis 1. However, the work settings of the participants in these studies were generally less arousing and stimulating than the work setting of the operators and crane drivers participating in the present study. Another argument supporting hypothesis 1 as well as hypothesis 2 is the following: Brandstätter (1994a) predicted and found better moods in extraverts (compared to introverts) in work situations only when the level of stimulation was above the average level of stimulation for work situations, and in leisure situations only when the level of stimulation was above the average level of stimulation for leisure situations. Thus, whether and how much extraverts feel better than introverts depends on the level of stimulation given in the situation.

Method

Procedure

A Time Sampling Diary, originally designed by Brandstätter (1977), was used for this field study carried out in a steel company. The participants were 12 crane drivers and 8 operators. All of the participants were full-time shift-workers between 25 and 55 years of age. For each employee, the shifts work schedule had a sequence of three early shifts (each from 6 A.M. to 2 P.M.), three late shifts (each from 2 P.M. to 10 P.M.), three night shifts (each from 10 P.M. to 6 A.M.), and three days off. The participants in the study had to record in the diary how they experienced their momentary situation, about four 4 times a day at randomly selected times.

Task Description

The following task description gives an impression of the kind of risks the two groups of workers have to cope with.

Crane Driver

Task and work environment.   The crane drivers have to transport fluid steel in a ladle from one part of a steel production hall to another. The weight of a full ladle is about 1000 t. Because of the steady amount of smoke in the factory, the view is somewhat impaired. The light in the factory during the day is a little bit brighter than during the night, and in general is backed up by big lamps. Sometimes, particularly in the summer, the temperature can reach 40° Celsius, despite the cooling equipment installed in each crane. Workers do not always use the cooler, and sometimes the cooler does not function properly. This work station was classified by the ergonomists to be in the low-noise category. Nevertheless, sometimes it can be very loud because of other working processes in the factory. Within the crane cabin, crane drivers have a communication system. They have to communicate with other stations in the factory to receive the orders on when and where to transport material. For special reasons there are also monitors in some of the cranes. These provide the crane driver with a better view down to the ground, from which he had to pick up a ladle. The crane drivers have different types of cranes to handle. Depending on the rotation design, a crane driver also executes different work schedules within a shift. Either he works three or nine consecutive days on the same crane, according to the decision of the work group supervisor. Each crane driver has a one-hour rest during his eight-hour work shift. There is one back-up crane driver (who drives the crane while the other driver is having his one-hour rest). The crane driver usually works alone in the cabin 20 m above ground. In general, the task as well the environment of the job station provides a very stimulating atmosphere: fire, engine noise, dim light in the hall, very bright light within the ladle from the fluid steel, and so on. The crane driver can communicate with others only by microphone, but he can watch all the activities of the other workers. This job is not only rather risky, but also quite stimulating and arousing.

Most critical incident.   The most dangerous occurrence during the transport would be the loss of the transport material, in whole or in part. In the worst possible case, fluid steel could run out of the ladle, in which case the workers below the crane would become the victims of the deadly material.

Operator

Task and work environment.   On a screen the operator has to watch the data of the steel cooling process on a steel production line. He has to observe a computer-guided process on the computer screen for any deviations from the programmed values. He is sitting in a kind of office, confronting a control panel. Also in front of him is a big window through which he can watch the ongoing steel cooling process within the hall. Because of the dangerous character of this process, this scene is in some way also arousing. At the operator's work station there are also monitors that allow the operator to view parts of the factory, which he can't look at directly. Within the same room as the operator, three other people (dispatchers) are working. They co-ordinate the schedule for the crane driver. The operator and the dispatcher can communicate directly. For communication with the people outside the office, the operator can use a telephone or a special radio system. The noise in the room only gets louder when a lot of people are gathered in the station and are talking to each other.

Most critical incident.   For the operator, the most critical incident would be to overlook an error-message on the computer screen, an explosion on the steel production line directly at a place where people are working would be the worst consequence. The lives of these people, therefore, depend on the attention and on the correct decisions of the operator. The nick-name given to this position is "water-man," because the worker is primarily responsible for the right quantity of water used for the cooling down process of the hot steel.

   In summary, both the crane driver and the operator are confronted quite frequently with situations where they have to decide, within only a short period of time, when to stop a running process. Making the right decision at the right time is, therefore, critical for the health and safety of many people, as well as for the efficiency of the production process.

Research-Instruments

Time Sampling Diary.   In each moment of observation the following questions have to be briefly answered:

1. How do I feel at the moment?
2. How can I describe my momentary mood state using one or two adjectives?
3. Why do I feel as I have indicated?
4. Where am I?
5. What am I doing?
6. Who else is present?
7. To what extent do I feel free to choose to stay or leave my present activity?

The following questions were added for the special purpose of the study:

8. How well have I got this situation under control?
9. What would the be consequences of an error of mine in this situation?
10. How much experience do I have with this kind of situation?
11. How dangerous is the situation in general?

Questionnaire.   In addition to the diary the participants answered an adjective version of Cattell's 16 PF questionnaire (Schneewind, Schröder, & Cattell, 1983), developed by Brandstätter (1988) for time-saving use in experiments and surveys. It allows to estimate the global personality dimensions self-control, emotional stability (the opposite of anxiety), independence, tough-mindedness, and extraversion.

Time Sampling Schedule

The schedule for the Time Sampling Diary, which was generated by a computer program, divided the 24 hours of the day into six segments of four 4 hours each and randomly chose one point of time within each segment. This schedule was printed on a sheet of paper and placed on the first page of the diary-booklet. Each sheet of the timetable included six entry times per day for a period of 12 days. In total there were 72 (12 × 6) times set for diary recordings. Taking an average sleeping time of eight hours, the expected number of records per day was four. Participants also received a wrist watch for programming the next time they had to write down how they were experiencing the momentary situation. They were told not to record remembered situations in case they had missed a scheduled observation. If a scheduled entry had been forgotten, the participants were instructed to take their notes as soon as they became aware of their omission. Whenever a pre-programmed time point occurred during sleeping time, it had to be marked after waking up as "sleeping." An average of four time sampling records per day were taken by each participant.

Coding of the Diary Records

At the end of the diary recording period, the participants were instructed to code their diary entries according to the following categories:

1. Time of observation
2. Mood
3. Time perspective (mood caused by a remembered, presently experienced or expected event)
4. Source of satisfaction/dissatisfaction
5. Actualized motives
6. Place
7. Activities
8. Other persons present
9. Perceived freedom
10. Control of the situation
11. Error consequences
12. Frequency of situation experience
13. General risk of danger
14. Adjectives describing the mood state

The participants were provided with a list of motives, places, activities, and persons to choose from in coding their diary entries. According to Brandstätter (1989), the list of 19 motives followed to some extent the motive classification by Murray (1938) and Lersch (1970).

The mood scale ranged from 1 to 5:

"− −"	=	very negative mood (1)
"−"	=	negative mood (2)
"0"	=	indifferent (3)
"+"	=	positive mood (4)
"+ +"	=	very positive mood (5)

For data analysis the scores 1, 2, and 3 were recoded as 0 (not positive), whereas 4 and 5 were recoded as 1 (positive). Subsuming the indifference-answer "3" under "not positive" is justified by the fact, that an indifference response often appeared together with negative adjectives and/or motive frustration. On the basis of this binary score, a general or situation specific mood ratio can be calculated, indicating the relative frequency of feeling good, generally or in a specific category of situations.

Results

The hypothesis is being tested with the individual's situation-specific mood ratio as dependent variable. The independent variables are position (crane driver vs. operator), personality (introversion vs. extraversion), and situation. Two kinds of situation comparisons are made, one for leisure versus work, and another one for less risky work situations versus particularly high-risk work situations. One should remember that the work of crane drivers and operators in a steel plant is

Table 7.1 Personality Values for Crane Drivers and Operators

	Crane drivers (N = 12)		Operators (N = 8)	
	M	SD	M	SD
Self-control	5.10	1.08	5.10	1.40
Emotional stability	5.16	1.81	5.37	2.26
Independence	5.98	1.42	5.33	1.14
Tough-mindedness	5.50	1.25	4.93	1.09
Extraversion	7.25	1.68	6.12	1.56

generally characterized by high risk and consequently by higher stimulation than workers' typical leisure activities.[1] Nevertheless, within the work in the steel plant, situations with low and moderate risk can be distinguished from situations with particularly high risk.

First, the means and standard deviations of the personality dimensions are presented for each working group (Table 7.1). There are no significant differences between crane drivers and operators. Compared to the general population (for which the scales are calibrated with M = 5.0 and SD = 2.0), both crane drivers and operators on the average have significantly higher scores on extraversion.

Testing hypothesis 1. Table 7.2 indicates the difference in mood between introverts and extraverts for leisure time and for work. The leisure mood ratios are based on about 24 observations per person, the work mood ratios on about 16 observations per person. It was expected that extraverts (crane drivers as well as operators) would feel better than introverts, more so during (generally rather risky) work than during leisure. This hypothesis was tested and confirmed by a 2 by 2 by 2 ANOVA (leisure/work by introversion/extraversion by crane driver/operator) with leisure/work as within-subject factor (Tables 7.2 and 7.3).

The extraversion by leisure/work interaction is significant ($F(1.16) = 5.32$, $p = 0.4$). Since the pattern of interaction had been predicted, a one-tailed test of the contrast is appropriate, which means that $p = .02$. The mood ratio of intro-

Table 7.2 Mood of Introvert and Extravert Crane Drivers and Operators during Leisure and Work

	Leisure			Work		
	M	SD	N	M	SD	N
Crane station						
Introverts	.70	.22	6	.29	.21	6
Extraverts	.87	.08	6	.67	.36	6
Operator station						
Introverts	.92	.09	4	.39	.19	4
Extraverts	.87	.08	4	.70	.14	4

Table 7.3 ANOVA (Position by Extraversion by
Leisure/Work) with Mood Ratio as Dependent
Variable

Source	d.f.	F(1.16)	p
Between-subjects effects			
Position *P*	1	1.48	.24
Extraversion *E*	1	8.21	.01
P by *E*	1	1.08	.31
Within-subject effect			
Leisure/Work *L/W*	1	28.61	.00
P by *L/W*	1	.12	.73
E by *L/W*	1	5.32	.04
P by *E* by *L/W*	1	.30	.59
Error	16		

verts and extraverts is .79 and .87 during leisure, but .33 and .68 during work
(weighted average of crane drivers and operators). Since the interactions with the
position (crane driver vs. operator) are by far not significant, hypothesis 1 is
equally supported by the data of crane drivers and of operators.

Testing hypothesis 2. It was further expected that the difference between extraverts and introverts would be higher in work activities with particularly high
risk than in work activities of relatively low risk. Two situation specific mood
ratios were calculated for each person, each based on about eight observations
per person, one for relatively low-risk work situations and one for particularly
high-risk situations.[2]

The risk classification was based on the participants' risk assessments as recorded in the diary for each time-point of observation on the way from home to
work, during work time, and after work time on the way to their home. All these
observations concern activities related to work. A separate median split was taken
for all the risk assessments of crane drivers and all the risk assessments of
operators. Below the median is defined as low risk, above the median as high
risk.

This hypothesis was tested and confirmed by a 2 by 2 by 2 ANOVA (low
vs. high risk work situations by introversion/extraversion by crane driver/opera-
tor) with low vs. high risk work situations as within-subject factor (Tables 7.4
and 7.5). In this case all measures for that time were taken, in which the worker
was out of home for work. The extraversion by risk interaction is marginally significant ($F(1.16) = 3.17$, $p = .09$). Again, since the pattern of interaction had
been predicted, a one-tailed test of the contrast is appropriate, which means
that $p = .04$. The mood ratio of introverts and extraverts averaged across both
work groups is .56 and .75 in low-risk work situations, but .22 and .64 in
high-risk work situations. Because the interactions with the position (crane driver
vs. operator) are again by far not significant, hypothesis 2 is also equally supported by the data of crane drivers and of operators.

Table 7.4 Mood of Introvert and Extravert Crane Drivers in Low- and High-Risk Work Situations

	Crane drivers			Operators		
	M	SD	N	M	SD	N
Low risk						
Introverts	.59	.34	6	.51	.36	4
Extraverts	.74	.26	6	.77	.29	4
High risk						
Introverts	.17	.16	6	.29	.29	4
Extraverts	.64	.39	6	.64	.28	4

Discussion

This study examined the covariation of introversion/extraversion and mood in work situations characterized by high risk. Previous research indicated that negative mood can hamper the quality of judgment and decision making in risky situations. The importance of mood for safety was, for example, stressed by pilots of a major airline, who stated that mood is a safety issue (Farthofer, 1992). There were complaints that nobody wants to know how the pilots feel while performing their highly responsible and risky jobs, although emotions in stressful situations are known not only to have long-term effects on well-being and health but to immediately influence the ongoing activities of coping with critical events and their outcome.

The first author's talks with people about their working experience in dangerous human-machine systems, on the one hand, and psychological research on the

Table 7.5 ANOVA (Position by Extraversion by Riskiness of Work Situations) with Mood Ratio as Dependent Variable

Source	d.f.	F(1.16)	p
Between-subjects effects			
Position P	1	.02	.90
Extraversion E	1	6.02	.03
P by E	1	.00	.99
Within-subject effect			
Riskiness R	1	13.84	.00
P by R	1	.52	.48
E by R	1	3.17	.09
P by E by R	1	.91	.35
Error	16		

relationship between mood and information processing, on the other hand, suggested the focus of this study on the combined effects of task and person characteristics on mood under safety relevant work conditions. It was anticipated that extraverts would feel better than introverts, more so during work than during leisure, if work is generally characterized as risky, and more so during work activities perceived as particularly high in riskiness than during work activities perceived as less risky. These hypotheses were based on the arousal theory of Eysenck (Eysenck & Eysenck, 1985), who postulates a higher need for stimulation for extraverts than for introverts.

The results of the time sampling study of emotions with 12 crane drivers and eight operators, both groups executing jobs with high potential of risk for health and safety, clearly confirm the predictions. The superiority in subjective well-being of extraverts to introverts is indeed more pronounced in work situations that generally bring about higher levels of risk than leisure situations, and more visible in work situations of high risk than in work situations of low risk. Whether one defines arousal in terms of situational characteristics—leisure (generally lower arousal) versus work (generally higher arousal)—or in terms of perceived risk at work—low risk (lower arousal) versus high risk (higher arousal)—the interaction of extraversion and environmental stimulation on mood follows the same pattern. The crucial point is the situation by person interaction: low versus high stimulation interacting with introversion/extraversion in creating good or bad feelings. Among others, Meyer and Shack (1989) and Larsen and Ketelaar (1991) report that extraverts feel generally better than introverts. This, however, needs some qualification. The superiority in the well-being of extraverts to introverts depends strongly on the circumstances, as Brandstätter (1994a) has shown.

The shortcomings of the study are rooted mainly in the small size of the sample, which, in addition, is barely representative. Only about one-third of the workers eligible for the study were ready to cooperate in the research effort. Statistical inferences and generalizations should, therefore, be drawn only with caution. In order to protect the anonymity of the responders, information on length of work experience and age was not ascertained, although these variables would have been valuable for covariance control. Further research with high risk workers should try to overcome some of these difficulties, although one has to acknowledge that time sampling studies will always be restricted to rather small and somewhat biased samples.

The study was undertaken under the premise that mood is important not only as an indicator of work satisfaction and subjective well-being but also as an influential condition of information processing and decision making under risk. This study focused on the combined effects of personality and environment on emotional responses to risky work situations. How mood eventually affects the performance of introverts and extraverts under different levels of risk has been left out of consideration. It could well be that extraverts generally feel better in risk-prone situations but that only stable extraverts perform better. Future studies will have to find an answer to this important question.

Experience with the Time Sampling Diary in the present study and in other studies (cf. Brandstätter, chapter 2 in this volume) suggests that participants, varying in age and education, are generally co-operative and careful in keeping the mood diary. Thus, one can trust that the data collected in the present study with this technique are reliable and valid and that time sampling, perhaps in combination with event sampling, will prove useful in future studies on affective reactions to dangerous work conditions and, in a second step, on performance in information processing and decision making.

Conclusion

Safety in hazardous work systems clearly depends on human performance. Limitations in cognitive capabilities and interference from affective arousal endanger the task accomplishment in such systems. The emotional experience of people working in hazardous work systems, although recognized as antecedent of more or less adequate information processing and task performance, still does not get enough attention in work design or in personnel selection and training, although there is ample research evidence that effective coping with stress is a matter of both selection and training (Hogan & Lesser, 1996; Hörmann & Maschke, 1996; Johnston & Cannon-Bowers, 1996; Keinan & Friedland, 1996; Pitz, 1992). Caring more about the causes and effects of people's emotions in work situations is supposed to support not only their well-being but also the system safety in general. The present study should be seen as a step in this direction.

Notes

1. That leisure activities of the participants in the present study are on average really less arousing than their work activities in the steel plant could be shown by comparing the relative frequencies of satisfaction and frustration of the need for sentience/activity (cf. Brandstätter, 1994a).

2. The time between leaving the home and arriving at the work station, not considered in the ANOVA of leisure versus work, was included in the analysis of low-risk versus high-risk work situations in order to keep the cell frequencies and the variation of experienced risk at a reasonable level.

References

Bless, H. (1997). *Stimmung und Denken. Ein Modell zum Einfluß von Stimmungen auf Denkprozesse* [Mood and thinking. A model of influence of mood on cognitive processes]. Bern: Huber.

Bless, H., & Fiedler, K. (1995). Affective states and the influence of activated general knowledge. *Personality and Social Psychology Bulletin, 21,* 766–778.

Bogner, M. S. (1994). *Human Error in Medicine.* Hillsdale, NJ: Lawrence Erlbaum.

Brandstätter, H. (1977). Wohlbefinden und Unbehagen. Entwurf eines Verfahrens zur Messung situationsabhängiger Stimmungen [Positive and negative mood. The design of a study for measuring mood changing with situations]. In W. H. Tack (Ed.), *Bericht über den 30 Kongreß der DGfPs in Regensburg 1976* (Vol. 2, pp. 60–62). Göttingen: Hogrefe.

Brandstätter, H. (1988). Sechzehn Persönlichkeits-Adjektivskalen (16 PA) als Forschungsinstrument anstelle des 16 PF [Sixteen Personality Adjective Scales (16 PA) as a substitute for the 16 PF in research settings]. *Zeitschrift für Experimentelle und Angewandte Psychologie, 35,* 370–391.

Brandstätter, H. (1989). Motives in everyday life situations. In F. Halisch & J. van den Bercken (Eds.), *International perspectives on achievement and task motivation* (pp. 327–349). Lisse: Swets & Zeitlinger.

Brandstätter, H. (1994a). Pleasure of leisure—Pleasure of work: Personality makes the difference. *Personality and Individual Differences, 16,* 931–946.

Brandstätter, H. (1994b). Well-being and motivational person-environment fit: A time-sampling study of emotions. *European Journal of Personality, 8,* 75–93.

Carayon, P. (1994). *A systems approach to reducing physical and psychological stress: Factors in organizational design and management—IV* (pp. 733–738). Amsterdam: Elsevier Science.

Clore, G. L., Schwarz, N., & Conway, M. (1994). Affective causes and consequences of social information processing. In R. S. Wyer, Jr., & T. K. Srull (Eds.), *Handbook of Social Cognition* (2nd ed., Vol. 1, pp. 323–417). Hillsdale, NJ: Lawrence Erlbaum.

Dunegan, K., Duchon, D., & Barton, S. (1992). Affect, risk, and decision criticality: Replication and extension in a business setting. *Organizational Behavior and Human Performance, 53,* 335–351.

Eysenck, H. J., & Eysenck, M. W. (1985). *Personality and individual differences.* New York: Plenum.

Farthofer, A. (1992). *Führungsfeld "Zwei-Mann-Cockpit"* [Leadership in High-Tech-Cockpits]. Unpublished master's thesis, University of Salzburg, Austria.

Hesse, F. W., & Spies, K. (1993). Möglichkeiten der Integration von Emotionen in theoretische Ansätze der Kognitionspsychologie [How to integrate emotions into theoretical approaches to cognitive psychology]. *Zeitschrift für Psychologie, 201,* 351–373.

Hesse, F. W., & Spies, K. (1996). Effects of negative mood on performance: Reduced capacity or changed processing strategy? *European Journal of Social Psychology, 26,* 163–168,

Hogan, J., & Lesser, M. (1996). Selection of personnel for hazardous performance. In E. Salas & J. E. Driskell (Eds.), *Stress and Human Performance* (pp. 195–222). Hillsdale, NJ: Lawrence Erlbaum.

Hörmann, H. J., & Maschke, P. (1996). On the relation between personality and job performance of airline pilots. *International Journal of Aviation Psychology, 6,* 171–178.

Isen, A. M., & Geva, N. (1987). The influence of positive affect on acceptable level of risk: The person with a large canoe has a large worry. *Organizational Behavior and Human Performance, 39,* 145–154.

Isen, A. M., & Patrick, R. (1983). The effect of positive feelings on risk taking: When the chips are down. *Organizational Behavior and Human Performance, 31,* 194–202,

Johnston, J. H., & Cannon-Bowers, J. A. (1996). Training for stress exposure. In E. Salas & J. E. Driskell (Eds.), *Stress and Human Performance* (pp. 223–256), Hillsdale, NJ: Lawrence Erlbaum.

Kahnemann, D., & Tversky, A. (1982). *Judgment under uncertainty: Heuristics and biases.* New York: Cambridge University Press.

Keinan, G., & Friedland, N. (1996). Training effective performance under stress: Queries, dilemmas, and possible solutions. In E. Salas & J. E. Driskell (Eds.), *Stress and human performance* (pp. 257–277), Hillsdale, NJ: Lawrence Erlbaum.

Kuhl, J. (1983). Emotion, Kognition und Motivation: II. Die funktionale Bedeutung der Emotionen für das problemlösende Denken und für das konkrete Handeln [Emotion, cognition, and motivation: II. The functional significance of emotions in problem solving and action]. *Sprache & Kognition, 4,* 228–253.

Larsen, R. J., & Ketelaar, T. (1991). Personality and susceptibility to positive and negative emotional states. *Journal of Personality and Social Psychologie, 61,* 132–140.

Lersch, P. (1970). *Aufbau der Person* [Structure of the person]. München: Barth.

Mann, J. (1992). Stress affect and risk taking. In J. F. Yates (Ed.), *Risk-taking behavior* (pp. 201–230). New York: Wiley.

Mano, H. (1992). Judgments under distress: Assessing the role of unpleasantness and arousal in judgment formation. *Organizational Behavior and Human Performance, 52*, 216–245.

Mano, H. (1994). Risk taking, framing effects, and affect. *Organizational Behavior and Human Performance, 57*, 38–58.

McFatter, R. M. (1994). Interaction in predicting mood from extroversion and neuroticism. *Journal of Personality and Social Psychology, 66*, 570–578.

Melton, R. J. (1995). The role of positive affect in syllogism performance. *Personality and Social Psychology Bulletin, 21*, 788–794.

Meyer, G. J., & Shack, J. R. (1989). Structural convergence of mood and personality: Evidence for old and new directions. *Journal of Personality and Social Psychology, 57*, 691–706.

Murray, H. A. (1938). *Explorations in personality.* New York: Oxford University Press.

Nygren, T., Isen, A. M., Taylor, P. J., & Dulin, J. (1996). The influence of positive affect on the decision rule in risk situations: Focus on outcome (and especially avoidance of loss) rather than probability. *Organizational Behavior and Human Decision Processes, 66*, 59–72.

Omodei, M. M., & Wearing, A. J. (1995). Decision making in complex dynamic settings: A theoretical model incorporating motivation, intention, affect, and cognitive performance. *Sprache und Kognition, 14*, 75–90.

Pitz, G. F. (1992). Risk taking, design, and training. In J. F. Yates (Ed.), *Risk-taking behavior* (pp. 283–320). New York: Wiley.

Reason, J. (1990). *Human error.* Cambridge: University Press.

Rusting, C. L. (1998). Personality, mood, and cognitive processing of emotional information: Three conceptual frameworks. *Psychological Bulletin, 124*, 165–196.

Salvendy, G. (1997). *Handbook of human factors and ergonomics* (2nd ed.). New York: Wiley.

Schneewind, K. A., Schröder, G., & Cattell, R. B. (1983). *Der 16-Persönlichkeits-Faktoren Test* [The 16-Personality-Factor-test]. 16PF. Bern: Huber.

Wickens, C. D. (1992). *Engineering psychology and human performance* (2nd ed.). New York: HarperCollins.

Wickens, C. D. (1996). Designing for stress. In E. Salas & J. E. Driskell (Eds.), *Stress and human performance* (pp. 279–295). Hillsdale, NJ: Lawrence Erlbaum.

Wickens, C. D., Stokes, A., Barnett, B., & Hymann, F. (1993). The effects of stress on pilot judgment in a MIDIS simulator. In O. Svenson & A. J. Maule (Eds.), *Time pressure and stress in human judgment and decision making* (pp. 271–292). New York: Plenum Press.

Wilpert, B., & Qvale, T. (1993). *Reliability and safety in hazardous work systems.* Sussex: HarperCollins.

8

Time Sampling of Unemployment Experiences by Slovak Youth

Jozef Džuka

Unemployment has been marking the life of many young people in industrialized Western countries (Roth, 1989; Kirchler, 1993). With an unemployment rate of more than 11% in 1996, Slovakia, though still at a lower level of industrial development than the industrialized Western nations, for some time now has had to struggle with the problem, too.

Unemployment and Its Effects on Slovak Youth

Research on the effects of unemployment in the Slovak Republic has provided ambiguous results. Adamovič, Kleinová, and Vonkomerová (1994) studied the effects of unemployment on a group of young people who had failed to find permanent jobs and had been registered with a Labor Exchange. They observed a relatively high percentage of symptoms indicating vegetative lability, neurotic fear, and reactions related to worry. Machalová (1994) compared unemployed university graduates with those graduates who had succeeded in getting jobs corresponding to their qualifications. She found "that for men unemployment was not a stronger stress factor than entering an occupation" (p. 33). Džuka and Pončáková (1994) compared unemployed secondary school leavers registered with a Labor Exchange and adolescents attending a secondary school with respect to subjective well-being. Their unemployed group had lower scores than the group of secondary school leavers in habitual satisfaction with life, but, paradoxically, the unemployed school leavers reported fewer emotional problems than the studying respondents. No differences were found in depressive mood, in the number of physical problems, or in self-esteem. All three studies were based on cross-sectional research strategies.

147

Short-Term and Long-Term Unemployment, and Their Effects on the Youth in Western Countries

Cross-sectional studies of unemployment in Western countries stress the detrimental effects of long-term unemployment. Franzkowiak and Stößel (1990) report a correlation between health-damaging group activities (including drug addiction) of youth and the length of unemployment. Kieselbach (1994) refers to a Finnish study that found a high incidence of an unhealthy life style—smoking, alcoholism, impairment of sleeping habits, and a lack of sport activities among the unemployed. Similar results were obtained by Australian researchers who compared groups of short-term and long-term unemployed young people. The long-term unemployed (more than five months) differed from the former in showing more of the following characteristics: physical inactivity, social isolation, impairment of sleeping and eating habits, increased consumption of alcohol and tobacco, and frequent visits to the physician (Turtle & Ridley, 1984, cited from Kieselbach, 1994). On the basis of these results, Kieselbach concludes that unhealthy behavior is conditioned by a certain length of unemployment. Stafford, Jackson, and Banks (1980), and Warr, Jackson, and Banks (1988) examined English youth and arrived at the conclusion that seven-month-unemployed school leavers showed more negative psychological symptoms than those who succeeded in getting jobs.

Contradictions in Available Findings

To summarize, the studies cited indicate the prevalence of negative psychical and behavioral symptoms in the long-term unemployed. Cross-sectional studies, however, are not conclusive as to whether the symptoms were caused by unemployment or had existed prior to unemployment (Winefield & Tiggemann, 1985). Longitudinal studies examining the relation between psychological symptoms, notably, subjective well-being, and unemployment in secondary school leavers are rare (Banks & Jackson, 1982; Donovan, Oddy, Pardoe, & Ades, 1986; Feather & O'Brien, 1986; Gurney, 1980; Patton & Noller, 1984; Winefield, Tiggemann, Winefield, & Goldney, 1993) and yield inconsistent results, as confirmed by Winefield, Tiggemann, Winefield, and Goldney (1991).

Methodological Limitations

For studies whose objective is to analyze the conditions of subjective well-being, people are usually asked to participate in interviews or complete questionnaires about their momentary experience or, more frequently, about how they generally felt during a given period of time (e.g., the last day, week, or month), and these responses are obtained either only once, or repeatedly. The questions concern happiness, satisfaction with one's life, satisfaction with oneself, anxiety, positive and negative affects, negative self-esteem, psychiatric symptoms, and so on. One hardly can contest these constructs of subjective well-being. What is called into question, however, is the measuring technique. For example, Smith (1979) and Mohr (1987) maintain that significant differences in answers are conditioned by the specific circumstances of completing a questionnaire, the particular wording of questions, or the order of questions within an interview. Judgments concerning one's mood over a longer period of time are not less questionable. "If we imagine the range of oscillation of mood in the course of a single day, we cannot be surprised at the fact that a particular person describes his/her mood during the previous two days both as very tense and rather relaxed." (Becker, 1988, p. 519). Furthermore, we cannot disregard Kozma and Stones's objection (1988). They say that measurements of subjective well-being tend to be impaired by respondents' giving socially required answers. And, last but not least, the measurement of emotional states without any possibility of checking their causes, as is the case when the participants describe their mood just with adjectives and without detailed reference to situations and events, cannot be regarded as compelling. Recently, Diener, Suh, Lucas, & Smith (1999) have given an overview of the theoretical issues and methodological problems in research on subjective well-being.

Time Sampling Diary and Process Approach

In his longitudinal study, Kirchler (1984) asked 33 unemployed respondents to record their mood in a Time Sampling Diary six times a day. This was done at ten-day intervals in the first, second, third, and sixth months following the beginning of the unemployment period. A similar strategy was employed by Windischbauer (1986) to analyze communication behavior of unemployed young people. Here, too, records were taken for ten days after three and six months of unemployment. Pelzmann (1988) used a daily retrospective diary with various groups, including a total of 300 unemployed respondents, some of them before the dismissal, others after the resumption of their jobs. They reported on their activities as well as on the occurrence of depressive moods.

These three research projects appear to be an appropriate alternative to questionnaire-based studies, since mood is diagnosed as an immediate reaction to the question "How am I feeling right now?" The aggregate data in the form of the average index of mood for a specific period of time are therefore not based on estimated mood reconstructed in the memory; on the contrary, they reflect immediate assessments of one's mood. In other words, the oscillation of mood, a source of error in surveys based on questionnaires or interviews (Schwarz, 1988), becomes an object of measurement.

Recently, strategies enabling young people to cope with unemployment have come under examination, too. A process-based approach shifts the focus of inquiry from the effects of unemployment to the active person who copes with his or her difficulties (Fraccaroli, Le Blanc, & Hajjar, 1994). These authors maintain that such research is expected to reveal factors that transform a potentially problematic situation. They draw on the model of social stress (Pearlin & Schooler, 1978) and assume that the existence and the intensity of the emotional effects of unemployment are a function of two factors: first, the quality of the participant's social interaction with family, friends, and institutions, and, second, social self-description (Sarchielli et al., 1991) (cited from Fraccaroli et al., 1994). The research of Fraccaroli et al. (1994), focused on French and Italian young people, shows that bad mood is characteristic of only those persons who miss social support and who have a poor self-image.

Hypotheses

The present research was aimed at comparing psychological effects of short-term (less than 7 months) and long-term (more than 12 months) unemployment on 18- to 22-year-old school leavers who had either failed in their attempts to continue their studies at a university level, or had not found any job. In accordance with Franzkowiak and Stößel (1990) and Kieselbach (1994), I assumed that long-term unemployment would have more adverse effects than short-term unemployment on the emotional sphere and on behavioral variables. In particular, the long-term unemployed were expected to experience more frequent and intensely negative mood; fear, loneliness, and stress; unhealthy behavior such as alcoholism, lack of physical activities, and disorganized eating habits; and diseases.

Method

Participants

Taking the average length (8.3 months) of youth unemployment in the district into account and following a contrast group design, the Labor Exchange office invited only those secondary school leavers to participate in the study who at that time were registered as having been unemployed for less than 7 months or more than 12 months. The sample includes only those secondary school leavers who had passed the school-leaving examinations. In total, 156 unemployed adolescents were interviewed on four consecutive days in an office of the Labor Exchange; 78 persons (50%) agreed to participate in the study after preliminary information. However, only 32 persons attended the first meeting scheduled for giving instructions. Two persons left the study due to health problems. In spite of my intention to take into consideration not only the length of unemployment but also the gender of the respondents (I attempted proportional representation of boys and girls), more girls than boys were finally willing to participate in the study. Thirty persons kept the Time Sampling Diary (TSD), including 23 girls and 7 boys. Twenty-six of their records could be included in the analysis: Two persons found a job in the course of this research, one boy took up studies, and the coding tables of one participant indicated that she had not observed sufficiently the instructions for keeping the Time Sampling Diary (all of them belonged to the under-7-month unemployment group). Thus, diary data from 26 participants could be processed (21 girls and 5 boys). Three boys and one girl were excluded randomly from the group of short-term unemployed, in order to have 10 girls and one boy in each group. The average unemployment length in the group of 11 less-than-seven-months unemployed was 6.0 months, and in the group of 11 more-than-12-month unemployed, 17.8 months. The age difference between the two groups was 2 years (18.6 and 20.5 years of age on the average, respectively).

Material

I used a Time Sampling Diary as specified by Brandstätter (this volume), with one exception: In the original format, the respondents generated their own adjectives for describing their mood and emotions without recoding them into standard categories. The research participants recoded their descriptions by means of a coding scheme that utilized "descriptive words" (including 12 emotional words): (1) I am afraid, I am scared; (2) I am angry, I am upset; (3) I am surprised; (4) I am sad, I am depressed; (5) I am pleased, I am glad; (6) I perceive something with interest, I am concentrated on something; (7) I feel ashamed, I am abashed; (8) I feel an aversion, I detest something; (9) I feel guilty; (10) I feel love for somebody; (11) I am tense, excited; (12) I am satisfied, I feel contented. The list of emotional words was completed by 12 non-emotional words: (13) I am cold; (14) I am warm; (15) I am in pain; (16) I am hungry, I am thirsty; (17) I am full; (18) I am tired; (19) I am intoxicated; (20) I feel comfortable; (21) I am ill, I am sick; (22) I am relaxed; (23) I am bored; (24) I am lazy. Respondents were asked to mark yes or no those words that in their meaning came closest to the self-generated adjectives. A theoretical starting point for the compiling of our list was the assumption that the mood of a person may result from psychological (emotional) and physical (non-emotional) components (see also Becker, 1991). The non-emotional words given in the coding scheme refer to bodily feelings. In compiling the adjective list, a reanalysis of some of Brandstätter's[1] Time Sampling Diary protocols proved useful.

In addition to the adjective coding of the participants, the author coded these emotional and non-emotional words in terms of their valence in order to (a) verify very quickly the prevailing mood component (psychical, physical) and the typical valence of emotions; and (b) to check the validity of answers, for instance, by matching the mood and the valence of the descriptive words used.

Procedure

The TSD data were collected from January through March 1996. Each of the participants kept the diary during 28 consecutive days, after a trial of one day. Before, during, and after this period, groups of participants met the researcher at the Labor Exchange for the sake of getting further instructions and to check whether they were completing the diaries appropriately. The meetings took place as follows:

First meeting: The participants were informed about the Time Sampling Diary and on the remuneration for participation in the research.

Second meeting: This session followed a one-day try of the diary keeping. Each participant received diary sheets for the period of 15 days, a random time schedule (in the diary), instructions for keeping the Time Sampling Diary, and a wrist watch with an alarm function. The alarm function (beep) was set up by each participant, according to the schedule, for each consecutive time at which they were to make a recording in the diary, with the exception of sleeping time. The participants had to countersign the receipt for the watch, thus promising to return the watch in case they would not complete the research.

Third meeting: After two weeks of keeping the diary, the participants encoded the diary records into coding tables, and passed them anonymously to the researcher.

Fourth meeting: This took place after another two weeks of diary keeping; during the meeting the participants encoded their records of the previous two weeks into coding tables.

Results

Twenty-two participants made a total of 2050 records during 28 days of research, with six records scheduled per day. Mood was recorded in the less-than-7-months unemployment group at 1016 time points (57.8%), and in the more-than-12-months unemployment group at 1034 time points (58.7%). The remaining scheduled time points fall into the hours of sleep or were omitted (42.2% and 41.3%, respectively).

Negative Emotions Dependent on the Length of Unemployment

On the basis of the answers to the question "How am I feeling right now?" I calculated the average index of mood rated on a five-point scale: 1—very good, 2—good, 3—indifferent, 4—bad, 5—very bad. The differences in mood between the less-than-7-months unemployed and the more-than-12-months unemployed were tested by a single factor analysis of variance: F (1,2048) = 6.3; p = .012. The compared groups show significant differences in mood, to the disadvantage of the more-than-12-months unemployed (average mood index: M = 2.38 and M = 2.50, respectively). The meaning of this difference is analyzed in this section.

The frequencies of four categories of descriptive words (positive vs. negative crossed with emotions vs. body feelings) are given in Table 8.1.

By logit transformation (Linder & Berchtold, 1976) I compared the relative frequencies of four descriptive word categories whose valence could be determined unambiguously. It follows from Table 8.1 that there is only one significant

Table 8.1 Description of Subjective Mood of the Less-Than-7-Months and More-Than-12-Months Unemployment Groups

Descriptions	Less than 7 months		More than 12 months		
	n	%	n	%	z
Positive emotional words	473	46.65	453	44.07	0.40
Negative emotional words	104	10.26	174	16.93	5.40**
Positive nonemotional words	115	11.34	145	14.11	1.85
Negative nonemotional words	107	10.55	104	10.12	0.11
False	65	6.41	125	12.16	
Indifferent	34	3.35	13	1.26	
Other	116	11.42	14	1.36	
Total	1014	100.00	1028	100.00	

The percentage data were transformed to logits, and the calculated test value z was compared to critical values $u_{0.05}$ = 1.960, and $u_{0.01}$ = 2.560, respectively.

False = a participant answered the question "How am I feeling right now?" positively, but in describing this state he/she selected a negative descriptive word, or vice versa. Indifferent = the answer was 0. Other = a participant encoded the description of his/her state by the category Other. Frequency differences in the false, the indifferent, and the other categories were not tested.

**p < .01

difference between the compared groups—the adolescents who have been unemployed more than 12 months report a significantly higher number of negative
emotions than those in the less-than-seven-months category ($z = 5.40$, $p < .01$).
No significant differences between the two groups were identified in the other
three categories—the number of positive emotions and the number of positive
and negative nonemotional states. Anger, sadness, and tension are the most frequently recorded emotions. They represent 22.56% of all (emotional and non-
emotional) descriptions in the more-than-12-months unemployment group, twice
as frequent as their occurrence in the less-than-7-months unemployment group
(10.46%). The two groups differ only slightly in the number of non-emotional
descriptions (subtotals 28.20% and 29.09%, respectively). The frequencies for
other positive (surprise, love) and negative emotions (fear, shame, aversion, and
guilt) approach 1% in both groups. Similarly, the share of non-emotional descriptions, including cold, warmth, pain, hunger, fullness, alcohol, disease, boredom,
and laziness, is about 1%. Taking all negative mood descriptions together (afraid,
angry, sad, ashamed, feeling aversion, feeling pain, feeling sick; that is, the "descriptive words" numbers 1, 2, 4, 7, 8, 9, 11, 15, and 21), one finds relative
frequencies of 29% vs. 14% for the long-term vs. the short-term unemployed.

Mood as Function of Unemployment Status, Emotional Stability, and Extraversion

Adding the unemployment status to emotional stability, extraversion,[2] and the
product of standardized scores of emotional stability and extraversion in predicting the relative frequency of those negative descriptive words increases the
explained variance from 15% to 41% (Table 8.2).

Figure 8.1 presents the relative frequencies of negative emotions estimated

Table 8.2 Hierarchical Regression Analysis: Predicting Relative Frequencies of
Negative Emotion from Emotional Stability, Extraversion, and Employment
Status (1 Short Term; 2 Long Term)

Model	Beta	p	R square	R square adj.
Model 1				
Stability (S)	−.34	.11		
Extraversion (E)	.00	.99		
			.12	.04
Model 2				
Stability (S)	−.37	.06		
Extraversion (E)	−.19	.37		
S x E	.42	.06		
			.26	.15
Model 3				
Stability (S)	−.33	.05		
Extraversion (E)	−.04	.83		
S x E	.33	.09		
Status	.52	.00		
			.50	.41

Emotional stability and extraversion are standardized scores (z-scores).

with the regression equation of Table 8.2 (model 3) for combinations of emotional stability (−1 unstable, +1 stable) and extraversion (−1 introvert, +1 extravert) and employment status. One can see that stable introverts (STABIN) have the lowest frequencies, unstable introverts (LABIN) the highest frequencies of negative emotions. Unstable extraverts experience negative emotions equally often as stable extraverts, which means that there is a marginally significant interaction between emotional stability and extraversion (cf. Figure 8.1 and Table 8.2).

Causal Attributions of Mood to Various Sources Dependent on Length of Unemployment

Table 8.3 presents the participants' subjective explanations of their mood states, that is, their casual attributions of mood to various sources, for both short-term and long-term unemployed.

The relative frequencies (%) of attributions and the respective average mood scores (M) show that the two groups differ in six out of the 12 most frequently mentioned attributive categories: the unemployed belonging to the more-than-12-months group specified their own character properties and their health condition as sources of their mood significantly more frequently than the members of the other group. The share of these two sources of all specified sources was 20.3% vs. 11.3%. In particular, as a separate analysis revealed (no table), negative emotions were more often internally attributed by the long-term unemployed than by the short-term unemployed (51.4% vs. 45.9%). The less-than-7-months group gave four other reasons as being mainly responsible for their mood: partner, friends, mass media, and the place of their immediate stay. The total percentage of attributions to these sources is 31.7% vs. 17.5%.

Occurrence and Experience of Behavior Settings Related to Length of Unemployment

At each time point of self-observation the participants recorded the place of their stay, their activities, and who else was present. In the following paragraph we look at differences between the two groups of unemployed youth in terms of the frequency with which they found themselves in the various behavior settings and with which they reported feeling good or bad in these settings.

Places. The following places were recorded with low frequencies (each with less than 3% of all records) by both groups: bathroom, bedroom, hospital, school, relatives, dining room, cafeteria, cinema, church, sports ground, shops, street, car, nature, hairdresser/barber, office. The categories exceeding 3% in both groups are grouped according to their common features. These are the three places "home," "friends/visit," and "entertainment" (Table 8.4).

It follows from Table 8.4 that the three categories of places—home, friends/visit, entertainment—represent more than 80% of all places specified by the participants. While the category "home" clearly dominates in both groups of the unemployed, the respective values are significantly higher for the more-than-12-months group. This significant difference in the frequency of answers, however, does not affect the differences in mood—both groups experience, on the average, slightly positive feelings at home, irrespective of the length of unemployment

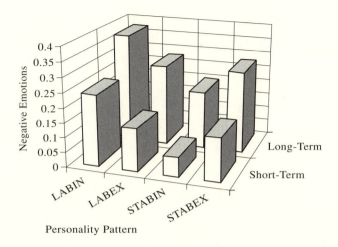

Figure 8.1. Frequency of negative emotions dependent on personality pattern (LABIN = unstable introverts; LABEX = unstable extraverts; STABIN = stable introverts; STABEX = stable extraverts) and unemployment status (short and long).

Table 8.3 Relative Frequencies of Causal Attributions to Various Sources of Mood (%) and Average Mood Score (M) Related to These Attributions for Short-Term and Long-Term Unemployed

Source	Less than 7 months		More than 12 months			
	M	%	M	%	t	z
1. My ability/inability	2.64	9.27	2.61	9.87	0.26	0.46
2. My character, properties	2.64	4.44	2.72	10.46	0.45	5.03**
4. My physical condition, my health	3.40	6.90	3.38	9.80	0.12	2.39*
5. My activities	2.02	11.44	2.10	11.05	0.65	0.32
6. Results of my work	2.34	4.83	2.10	3.81	1.15	1.32
7. Partner	1.89	7.30	2.25	3.13	1.61	4.79**
8. Parents	2.47	5.42	2.53	6.55	0.31	1.46
9. Siblings	2.83	4.73	2.42	3.23	1.38	1.65
11. Friends	1.78	5.62	2.25	3.13	2.26*	2.71**
22. Radio, TV, books, magazines	2.36	10.65	2.01	6.65	2.57**	4.70**
25. Place of my present stay	2.15	8.09	2.21	4.59	0.11	4.60**
28. Food	2.11	3.35	2.13	3.71	1.10	0.57
30. Other		5.23		3.62		1.78
Categories under 3%		12.72		20.40		
Total		100.00		100.00		

The percentage data were transformed to logits, and the calculated test value z was compared to critical values $u_{0.05} = 1.960$, and $u_{0.01} = 2.560$, respectively. t refers to differences in means, z refers to differences in relative frequencies.

*$p < .05$
**$p < .01$

Table 8.4 Dependence of Mood on Places of Participants' Stay and Length of Unemployment

Places	Less than 7 months		More than 12 months			
	M	%	M	%	t	z
1. Home	2.48	68.66	2.50	84.32	0.38	8.24**
2. Friends/visit	1.84	4.92	2.36	1.07	1.64	4.70**
3. Entertainment	2.01	10.14	2.10	0.97	0.25	8.60**
Total 1, 2, 3		83.72		86.36		
Categories under 3%		16.28		13.64		

*$p < .05$
**$p < .01$

($M = 2.48$ vs. $M = 2.50$). The time spent outside participants' home clearly depends on the length of unemployment: the less-than-seven-months group visits partners and/or friends significantly more frequently and/or spends more time at various places of entertainment (cinema, café, sportsground). Again, no statistically significant differences in mood were found.

Activities. The answers to the question "What am I doing right now?" enabled us to study the activities of the respondents at scheduled time points, as well as their feelings at that time. Activities whose occurrence exceeded 3% of the total number of cases were grouped into broader categories (Table 8.5).

The most frequent activities include mass media consumption (radio, TV, reading) and housework. These two categories represent more than 55% of all the activities in each of the compared groups. The length of unemployment does not seem to affect significantly the frequency of these two main categories. The frequencies in the category "Active relaxation" differ—the less-than-seven-months group is more active than the other group (9.44% vs. 6.91%, $p < .05$), which, however, does not apply to mood: both groups experience equally positive feel-

Table 8.5 Dependence of Mood on the Activities Grouped into Categories and Length of Unemployment

Groups of activities	Less than 7 months		More than 12 months			
	M	%	M	%	t	z
1. Housework	2.44	21.46	2.63	20.83	1.88	0.24
2. Mass media	2.45	34.96	2.36	33.98	1.19	0.21
3. Active relaxation	2.41	9.44	2.46	6.91	0.37	2.06*
4. Idling	3.07	5.46	2.79	11.00	1.46	4.46**
Total 1, 2, 3, 4		71.30		72.73		
Other		9.83		8.67		0.90
Categories under 3%		18.87		18.60		

*$p < .05$
**$p < .01$

Table 8.6 Dependence of Mood on Present Persons and Length of Unemployment

Present persons	Less than 7 months		More than 12 months		t	z
	M	%	M	%		
1. Alone	2.55	35.27	2.59	30.44	0.47	2.01*
2. Partner	1.87	8.97	2.32	5.71	2.32*	2.80*
3. Siblings	2.48	22.76	2.34	24.33	0.18	1.70
4. Mother	2.37	12.12	2.62	21.48	2.20*	5.45**
5. Father	2.45	3.05	2.45	2.17	0.11	1.12
7. Friends	2.06	12.02	2.32	3.35	1.31	6.20**
Total		94.19		87.48		
Categories under 3%		5.81		12.52		

*p < .05
**p < .01

ings (M = 2.41 vs. M = 2.46) during active relaxation. The last category to be mentioned is "Idling." This category has not been included in any of the other categories because of its ambiguity. Though idling is more frequent in the more-than-12-months group than in the less-than-seven-months one (11.00% vs. 5.46%), the difference in mood is again not significant (M = 2.79 vs. M = 3.07, p = .15).

Other persons present. At each scheduled time point, the participants had to answer the question "Who else is present?" The frequencies for these categories, and respondents' mood at the time of answering the question, are given in Table 8.6.

Table 8.6 illustrates what kinds of persons the two groups of the unemployed met, the length of time spent with them, and the participants' mood at that time. The presence of partners and of mothers makes a difference in mood: When partners are present, respondents' mood is significantly more positive in the less-than-seven-months group. In addition, the members of this group spend significantly more time with their partners than the members of the more-than-12-months group (M = 1.87 vs. M = 2.32, p < .05; 8.97% vs. 5.71%, p < .01). Both groups spend much time with their mothers, but the members of the more-than-12-months group were with their mothers significantly more frequently than the other group (21.48% vs. 12.12%, p < .01). In addition, mood of the more-than-12-months group is significantly worse when spending time with their mothers than among the less-than-seven-months group (M = 2.62 vs. M = 2.37, p < .05).

Discussion

Some limitations of the TSD. Since the Time Sampling Diary is a costly and demanding technique of data collection, it does not allow studying large representative samples, but it is a valuable approach to representative samples of situations. Moreover, restrictions should be taken into account that follow from the way of recruiting volunteers for the present research—only those unemployed were included who were willing to keep the Time Sampling Diary for the required period of time. And, finally, it should be noted that the compared groups could not be balanced in terms of age (average: 18.6 vs. 20.5). However, it is unlikely that the age difference, and not the unemployment status, is responsible for the differences found between the two groups.[3] Banks and Jackson (1982) compared several thousand school leavers, notably their emotional disturbance before they left school and then one to two years later. Emotional disturbance scores of those who failed to find jobs increased, while the data for those who succeeded in getting jobs decreased. The comparison of the examined unemployed after one year and two years, respectively, indicated that the length of unemployment made no difference. This conclusion is supported by a meta-analysis of subjective well-being studies (Stock, Okun, Haring, & Witter, 1983): "Meta-analysis of studies conducted prior to 1980 revealed that the correlation between age and SWB was near zero, regardless of whether other variables were controlled" (cited from Diener, 1984, p. 554).

Emotions. Generally, the unemployed youth, like most other groups studied with the TSD, experience positive moods more often than negative moods. The difference between average mood indexes is, however, statistically significant to the disadvantage of the more-than-12-months group ($M = 2.38$ vs. $M = 2.50$, $p. = .012$; remember that 1 means very good, and 5 very bad mood). A more profound analysis of mood based on descriptive words makes it possible to draw the following conclusions: The frequencies of positive emotions are the same for both groups and considerably exceed the respective frequencies of negative emotions. However, the frequency of negative emotions is statistically much higher in the more-than-12-months group (Table 8.1 and 8.2). To put it differently, while there are no differences between the two groups of unemployed in terms of the frequency of experiencing positive emotions, negative emotions are experienced by the more-than-12-months unemployed significantly more frequently than by the less-than-seven-months group. A more profound analysis indicates that the differences pertain to three specific emotions—anger (7.39% vs. 4.64%), sadness (8.85% vs. 3.65%), and tension (6.32% vs. 2.17%). It is very likely that this is indeed an effect of the duration of unemployment, and not an effect of a personality characteristic like "negative affectivity" (Watson & Clark, 1984), which in turn might contribute to the difficulty of finding a job or getting admission to a university, because short-term and long-term unemployed show no significant differences in the global 16 PF personality dimensions. However, only a longitudinal study, starting before a person faces unemployment and extending over a longer period of time, would provide a clearer picture of the causal paths.

Attributions. With the exception of two attributed mood causes (friends and mass media), no differences were found between the two compared groups in terms of the index of mood (Table 8.3). It should be noted, however, that attributions to one's health were usually connected with negative mood, whereas attributions to other causes were predominantly associated with positive mood. That the frequency of health attributions is higher in the more-than-12-months group (9.80% vs. 6.90%) could mean that this group had indeed more health problems. This conclusion is supported by a somewhat (statistically not significant) higher frequency of recording "I am in pain" and "I am sick" in the long-term unemployed (4.1 vs. 2.8 percent).

Personality and emotions. The emotion words give additional valid information on a person's affective states. Without going into details, it should be mentioned here that emotional stability predicts the relative frequency of negative words (*beta* = -0.31; p = .080), whereas extraversion predicts the relative frequency of positive words (*beta* = 0.40; p = .056) (cf. also DeNeve & Cooper, 1998). A closer look, however, shows that the first relationship is more pronounced with introverts than with extraverts, and the second relationship more with emotionally unstable participants than with emotionally stable ones. This interaction between emotional stability (the opposite of neuroticism) and extraversion is in line with findings of McFatter (1994).

Activities. Sportsgrounds and nature were rarely frequented by the participants. They spent almost all their time at home. This is not to say that they were not physically active, But doing nothing is significantly more frequent in the more-than-12-months group (11.00% vs. 5.46%). A symptom of low social interaction (the term "social isolation" can hardly be used, though) is indicated by the fact that the less-than-7-months unemployed spent more time with friends (12.02% vs. 3.35%) or partners (8.97% vs. 5.71%), and they devoted much more time to entertainment (10.14% vs. 0.97%).

Conclusions

To summarize: We found out that tension, as one of the possible symptoms of frequently experienced stress, as well as sadness and anger, are experienced more frequently by the more-than-12-months unemployed than by the other group examined. In addition, the more-than-12-months unemployed are found to be both in situations of social interaction and in situations of active relaxation less frequently, and they are more often sick. The frequency of alcohol and drug consumption is generally very low, with no difference between the two groups. Both groups spent most of their time at home (see Table 8.4). They devoted equal time to housework and mass media—the latter two activities represent more than 55% of all the activities for both of the compared groups. Social support by the family may have helped both groups to cope with the hardships of being unemployed. Arguments in favor of this assumption are presented, for example, in Gluchman's research (1996) into the value orientation of young people in Slovakia. Fraccaroli et al. (1994) are also of the opinion that favorable family relations facilitate young unemployed people's coping with the impacts of unemployment. Gluchman found out that Slovak youth, when asked about their values, cite health and family happiness as their first priority (79.9% and 77.2% of respondents, respectively). A good job is an important value for less than 25% of this group. In addition, only 5% of research participants are apprehensive of failing at work and/or becoming poor. In other words, family provides the unemployed with an emotional background and can function as a buffer against fear and misgivings. Fraccaroli et al. (1994) also maintain that family provides the unemployed youth with both emotional and instrumental (job-seeking) support in coping with problems. Less compatible with this interpretation is the fact that the long-term unemployed in the present study have lower values of mood when they spend time with their mothers. The high frequency of watching TV could be another way of avoiding negative mood. Positive effects of the mass media upon mood of the unemployed youth were also reported by Windischbauer (1986).

Future research should compare the daily experiences of adolescents who succeeded in getting jobs after leaving secondary school or in passing university entrance exams with the experience of adolescents of the same age who were less successful in finding jobs or gaining admission to a university. Such a comparison would further clarify the interactive effects of personality characteristics and career opportunities on the subjective well-being of adolescents during a particularly critical period of their lives.

Notes

This research was implemented during the present author's study stay in Austria supported by the Scientific Research Foundation (FWF) of the Austrian Republic. I express my gratitude to Prof. Dr. Hermann Brandstätter for his assistance in and support of the implementation of the research.

1. The author expresses his thanks to Hermann Brandstätter for the data provided.
2. The scores on these dimensions were derived from the answers to a Slovac version of the 16 PA (Brandstätter, 1988).
3. Controlling for age in group comparisons did only marginally affect the results.

References

Adamovič, K., Kleinová, R., & Vonkomerová, R. (1994). Psychické prežívanie nezamestnanosti absolventov stredných škôl. [Psychical experiences with unemployment in secondary school leavers]. *Psychológia a patopsychológia diet'at'a, 29*, 115–125.
Banks, M. H., & Jackson, P. R. (1982). Unemployment and risk of minor psychiatric disorder in young people. *Psychological Medicine, 12*, 789–798.
Becker, P. (1998). Ein Strukturmodell der emotionalen Befindlichkeit [A structural model of emotional mood]. *Psychologische Beiträge, 30*, 514–536.
Becker, P. (1991). Theoretische Grundlagen [Theoretical foundations]. In A. Abele & P. Becker (Eds.), *Wohlbefinden. Theorie—Empirie—Diagnostik*. (pp. 13–49). München: Juventa.
Brandstätter, H. (1988). Sechzehn Persönlichkeits-Adjektivskalen (16 PA) als Forschungsinstrument anstelle des 16 PF [Sixteen Personality Adjective Scales (16 PA) as a substitute for the 16 PF in research settings]. *Zeitschrift für Experimentelle und Angewandte Psychologie, 35*, 370–391.
DeNeve, K. M., & Cooper, H. (1998). The happy personality: A meta-analysis of 137 personality traits and subjective well-being. *Psychological Bulletin, 124*, 197–229.
Donovan, A., Oddy, M., Pardoe, R., & Ades, A. (1986). Employment status and psychological effects. A longitudinal study of 16-year-old school leavers. *Journal of Child Psychology and Psychopathology, 1*, 67–76.
Diener, E. (1984). Subjective well-being. *Psychological Bulletin, 95*, 542–575.
Diener, E., Suh, E. M., Lucas, R. E., & Smith, H. L. (1999). Subjective well-being: Three decades of progress. *Psychological Bulletin, 125*, 276–302.
Džuka, J., & Pončáková, K. (1994). Subjektívna pohoda u nezamestnaných absolventov stredných škôl [Subjective well-being of umemployed secondary school leavers]. *Psychológia a patopsychológia diet'at'a, 4*, 334–344.

Feather, N. T., & O'Brien, G. E. (1986). A longitudinal study of the effects of employment and unemployment on school leavers. *Journal of Occupational Psychology, 59*, 121–144.

Fraccaroli, F., Le Blanc, A., & Hajjar, V. (1994). Social self-description and affective well-being in young unemployed people. A comparative study. *European Work and Organisational Psychologist, 4*, 81–100.

Franzkowiak, P., & Stößel, U. (1990). Jugend und Gesundheit [Youth and health]. In Sachverständigenkommision 8. Jugendbericht (Eds.), *Risiken des Heranwachsens. Probleme der Lebensbewältigung im Jugendalter* (Vol. 3, pp. 53–101). Augsburg: Verlag Deutsches Jugendinstitut.

Gluchman, V. (1996). Hodnoty a mravné hodnoty slovenských vysokoškolákov [Values and moral values in Slovak undergraduates]. *Pedagogická revue, 35*, 237–246.

Gurney, R. M. (1980). The effects of unemployment on the psychosocial development of school leavers. *Journal of Occupational Psychology, 53*, 205–213.

Kieselbach, T. (1994). Arbeitslosigkeit als psychologisches Problem—auf individueller und gesellschaftlicher Ebene [Unemployment as a psychological issue—at the individual and social level]. In L. Montada (Ed.), *Arbeitslosigkeit und soziale Gerechtigkeit.* (pp. 233–263). Frankfurt/Main: Campus.

Kirchler, E. (1984). *Arbeitslosigkeit und Alltagsbefinden. Eine sozialpsychologische Studie über die subjektiven Folgen von Arbeitslosigkeit* [Unemployment and subjective mood. A sociopsychological study on subjective impacts of unemployment]. Linz, Austria: Trauner.

Kirchler, E. (1993). *Arbeitslosigkeit. Psychologische Skizzen über ein anhaltendes Problem* [Unemployment. A psychological outline of a persisting problem]. Göttingen: Hogrefe.

Kozma, A., & Stones, M. J. (1988). Social desirability in measures of subjective well-being: Age comparisons. *Social Indicators Research, 29*, 1–14.

Linder, A., & Berchtold, W. (1976). *Statistische Auswertung von Prozentzahlen. Probit- und Logitanalyse mit EDV* [Statistical percentage evaluations. PC-based Probit and Logit analyses]. Basel: Birkhäuser.

Machalová, M. (1994). Psychické stavy absolventov vysokých škôl v tranzite zo školy do zamestnania [Mental states in university graduates during the transition from school to work]. *Psychológia a patopsychológia diet'at'a, 1*, 26–34.

McFatter, R. M. (1994). Interactions in predicting mood from extraversion and neuroticism. *Journal of Personality and Social Psychology, 66*, 570–578.

Mohr, H. M. (1987). Analysen zur Vergleichbarkeit von Zufriedenheitsmessungen [Analyses of the comparability of satisfaction measurements]. *Zeitschrift für Psychologie, 18*, 160–168.

Patton, W., & Noller, P. (1984). Unemployment and youth: A longitudinal study. *Australian Journal of Psychology, 42*, 399–413.

Pearlin, L. I., & Schooler, C. (1978). The structure of coping. *Journal of Health and Social Behaviour, 19*, 2–21.

Pelzmann, L. (1988). *Individuelle Folgen von Arbeitslosigkeit* [Individual impacts of unemployment]. Heft 33, Linz: Österreichisches Institut für Arbeitsmarktpolitik.

Roth, R. (1989). *Jugendarbeitslosigkeit und politische Kultur: Eine Regionalstudie zur Untersuchung politischer Einstellungen bei beschäftigten und arbeitslosen Jugendlichen* [Unemployment of youth and political culture: A regional research into political attitudes of the employed and unemployed youth]. Passau: Passavia-Uni-Verlag.

Schwarz, N. (1988). Stimmung als Information [Mood as information]. *Psychologische Rundschau, 39*, 148–159.

Smith, T. H. (1979). Happiness: Time trends, seasonal variations, intersurvey differences, and other mysteries. *Social Psychology Quarterly, 42*, 18–30.

Stafford, E. M., Jackson, P. R., & Banks, M. H. (1980). Employment, work involvement and mental health in less qualified young people. *Journal of Occupational Psychology, 53*, 291–304.

Stock, W. A., Okun, M. A., Haring, M. J., & Witter, R. A. (1983). Age and subjective well-being: A meta-analysis. In R. J. Light (Ed.), *Evaluation studies: Review annual* (Vol. 8, pp. 279–302). Beverly Hills, CA: Sage.

Warr, P., Jackson, P., & Banks, M. (1988). Unemployment and mental health: Some British studies. *Journal of Social Issues, 44*, 47–68.

Watson, D., & Clark, L. A. (1984). Negative affectivity: The disposition to experience aversive emotional states. *Psychological Bulletin, 96*, 465–490.

Windischbauer, A. (1986). *Arbeitslos—kommunikationslos? Veränderungen im Kommunikationsverhalten bei langzeitarbeitslosen Jugendlichen in Salzburg* [No job— No communication? Changes in communication behaviour in the long-term unemployed youth in Salzburg]. Unpublished doctoral dissertation, University of Salzburg, Austria.

Winefield, A. H., & Tiggemann, M. (1985). Psychological correlates of employment and unemployment: Effects, predisposing factors and sex differences. *Journal of Occupational Psychology, 58*, 229–242.

Winefield, A. H., Tiggemann, M., Winefield, H. R., & Goldney, R. D. (1991). A longitudinal study of the psychological effects of unemployment and unsatisfactory employment on young adults. *Journal of Applied Psychology, 3*, 424–431.

Winefield, A. H., Tiggemann, M., Winefield, H. R., & Goldney, R. D. (1993). *Growing up with unemployment: A longitudinal study of its psychological impact.* London: Routledge.

9

Everyday Life of Commuters' Wives

Christa Rodler & Erich Kirchler

Previous Research

Housework

Early studies of the psychological consequences of wives' work often indicated that working outside the home is generally more emotionally fulfilling than being a full-time housewife. Recent studies (Barnett & Baruch, 1985; Brandstätter & Wagner, 1994), however, paint a more complex picture. The characteristics of housework need to be considered very closely. Studies dealing with housework and its influence on the well-being of women have investigated housework from the perspective of work psychology (Orendi & Rückert, 1982). They propose that well-being depends on the positive or negative effect of various work characteristics: autonomy, fragmentation of work, routine, and rewards.

Enjoying *autonomy*, including the lack of supervision and the possibility of planning and goal-setting, were often mentioned as major positive aspects of housework and family care (Bird & Ross, 1993). But there are other time-related features that restrict autonomy within the household: First, the sequence of specific tasks is logically fixed if housework is to be done efficiently (Berk & Berk 1979). Second, the husband's work or the children's school is what determines a housewife's schedules. Daily schedules of family members restrict housewives in arranging their time freely and in drawing a clear line between work and leisure.

Fragmentation of housework is a feature often mentioned as negatively affecting well-being. Interruptions are often caused by children who express their needs insistently regardless of what their mother happens to be doing at the time (Rerrich, 1983). Since most couples want children, the idea of raising children promises fulfillment and a more satisfying life. Empirical findings contradict this belief.

163

The presence of children under the age of 18 living in the household was consistently reported as having a negative effect on women's individual and marital well-being (Erickson, 1993; McLanahan & Adams, 1987). Since mothers spend a lot of time solely in the company of their children (Baruch & Barnett, 1986; Thompson & Walker, 1989), one central focus of this study should be the presence of children and the relationship of their absence or presence to the well-being of housewives. For example, Ochel (1989) found that the extensive limits placed on mother-child communication in everyday life was an important source of dissatisfaction for housewives.

Although housewives are responsible for a wide range of tasks, most studies describe housework as *routine and monotonous* (Berheide, 1984; Bird & Ross, 1993). Housework is never finished: Cooking, shopping, child care, laundry, and tidying up are all tasks that usually have to be repeated the next day or sooner. Housewives report that their work does not offer much opportunity for the expression and development of their own abilities and talents (Bergmann, 1986; Berheide, 1984). The feeling that their work gives them a chance to do things they enjoy, to develop personally, and to learn new skills are the very aspects of work fulfillment that Bird & Ross (1993) found that housewives miss the most as compared with paid workers.

Housewives don't earn *income* directly from their work but receive goods and services indirectly from someone else, usually their husbands. Bird & Ross (1993) describe housework as ungratifying and unrewarding. It was found that housewives are thanked least for a job well done. Housewives are dependent on the gratitude of their husbands and their family, which is their main source of reward. Full-time housewives' well-being is therefore especially closely related to the quality of the marriage as well as to the specific life situations of their husbands, ranging from matters of income to his work conditions. The influence of husbands' work conditions on housewives' well-being has been rarely investigated.

Commuter Families

A commuter is a person who travels to work over an appreciable distance, usually from the suburbs to the center of the city. A variety of circumstances can require persons to commute: Mainly it depends on the fact that the regional labor market cannot provide (a) enough jobs for the inhabitants who wish to be employed, (b) highly paid jobs, (c) jobs that match the professional educations of local residents, (d) jobs that meet individuals' personal expectations of a job.

Throughout history there have always been various circumstances that have required married couples to live apart for some time. Examples include business and military personnel, immigrants, and traveling merchants, as well as the types of commuters who live apart in order to take advantage of career opportunities or just in order to have a job if there are none close to home. All of these individuals spend substantial periods of time away from their own homes. Observers describe such couples as "two-location," "long-distance," or "weekend" marriages (Peuckert, 1991).

With the improvement of transportation facilities and the shortening of weekly working hours in the twentieth century, it has become possible for many to commute daily and to reconcile their work with family life. Traditionally, wives have been expected to remain in the family home and have usually been excluded from tasks involving geographic mobility, especially over long distances.

Only a few studies in social psychology and sociology in which male samples were used give us insight into individual motives of commuters and the consequences commuting has for their families (Hiebler, 1988; Karner, 1988; Kleppe & Gronhaug, 1997; Wedral, 1991). Gerstel and Gross (1984) investigated a recent form of commuter marriage in which commuting is necessary because both partners are pursuing their own careers. In their study they compared a "dual-career" sample with the traditional husband-dominated marriage of merchant marines. Although either form has its own characteristic set of costs and benefits and differs in the pattern of values, expectations, and resources typically associated with it, these researchers found that there are some problems common to both forms regardless of the motives for commuting. Commuter couples reported missing informal conversation, the sharing of trivia, spontaneous leisure, the physical presence of the husband, and the availability of the partner to serve as a sounding board. They also reported tensions in their relationship as a couple that arise from repeated separations and reunions. Further problems can be seen in the couple's need to organize daily commitments around each other's schedules and to share child care tasks. Young couples in particular are afraid of drifting apart (Farris, 1978) as a result of the spouse's being absent for extended periods. Dissatisfaction tends to increase with the presence of young children, with increasing length of time apart, and with irregularity of reunions (Macklin, 1987).

Wives' Well-Being According to Husbands' Presence in or Absence from the Home

Kirchler (1989) found, in a study conducted with a couple-interaction diary, that in day-to-day interactions the presence of the spouse was especially rewarding to husbands, independent of the quality of marriage, whereas wives felt equally good in certain situations regardless of whether the husband was present or absent. Kirchler (1989) argues that the wife's presence usually means leisure time for the husband, whereas the husband's presence does not necessarily mean leisure time for the wife. When husbands return home from daily work, their leisure time begins, whereas the wives have to keep on working (e.g., cooking, washing up, taking care of the children). Brandstätter & Wagner (1994) also report that the wife's mood does not necessarily improve if the spouse is present while she is doing housework. On the contrary, Brandstätter, Barthel, & Fünfgelt (1984) found that the presence of the husband while the wife was doing housework actually decreased her feeling of well-being. The opposite was found in leisure time situations: The presence of the husband led to an increase in the wife's sense of well-being. These findings indicate that women's subjective feelings in everyday life must be assessed by taking into account the social context involved.

The most obvious feature of commuter families is the reduction in the amount of time both spouses are home together. Gerstel & Gross (1984) also emphasized that the major structural difference between a "normal" family and a commuter family is the degree of physical proximity among family members. Time spent working and traveling is time not spent with family members or performing family functions. Several findings show that the number of hours spent at work is associated with work-family conflict and with difficulties in managing personal and family activities (Piotrkowski, Rapoport, & Rapoport, 1987). The question arises as to what extent a wife's well-being is affected by the commuter status of her husband, first, if he is absent for at least a few days a week and, second, in the case of long-distance daily commuters, when the available time together during the week is reduced, because of early morning departures and late evening returns.

Husbands' Support for Their Wives

The marital relationship is typically a major source of social support for most people (Coyne & DeLongis, 1986; Cutrona, 1996). Within the multidimensional concept of social support, perceived support is defined as "the belief that, if the need arose, at least one person in the individual's circle of family, friends and associates would be available to serve one or more specific functions" (Cutrona, Suhr, & McFarlane, 1990, p. 31). Pina and Bengston (1993) point out that the marital and personal well-being of housewives in their study was directly influenced by the subjective feeling of being supported by their husbands and only indirectly influenced by their husbands' *instrumental support*, that is, the amount they actually helped with housework.

Husbands' performance of family work has often been found to have a positive effect on women's well-being (Erickson, 1993; Staines & Libby, 1986). However, it can be assumed that full-time housewives don't expect a great amount of help from their spouses in performing household duties. Full-time housewives seem to be dissatisfied with husbands who do not provide a just amount of instrumental support mainly when these husbands are absent in the evening or on weekends, enjoying their own leisure time, while their wives are still performing household duties or need to care for the children (Pleck, 1985).

Besides instrumental support, social and emotional support are also important. *Social support* is related to communication between spouses, an aspect said to be one of the main features of a satisfying relationship (Stroebe & Stroebe, 1991). Duck (1986), Kirchler (1989) and others found a positive correlation between the amount of conversation between couples and their marital satisfaction. Daily face-to-face interaction between spouses fosters emotional intimacy and coherence in family life (Kirschner & Walum, 1978). The more shared activities and the less physical separation, the greater marital quality was found to be. Commuting to work reduces the possibilities for daily face-to-face communication between spouses. Even though there are a lot of possibilities to replace face-to-face interaction thanks to modern telecommunication, Gerstel & Gross (1984, p. 54) think that such substitutions are insufficient for commuter families where couples are separated more often than other families in which couples spend time together every day. "Sharing 'trivia' is an essential aspect of the emotional content of marriage according to many commuters."

Emotional support denotes behavior that increases another's emotional well-being. Erickson (1993) emphasizes that emotional support is an important part of family work. She found that the effect of a husband's "emotional work" had a greater impact on a woman's perception of her well-being than did housework or child-care tasks.

The amount of time husbands are available to comply with their wives' requests and wishes in their role as intimate partner and father is reduced in commuter families. Daily commuters are present mainly in the early morning and the late evening; weekly commuters are present on weekends only. Cohen (1977) found that young fathers who traveled frequently or worked long hours did not play significant roles as companions or disciplinarians for their children. At the very least, this means mothers are primarily responsible for child-rearing. Difficult situations in everyday life that require decision-making or dealing with conflicts is part of everyday life with children. In many cases, action is required immediately. Baruch, Biener, & Barnett (1987) argued that parenting is particularly stressful for women and that parental stress undermines women's well-being. It appears plausible that women often desire someone who will help them find a good solution or at least confirm that they have done the right thing. Piotrkowski et al. (1987) report several research findings that showed that the absence of fathers also has negative effects on children. These researchers assume that difficulties may be related not only to paternal absence per se but also to changes in the relationship between mothers and children that are related to fathers' absences. In a study by Gerstel & Gross (1984), commuter's wives mentioned that they often felt like single parents, particularly in matters concerning child care. This may be the case because many problems either lose their urgency by the time the husband returns home or have already been resolved and may not be thought to be important enough to be brought up again.

In many studies, women, not men, were found to be the primary providers of socio-emotional support for their families (Kessler & McLeod, 1984). It can be assumed that wives are considerate about their husbands' need to relax when at home. They are aware that commuting is stressful and that they should not burden their husbands with trivial things that may have happened during the day, even though they may have been exciting at the time. Karner (1988) found that 52% of the daily commuters reported that daily commuting can be as stressful as work itself. Sixty-two percent of the commuters who came home once a week said that commuting reduced their quality of life and placed a great burden on them.

A husband's stress may also affect his wife's emotional state. According to the assumptions of the so-called spill-over model, unpleasant work conditions can be expected to have a negative effect on family life (Bolger, DeLongis, Kessler, & Schilling, 1989; Brandstätter & Wagner, 1994; Repetti, 1989; Rook, Dooly, & Catalona, 1991).

The present study explores the well-being felt in everyday life experiences by spouses of commuting husbands. It can be assumed that commuting has different effects on various aspects of life of commuters and their families, depending on the distance to the workplace, the frequency of commuting (e.g., once a day, once a week), and the time needed to reach the workplace. It is assumed that commuter status affects housewives' daily activities, social contacts, needs, and moods, as well as the factors to which they attribute their moods.

Table 9.1 Sociodemographic Characteristics and Classification of Participants by Husbands' Commuter Status

	Husband not commuting		Husband commuting daily		Husband commuting weekly	
Husbands' distance to workplace	5–25 km		70–100 km		70–100 km	
Time husbands need to reach their workplaces	15–20 min		90–150 min		90–150 min	
N	12		7		11	
	Mean	*SD*	*Mean*	*SD*	*Mean*	*SD*
Age	30.33	7.92	27.84	4.95	28.00	5.66
Completed years of education	10.58	1.67	9.43	1.13	10.36	1.56
Number of children at home	2.00	.74	1.57	.53	2.09	.54
Monthly family income in thousands of US $	2.23	.64	2.21	.46	2.14	.50

Method

Participants

Overall, 30 wives, ages 20 to 49, participated in the study. All women were married, took care of at least one child of preschool-age or school-age, and were housewives. All were living in a small Austrian village 100 km from Vienna. The village itself did not provide enough jobs for local residents. Most of the inhabitants commuted to their workplaces outside the local county. Participants differed in their husbands' commuter status: Eleven husbands traveled 70 to 100 km, returning home on a weekly basis. This group is labeled "husband commutes weekly." Seven husbands traveled 70 to 100 km but returned home every day ("husband commutes daily"). The time that commuters needed to reach their workplaces depended on the means of transport they used. Twelve husbands worked close to home (5 to 25 km) and required 15 to 20 minutes by car to get to work ("no commuter husband"). Socio-demographic features of the participants are presented in Table 9.1 by commuter status.

Material

Diary. A Time Sampling Diary designed by Brandstätter (1977) and presented in this volume by Brandstätter was used. Entries were recorded over a period of 30 days.

The participants were asked to cooperate as "co-investigators." They were instructed to analyze the contents of their diaries themselves after a certain recording period, employing a coding scheme designed together with the participants. The following categories were used to describe the situations recorded in the diary:

1. *Hour and date of entry.*
2. *Well-being.*
3. *Time perspective* to indicate whether their momentary well-being derived from past, present, and/or future events.
4. *Sources of well-being.* Sixty-five sources were categorized according to previous studies (Kirchler, 1985, 1989) in the following classes "self," "family" (e.g., husband, children), "social sources" (e.g., relatives or, friends), "activity" (e.g., the result of work, the performance of an activity), and "other sources" (e.g., the car, the weather).
5. *Motives.* Nineteen motives were assigned to six categories according to Brandstätter (1983): need for physical comfort; need for affiliation (e.g., needs for affiliation, sex, love, and nurturance); power motives (e.g., needs for self-esteem, revenge, independence); achievement motives; needs for activity and new experiences (sentience); higher-order motives (such as needs for order, aesthetic and ethical values, religion, and understanding).
6. *Locations.* Overall, 58 places were clustered into the categories "private rooms," including one's own living room, or kitchen; "semi-private rooms," such as the home of friends, and the area near the house; and "public rooms" such as the supermarket or the school.
7. *Activity currently being performed.* Sixty-seven different activities were distinguished according to the lifetime model of Opaschowski (1988) into "work" (housework, child care), "obligation" (self maintenance, eating), and "recreation" (active leisure activities, passive leisure activities).
8. *Other persons present.* The participants mentioned a total of 57 different persons who were present throughout the period of the study. These were classified according to intimacy: "none," "husband only," "child/ren only," "family" (being together with the husband and at least one of the children, while no others are present), and the categories "relatives," "friends," and "others" (these do not necessarily exclude family members)
9. *Topics of conversation.* Those were categorized into "public topics" (e.g., politics; environment), "private topics" (e.g., dreams, personal problems), and "small talk" (e.g., acquaintances, birthday party). Overall, 55 topics were mentioned; the category "no conversation in the presence of other people" was added for specific analysis.
10. *Perceived power or ego-strength* ("How strong do I feel at the moment")
11. *Freedom of choice* ("How free do I feel at the moment")

Questionnaires. Two questionnaires were distinguished to assess personality characteristics and satisfaction with life. The 16 PA (Brandstätter, 1988) was used to measure participants' personality structure. Satisfaction with various aspects of life was assessed by means of satisfaction questionnaire (Borg, 1978). A set of questions concerning experiences with the diary was also included.

Procedure

The investigation was conducted in May 1993. The participants were visited at home, were individually informed about the aim of the study, and were instructed on how to complete the diary. They had two days in which to become familiar with the diary. They also answered the questionnaires at the outset of the study. At a subsequent meeting, all the participants were brought together and had the opportunity to ask technical questions about the diary method. In this session, content analysis was explained on the basis of the first two-day recording period, and a classification system was set up together with the participants to allow meaningful comparisons of diary entries among the participants. Twice, after two weeks in the middle of the recording period and after four weeks at the end of the recording period, the participants met with the investigator and analyzed their entries themselves. The complete privacy and anonymity of the diary entries were guaranteed. The diary study took four weeks. During this period the participants were in close contact with the investigator. At the end of the recording period, participants filled out the questionnaires a second time. The participants also completed an additional questionnaire on their attitudes toward the study.

Results

Overview

The number of observations totaled 5400 entries. Thirty-eight percent of the scheduled times fell under the category "sleep" when no notes were taken; 1% of the entries were missing; that left 61% for analysis. Seventy-five percent of the diary entries were recorded punctually at the scheduled time; 25% of diary entries were delayed, mainly because the participants were not able to record them at the scheduled time, for example, because they were driving a car or couldn't interrupt whatever they were doing at the time. In these latter cases (12%), participants noted the experience they were having at the scheduled time and filled out the diary sheet as soon as they could later on. If they had skipped a recording time (13%), they wrote down the entries as soon as they became aware of the omission. The participants indicated the mode of the given recording, as explained earlier, on their diary sheet.

The analysis focused on group differences in well-being between wives whose husbands had a workplace near home (non-commuter group), wives whose husbands commuted daily (daily commuter group), and wives whose husbands stayed outside the home for at least a few nights a week (weekly commuter group).

Well-Being in General

Because the individual diary entries draw relationships between single events, data analyses on the event level would have led to severe shortcomings had we used conventional procedures for data analysis. Therefore, each person's diary entries were averaged and analyzed at this aggregate level. This type of analysis is in the line with the data handling techniques used in similar studies (e.g., Brandstätter, 1983; Csikszentmihalyi & Larson, 1984; Hormuth, 1986; Kirchler, 1989).

Well-being was coded +1 if clearly positive, +0.5 if rather positive; −1 if clearly negative, −0.5 if rather negative, and 0 if indifferent. The average well-being index was $M = .41$; $SD = .55$; $n = 30$. Data about perceived ego-strength and freedom in choosing the performed activity were coded in the same way as well-being.

The correlations between well-being and freedom of choice ($r = .59$), and between well-being and ego-strength ($r = .57$) are high; for further analysis only the well-being index was used.

Neither self-control ($r = .05$), emotional stability ($r = .23$), independence ($r = .17$), tough-mindedness ($r = -.02$), nor extraversion ($r = -.19$), as measured by Brandstätter's 16 PA, was significantly correlated with the average well-being.

The correlation ($r = .48$) between general satisfaction with life, as assessed by the questionnaire of Borg (1978), and current well-being, as assessed by the Time Sampling Diary, also indicates the small amount of common variance (23%) and emphasizes the usefulness of different measurements in a study about everyday life experiences.

Wives' Well-Being, Commuter Status of Husbands, and Characteristics of Situations

In the first step of the analysis, six ANOVAs (two-way, random model) were performed with well-being as dependent on (a) the commuter status and (b) places, (c) activities, (d) other persons present, (e) topics of conversation, (f) needs actualized, or (g) attributions. Table 9.2 presents an overview of the objective and subjective situational characteristics and of well-being, which is related to these variables, as well as of the relative frequencies of observations. F-values for the main effects of the situational variables and commuter status are also included. In no case did significant two-way interactions result.

The 3 (commuter status) by 3 (places) ANOVA indicated a significant main effect ($F(2,81) = 6.28$; $p = .003$) for the places, but not for the commuter status. The housewives were in a better mood outdoors (semi-private: $M = .54$, public: $M = .53$) than at home ($M = .36$). Housewives stayed at home about 70% of the time. About 16% of the time, they were visiting at the homes of friends or relatives, and 15% of the time they were in shops or, restaurants or on the street.

In a 3 (commuter status) by 3 (activities) ANOVA, the main effect of activities ($F(2,89) = 11.09$; $p < .001$) was significant, whereas the main effect of commuter status ($F(2,89) = .72$; $p = .491$) was not significant. The women reported feeling better during leisure ($M = .57$) and obligation time ($M = .49$) than they did while performing housework ($M = .30$). As can be seen in Table 9.2, weekly commuters' wives were occupied with housework slightly more (60%) than the other two groups (53 and 56%, respectively). Leisure time accounted for a reported 25% of total time for weekly commuters' wives; 29% for daily commuters' wives, and 30% for women whose husbands had workplaces close to home. Women spent about 15% of their time on obligatory tasks, such as body care or having meals.

In a 3 (commuter status) by 7 (persons present) ANOVA, the main effects were significant (commuter status: $F(2,185) = 3.87$; $p = .024$; person present: $F(6,185) = 9.00$; $p < .001$). As can be seen in Table 9.2, wives whose husbands commuted daily reported having negative feelings in the presence of children or in the presence of their family (husbands and children) more often than the non-commuter group. The means for the weekly commuter group did not differ significantly from

Table 9.2 Well-Being by Commuter Status Related to Objective and Subjective Features of Various Situations (Means, Relative Frequencies, n of Subjects, F-values of Main Effects)

	Husband not commuting			Husband commutes daily			Husband commutes weekly			F of situational variable	F of commuter status
	M	f	n	M	f	n	M	f	n	F (df); p	F (df); p
Places										6.28 (2,81); .003	1.51 (2,81); .226
At home	.44	.71	(12)	.24	.71	[7]	.35	.71	[11]		
Semiprivate	.56	.17	(12)	.54	.16	[7]	.51	.15	[11]		
Public	.58	.13	(12)	.57	.14	[7]	.46	.15	[11]		
Activities										11.09 (2,89); < .001	.72 (2,89); .491
Housework	.40	.53	(12)	.15	.56	[7]	.31	.60	[11]		
Obligation	.49	.17	(12)	.57	.15	[7]	.48	.15	[11]		
Recreation	.60	.30	(12)	.55	.29	[7]	.55	.25	[11]		
Other persons present										9.00 (6,185); < .001	3.87 (2,185); .024
None present	.37	.20	(12)	.21	.26	[7]	.28	.24	[11]		
Husband	.53	.08	(12)	.38	.10	[7]	.53	.07	[11]		
Child/ren	.38[a]	.20	(12)	.10[b]	.21	[7]	.27[ab]	.26	[11]		
Family	.55[a]	.17	(12)	.29[b]	.13	[7]	.50[ab]	.10	[11]		
Relatives	.56	.18	(12)	.51	.15	[7]	.47	.19	[11]		
Friends	.67	.08	(12)	.69	.07	[7]	.65	.07	[11]		
Others	.56	.10	(12)	.64	.08	[7]	.39	.08	[11]		
Topics of conversation										3.77 (3,103); .012	3.30 (2,103); .041
Private	.51	.17	(12)	.44	.23	[7]	.39	.17	[11]		
Small talk	.54	.57	(12)	.41	.48	[7]	.45	.58	[11]		
Public	.68[a]	.04	(11)	.31[b]	.04	[6]	.68[a]	.03	(8)		
No conversation in the presence of others	.41	.22	(12)	.29	.25	[7]	.31	.22	[11]		

Motives

Physical comfort	.48	.13	[12]	.29	.13	[7]	.29	.11	[11]	5.40 (5,162); < 001	4.06 (2,162); .019
Power	.38	.27	[12]	.24	.28	[7]	.30	.27	[11]		
Affiliation	.65	.20	[12]	.63	.15	[7]	.60	.23	[11]		
Sentience	.39	.16	[12]	.47	.22	[7]	.33	.11	[11]		
Achievement	.45	.12	[12]	.21	.14	[7]	.39	.10	[11]		
"Higher" motives	.48[a]	.12	[12]	.18[b]	.07	[7]	.34[ab]	.18	[11]		

Attributions

Self	.34	.33	[12]	.23	.28	[7]	.23	.29	[11]	9.00 (4,135); <.001	4.65 (2,135); .011
Family	.49	.14	[12]	.26	.15	[7]	.38	.18	[11]		
Husband	.62	.04	[12]	.36	.05	[7]	.40	.05	[11]		
Child/ren	.44	.10	[12]	.23	.10	[7]	.35	.13	[11]		
Other social sources	.60	.23	[12]	.51	.26	[7]	.56	.20	[11]		
Activity	.52[a]	.21	[12]	.29[b]	.21	[7]	.42[ab]	.25	[11]		
Other sources	.63	.10	[12]	.52	.10	[7]	.62	.08	[11]		

Means not sharing a common superscript within rows are different at $p < .05$.

those for the other groups. The relative frequencies in Table 9.2 show that weekly commuters' wives were more often alone with their children (26%) and less often together with their whole family (10%). Wives whose husbands had workplaces close to home were alone 20% of the time and together with their family 17% of the time.

In a 3 (commuter status) by 4 (topics) ANOVA, the main effects were significant (commuter status: F (2,103) = 3.30; p = .041; topics: F (3,103) = 3.77; p = .012). When talking about public issues, like the environment or politics, the mood of daily commuters' wives was worse (M = .31) than the moods of the other groups. On average across groups, participants reported having engaged in small talk with others in 55% of the situations; having talked about personal issues, such as their moods, their dreams, or their marriages (private) in up to 18% of the situations; and having had no conversation in the presence of other persons in 23% of the situations.

The 3 (commuter status) by 6 (motives) ANOVA yielded significant main effects (commuter status: $F(2,162)$ = 4.06; p = .019; motives: $F(5,162)$ = 5.40; $p < .001$). Wives whose husbands commuted daily reported a lower degree of well-being (M = .18) when "higher-order" motives were noted. As Table 9.2 reveals, participants, in the three groups referred frequently to power motives and affiliation motives. The need for power was often related to negative feelings, whereas the need for affiliation was frequently related to a positive mood.

In a 3 (commuter status) by 5 (attributions) ANOVA, the main effects were significant (commuter status: F (2,135) = 4.65; p = .011; attributions: F (4,135) = 9.00; $p < .001$). Out of all the factors to which well-being was attributed, participants noted "self" in about one-third of the recorded situations. Wives seldom felt happy when they attributed their well-being to themselves. Social sources (e.g., spending pleasant time with friends or relatives) led to positive feelings in most cases. As compared with the other groups, the daily-commuter group reported a lower degree of well-being (M = .29) when they felt that their current activity was the reason for their mood. No differences between commuter groups were found with regard to attributing well-being to the husband or children.

Wives' Well-Being, Commuter Status of Husbands, Daily Activities, and Motives

To give an impression of the housewives' daily activities, Figure 9.1 shows the time spent by all respondents doing various tasks (as bars) and the average well-being (as a line) during the performance of various activities. Estimation of the time spent on various activities is based on relative frequencies as indicated in the diary entries. Because of the random distribution of the times of the diary entries and the assumption that on average the participants were awake 1000 minutes per day, a relative frequency of 10% corresponds to 10 minutes per day (for detailed information concerning the estimation of time see Brandstätter & Wagner, 1994).

Figure 9.1 shows that the housewives in the study spent an average of two hours a day preparing meals and tidying the home (119 minutes versus 102 minutes). Doing laundry took 59 minutes a day. Activities relating to child care took 103 minutes. Leisure time was split between socializing with other people

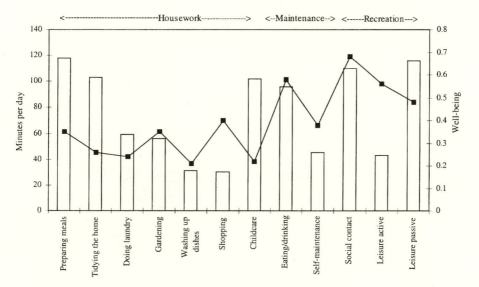

Figure 9.1. Well-being and time spent on various activities.

(103 minutes), spending leisure time actively (e.g., with sports, 56 minutes) or passively (just doing nothing or watching TV, 107 minutes). A lower degree of well-being was reported during housework and child care, whereas eating and drinking, as well as recreation activities, especially social contacts, led to a strong sense of well-being.

With regard to the validity of the diary data, it seems remarkable that the findings of a representative study of the Austrian Census Office (Österreichisches Statistisches Zentralamt, 1992) reports quite similar results for the way housewives budget their time, for example, 108 minutes for preparing meals, 102 minutes for child care tasks, and 30 minutes for shopping.

To assess how housewives' well-being is related to the satisfaction of needs when the housewives are performing everyday activities, the dependency of well-being on activities (A) and needs (B) and commuter status (C) was investigated by a 4 × 6 × 3 analysis of variance, which revealed significant main effect (F_A (3,538) = 14.175; $p <$ .001; F_B (5,538) = 7.872; $p <$. 001; F_C (2,538) = 5.424; $p =$ .005). The interaction between activities and commuter status also turned out to be significant (F (6,538) = 2.273; $p =$ .036) indicating that the noncommuter group felt better ($M =$ .42) than the daily commuter group ($M =$ .15) when performing housework. No other two-way or three-way interaction effect proved to be significant (all $F <$ 1). Figure 9.2 and Figure 9.3 present the average well-being as dependent on six categories of motives present when the wives performed housework and child care tasks, respectively.

During the *performance of housework* the wives felt quite good when affiliation motives came into play. Also, the need for sentience was satisfied in housework situations. A lower degree of well-being was reported when the motive of physical comfort or power motives came into play. In terms of group differences, Figure 9.2 indicates that the daily commuter group felt worse ($M =$ .09) than the

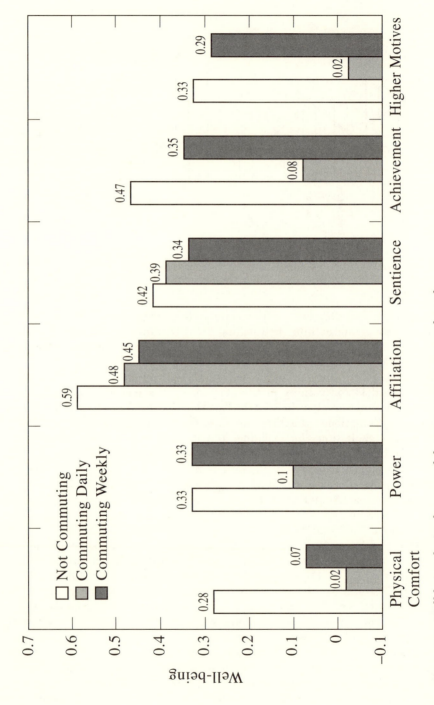

Figure 9.2. Well-being during housework by commuter status and needs.

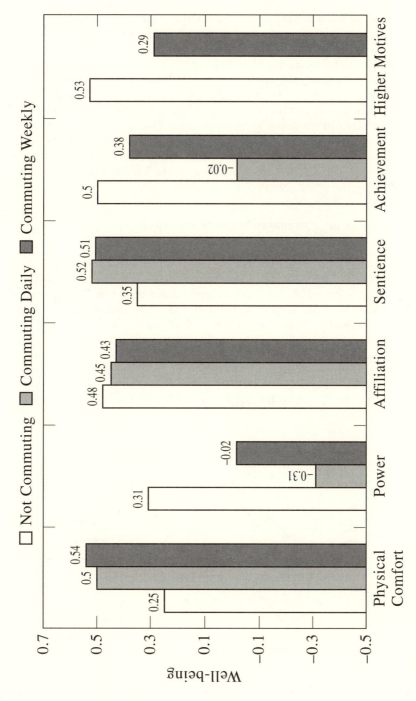

Figure 9.3. Well-being during child care by commuter status and needs.

non-commuter group ($M = .47$) in that they reported having the feeling of not performing their work well (frustration of the achievement motive). Weekly commuters' wives did not differ significantly from the other two groups. When higher-order motives came into play, the average well-being index ($M = .02$) of the daily commuters' wives differed from both other groups (non-commuter husband: $M = .33$; weekly commuter husband: $M = .29$).

In *child care* situations (Figure 9.3), it is remarkable that both groups of commuters' wives (daily: $M = -.31$ and weekly: $M = -.02$) reported a low degree of well-being when power motives came into play, noting that they often had the feeling that others did not listen to them. Wives whose husbands had their work close to home felt significantly better with regard to the power motive in child care situations ($M = .31$). In terms of the achievement motive, daily commuters' wives reported a lower degree of well-being while looking after their children ($M = -.02$) than the other groups did.

Wives' Well-Being, Commuter Status of Husbands, and Daily Interactions

Perceived support in specific work situations was the next factor analyzed. A 3 by 4 by 7 analysis of variance with the commuter status (A), activities performed (B), and persons present (C) as independent variables and well-being as a dependent variable revealed significant main effects (F_A (2,258) = 5.291; $p = .005$; F_B (3,558) = 14.966; $p < .001$; F_C (6,558 = 8.177; $p < .001$) and a significant interaction effect for commuter status and activities (F_{AxB} (6,558) = 2.113; $p = .050$), indicating that the non-commuter group felt better than the daily commuter group when performing housework ($M = .44$; $M = .25$, respectively) and child care ($M = .42$; $M = .14$, respectively).

Figure 9.4 presents moods felt by wives while *performing housework* alone

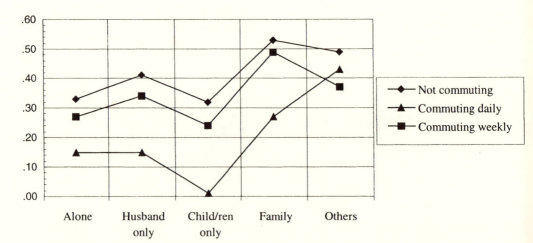

Figure 9.4. Well-being during housework by commuter status based on the other persons present or not present.

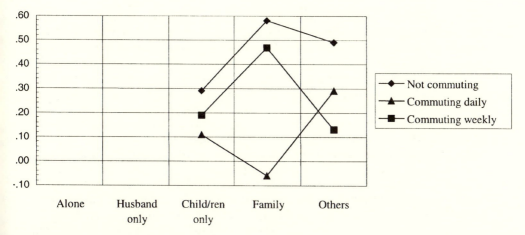

Figure 9.5. Well-being during child care by commuter status based on the other persons present or not present.

and while others were present. Figure 9.5 depicts well-being during child care while being alone with the children and while being together with the family or with other persons. As confirmed by a Duncan test, non-commuters' and weekly commuters' wives ($M = .32$ and $M = .24$, respectively) felt better doing housework when their children were present than daily commuters' wives did ($M = .08$).

When the daily commuter group recorded *child care* in the presence of their family as their current activity, they also frequently reported being unhappy ($M = -.06$). Non-commuters' wives ($M = .58$) and weekly commuters' wives ($M = .47$) felt significantly better in child care situations when their husbands were at home (presence of family).

Conclusion

The aim of the study was to provide insights into the everyday sense of well-being experienced by housewives married to commuting husbands. Results show that daily activities of housewives as well as the fact of having commuting husbands influenced wives' well-being, especially their moods in conjunction with daily interactions with the children.

The results of this study correspond to other findings on the well-being of housewives in everyday situations (e.g., Brandstätter et al., 1984). A closer look at the husbands' commuter status reveals further information about the conditions of life in the two types of commuter families. Wives whose husbands work fairly close to home reported the highest sense of well-being throughout the study, whereas daily commuters' wives reported negative feelings frequently. Weekly commuters' wives felt quite good in most everyday situations. What turned out to be a problem for women in commuter families were the daily hassles with the children. Both the daily and the weekly commuters' wives reported negative feelings when they were alone with their children performing daily household tasks.

Housewives' most frequent everyday situation is to be alone or to be solely in the company of their children; both of these situations are related to relatively poor mood. Contrary to expectations, the commuter groups differed only slightly in terms of the frequency with which husbands were present. Individual preferences as to whether to enter or avoid a specific social situation may serve as an explanation here. Mothers may not be able to avoid being solely in the company of their children during the week, but if, for example, a weekly commuter's wife has a chance to be alone with her husband when he is at home, she may choose this option as often as possible. Having children at home was often found to decrease parental well-being (Erickson, 1993; McLanahan & Adams, 1987). Being in charge of caring for the children was found to influence the commuters' wives moods negatively (Gerstel & Gross, 1984; Macklin, 1987). In this study, the daily commuters' wives in particular reported having the lowest sense of well-being when in the presence of their children.

Negative emotions resulted from frustration about power motives that came into play when the commuters' wives had to perform child care duties. These frustrations stemmed from the children's not listening to them and resulted in daily conflicts, which were found to affect parental well-being. The low degree of well-being reported by commuters' wives in relation to daily anger with their children is probably linked to the wives' feeling of being given inadequate support in such situations. As noted in the findings of Pina and Bengston (1993), the women may not have missed instrumental support, such as direct help with the children, as much as they did emotional support in coping with unpleasant daily experiences.

In previous studies it was observed that the presence of the husband did not lead to an improvement in the wife's well-being (Brandstätter & Wagner, 1994; Kirchler, 1989). This was especially true in housework situations. Results of the present study confirm these findings. The average mood of the participants while performing housework with their husbands present did not differ from their feelings when they were alone. The presence of the children seemed to worsen the wives' moods while the women were performing daily housework. The fragmentation of housework caused by the interruptions of the children, a factor often mentioned in the housework literature as having a negative influence on housewives' well-being (Rerrich, 1983), could also serve as an explanation. This was especially true for the daily commuters' wives in the study as compared with the other groups.

Whereas the mood of the non-commuter group and the well-being of the weekly commuter group increased when they were together with their husbands looking after the children, daily commuters' wives reported negative feelings frequently. The non-commuter group and the weekly commuter group felt supported in child care matters when the spouse was at home. The low well-being of the daily commuters' wives indicates that their husbands did nothing to improve the wives' well-being. It can be assumed that a daily commuter has a great need to relax when he returns home from work in the evening and is therefore not able or willing to provide the necessary support, although his wife expects at least some help with the children. This could be explained first of all, as in Kirchler

(1989), by a lack of understanding about the partner's unpleasant experiences during the day. Second, it can be assumed that the daily commuter comes home tired and is not able to provide the necessary support. Traveling long distances to work daily leads to feelings of distress and overload (Karner, 1988), which also probably influences the wife's emotional state negatively (Almeida & Kessler, 1998; Bolger et al., 1989; Brandstätter & Wagner, 1994).

Weekly commuters' wives reported being in relatively good moods in most everyday situations. Only in situations when they reported anger while being alone with the children were they rather unhappy. But their increased average well-being in child care situations when their husbands were present indicates that weekly commuters' wives felt they received support when husbands were at home. All things considered, it can be assumed that they have a clear-cut weekly schedule. Because of the regular absence and presence of their husbands, it may be easier for this group to draw a line between work and leisure time. This regularity may also help them to adjust to the life of a commuter's wife. During the week they expect no support from their husbands, and on the weekends the family enjoys leisure and recreation time together.

Because of the present situation in the labor market, more and more people are being forced every year to start commuting, making commuting itself an increasingly relevant topic for psychological research. Although the present study considered only one side of the coin, namely the experiences of commuters' wives, findings of this study provide information about certain situational patterns within commuter families. Subsequent investigations should seek to take into account both partners' perspectives.

References

Almeida, D. M., & Kessler, R. C. (1998). Everyday stressors and gender differences in daily distress. *Journal of Personality and Social Psychology, 75*, 670–680.

Barnett, C., & Baruch, G. K. (1985). Women's involvement in multiple roles, role strain, and psychological distress. *Journal of Personality and Social Psychology, 49*, 135–145.

Baruch, R., & Barnett, G. K. (1986). Consequences of father's participation in family work. *Journal of Personality and Social Psychology, 51*, 983–992.

Baruch, R., Biener, L., & Barnett, G. K. (1987). Woman and gender in research work and family stress. *American Psychologist, 42*, 136–136.

Bergmann, B. (1986). *The economic emergence of women.* New York: Basic Books.

Berheide, C. W. (1984). Woman's work in the home: Seems like old times. In B. B. Hess & M. B. Sussman (Eds.), *Woman and the family: Two decades of change* (pp. 37–55). New York: Hawthorne Press.

Berk, R., & Berk, S. F. (1979). *Labour and leisure at home: Content and organization of the household.* Beverly Hills: Sage.

Bird, C. E., & Ross, C. E. (1993). Houseworkers and paid workers: Qualities of the work and effects on personal control. *Journal of Marriage and the Family, 55*, 913–925.

Bolger, N., DeLongis, A., Kessler, R. C., & Schilling, E. A. (1989). The effects of daily stress on negative mood. *Journal of Personality and Social Psychology, 57*, 808–818.

Borg, I. (1978). Ein Vergleich verschiedener Studien zur Lebensqualität [A comparison of various studies on the quality of life]. *Zeitschrift für Sozialpsychologie, 9*, 152–164.

Brandstätter, H. (1977). Wohlbefinden und Unbehagen. Entwurf eines Verfahrens zur

Messung situationsabhängiger Stimmungen [Positive and negative mood. The design of a study for measuring mood changing with situations]. In W. H. Tack (Ed.), *Bericht über den 30. Kongreß der DGfPs in Regensburg 1976* (Vol. 2, pp. 60–62). Göttingen: Hogrefe.

Brandstätter, H. (1983). Emotional responses to other persons in everyday life situations. *Journal of Personality and Social Psychology, 45*, 871–883.

Brandstätter, H. (1988). Sechzehn Persönlichkeits-Adjektivskalen (16 PA) als Forschungsinstrument anstelle des 16 PF [Sixteen Personality Adjective Scales (16 PA) as a substitute for the 16 PF in research settings]. *Zeitschrift für Experimentelle und Angewandte Psychologie, 35*, 370–391.

Brandstätter, H., Barthel, E., & Fünfgelt, V. (1984). Beruf "Hausfrau." Eine psychologische Studie mit dem Zeitstichprobentagebuch ["Housewife" by occupation. A psychological study with the Time Sampling Diary]. In R. Blum & M. Steiner (Eds.), *Aktuelle Probleme der Marktwirtschaft aus einzel- und gesamtwirtschaftlicher Sicht* (pp. 407–431). Berlin: Duncker & Humblot.

Brandstätter, H., & Wagner, W. (1994). Erwerbstätigkeit der Frau und Alltagsbefinden von Ehepartnern im Zeitverlauf [Employment status of the wife and marital partner's well-being in the course of time]. *Zeitschrift für Sozialpsychologie, 25*, 126–146.

Csikszentmihalyi, M., & Larson, R. (1984). *Being adolescent.* New York: Basic Books.

Cohen, G. (1977). Absentee husbands in spiralist families: The myth of the symmetrical family. *Journal of Marriage and the Family, 39*, 595–604.

Coyne, C., & DeLongis, A. (1986). Going beyond social support: The role of social relationships in adaption. *Journal of Consulting and Clinical Psychology, 54*, 454–460.

Cutrona, C. E. (1996). *Social support in couples.* Thousand Oaks, CA: Sage.

Cutrona, C. E., Suhr, J. A., & McFarlane, R. (1990). Interpersonal transactions and the psychological sense of support. In S. Duck & R. C. Silver (Eds.), *Personal Relationships and Social Support* (pp. 30–45). London: Sage.

Duck, S. (1986). *Human Relationships: An Introduction to Social Psychology.* London: Sage.

Erickson, R. J. (1993). Reconceptualizing family work: The effect of emotion work on perceptions of marital quality. *Journal of Marriage and the Family, 55*, 888–900.

Farris, A. (1978). Commuting. In R. Rapoport, R. N. (Eds.), *Working couples* (pp. 100–107). New York: Plenum.

Gerstel, N., & Gross, H. (1984). *Commuter Marriage. A Study of Work and Family.* New York: Guilford Press.

Hiebler, H. (1988). *Wochenpendler Selbst-Fremdbild. Einstellung zu Ehe und Familie und Vaterschaft* [Weekly commuters perceived by themselves and others. Attitude toward marriage, family, and fatherhood]. Unpublished master's thesis. University of Graz, Austria.

Hormuth, S. E. (1986). The sampling of experiences in situ. *Journal of Personality, 54*, 262–293.

Karner, G. (1988). *Soziale und kulturelle Aspekte der Pendelwanderung. Eine Untersuchung im Auspendlerraum Burgenland* [Social and cultural aspects of commuting. A study in the commuter region of Burgenland]. Unpublished master's thesis. University of Vienna.

Kessler, R. C., & McLeod, J. D. (1984). Sex differences in vulnerability to undesirable life events. *American Sociological Review, 49*, 620–631.

Kirchler, E. (1985). Job loss and mood. *Journal of Economic Psychology, 6*, 9–25.

Kirchler, E. (1989). Everyday life experiences at home: An interaction diary approach to assess marital relationships. *Journal of Family Psychology, 3*, 311–336.

Kirschner, B., & Walum, L. (1978). Two location families: Married singles. *Alternative Lifestyles, 1*, 513–525.

Kleppe, I. A., & Gronhaug, K. (1997, September). *Life-events during the first stage of the family life cycle: Experienced stress and adjustments.* Paper presented at the Twenty-second IAREP conference, Valencia, Spain.

Macklin, E. D. (1987). Nontraditional family forms. In M. B. Sussman & S. K. Steinmetz (Eds.), *Handbook of Marriage and the Family* (pp. 317–353). New York: Plenum.

McLanahan, S., & Adams, J. (1987). Parenthood and psychological well-being. *Annual Review of Sociology, 5*, 237–257.

Ochel, A. (1989). *Hausfrauenarbeit* [The work of housewives]. München: Profil.

Opaschowski, H. (1988). *Psychologie und Soziologie der Freizeit* [Psychological and sociological aspects of leisure time]. Opladen: Leske & Budrich.

Orendi, B., & Rückert, D. (1982). Nichterwerbstätige Frauen—ihre Arbeits-und Lebenssituation [Women not gainfully employed—their work and life situation]. In G. Mohr, D. Rückert, & M. Rummel (Eds.), *Frauen. Psychologische Beiträge zur Arbeits- und Lebenssituation* (pp. 38–54). München: Urban & Schwarzenberg.

Österreichisches Statistisches Zentralamt (1992). Zeitverwendung 1992/1981. Ergebnisse des Mikrozensus [Use of time 1992/1981. Survey results]. *Beiträge zur Österreichischen Statistik, 171*, (1).

Peuckert, R. (1991). *Familienformen im sozialen Wandel* [Family types under social change]. Opladen: Leske & Budrich.

Pina, D. L., & Bengston, V. L. (1993). The division of household labour and wives' happiness: Ideology, employment, and perceptions of support. *Journal of Marriage and the Family, 55*, 901–912.

Piotrkowski, C. S., Rapoport, R. N., & Rapoport, R. (1987). Families and work. In M. B. Sussman & S. K. Steinmetz (Eds.), *Handbook of Marriage and the Family* (pp. 251–283). New York: Plenum.

Pleck, J. H. (1985). *Working wife/working husband.* Beverly Hills, CA: Sage.

Repetti, R. L. (1989). The effects of daily work overload on subsequent behaviour during marital interaction: The roles of social withdrawal and spouse support. *Journal of Personality and Social Psychology, 57*, 651–659.

Rerrich, M. S. (1983). Veränderte Elternschaft. Entwicklungen in der familären Arbeit mit Kindern seit 1950 [Changing roles of parents. Developments of family child care since 1950]. *Soziale Welt, 34*, 420–449.

Rook, K., Dooly, D., & Catalona, R. (1991). Stress Transmission: The effects of husbands' job stressors on the emotional health of their wives. *Journal of Marriage and the Family, 53*, 165–177.

Staines, G. L., & Libby, P. L. (1986). Men and women in role relationships. In R. D. Ashmore & F. K. Del-Boca (Eds.), *The Social Psychology of Female-Male Relations: A Critical Analysis of Central Concepts* (pp. 211–258). New York: Academic Press.

Stroebe, W., & Stroebe, M. (1991). Partnerschaft, Familie und Wohlbefinden [Partnership, family, and well-being]. In A. Abele & P. Becker (Eds.), *Wohlbefinden. Theorie-Empirie-Diagnostik* (pp. 155–174). Weinheim: Juventa.

Tompson, L., & Walker, A. J. (1989). Gender in families: Women and men in marriage, work and parenthood. *Journal of Marriage and the Family, 51*, 845–871.

Wedral, H. (1991). Pendelwanderung, Abwanderung und die Situation auf dem burgenländischen Arbeitsmarkt [Commuting, moving away, and the job market in Burgenland]. In T. Horvath & R. Münz (Eds.), *Migration und Arbeitsmarkt* (pp. 18–31). Eisenstadt: Prugg.

PART IV

WELL-BEING DURING AN INTERNATIONAL SUMMER SCHOOL

10

Correspondence Analysis of Everyday Life Experience

Tiziana Mancini & Paola Bastianoni

In recent years a growing number of studies on person-environment transactions have been carried out (see Canter, 1977; Stockols & Altman, 1987; Sundstrom, Bell, Busby, & Asmus, 1996).

The present study focuses on the external (environmental) conditions of emotional responses to everyday life situations. Data were collected using the Time-Sampling-Diary (TSD) designed by Brandstätter (1977). Multiple Correspondence Analysis was applied to analyze the data. Acknowledging that MCA is predominantly a technique for exploratory data analysis and visual representation of the contingencies (dependencies) of categorical data, we do not test any specific hypotheses, but we want to give an example of how MCA can be used in defining behavior settings and in making visible the dependence of mood variation on these behavior settings.

Method

Participants

The study involved 11 graduate students in a social psychology Summer School (nine females, two males)[1] from seven different European countries who participated in a workshop titled "Ecological Approach to the Study of Emotions."

The Time Sampling Diary

Following the procedure of the Time Sampling Diary (Brandstätter, 1977; for variations of the technique see Csikszentmihalyi & Larson, 1987; Hormuth, 1986), the participants took notes on their momentary experiences about eight times a day during a period of three weeks (two weeks at the summer school and the following third week back home) at randomly selected points of time. The random time samples were different for each day and each person. In each recording, each participant noted his or her momentary mood (negative, neutral, or positive), the place, activity being performed and other persons present. The participants also answered an English adjective version of Cattell's 16 PF (Barton, 1986, p. 255) and a value questionnaire (Schwartz & Bilsky, 1990). In this chapter we are not reporting data on personality and value scales (see Kiss, Dornai, & Brandstätter, this volume).

Coding the Diary Records

Following Brandstätter's suggestions, the diary notes were coded by the participants themselves to make sure that all data would be completely anonymous, and to preserve the personal structuring of experience. The list of categories was constructed by the participants themselves on the basis of categories provided by a prior study (Brandstätter, 1994). The categories are : (a) time of note; (b) mood state (negative, indifferent, positive); (c) adjectives describing the mood state; (d) "affect grid" (Russell & Pratter, 1980) rated both for the personal mood and for the environment; (e) sources of satisfaction/dissatisfaction; (f) motives involved in the emotional experience; (g) places; (h) activities; (i) other persons present; and (j) perceived external and internal freedom.

In this study we consider only the following variables: motives, places, persons, activities, and momentary mood. *Places* are categorized into home, workplace and other places. Home includes kitchen, living room, bedroom, and other private places. Work includes university and other workplaces. Other places are public places such as parks, cinemas, churches, and restaurants.

For *persons present* we used the categories alone, relatives (parents, children, sisters and brothers, friends), colleagues, and strangers.

Activities are divided into self-care or maintenance (cooking, shopping, sleeping, taking care of oneself or others), work (individual or collective work activities), and leisure activities (chatting, dancing, participating in cultural activities, watching television, reading newspapers).

Actualization of motives is derived from statements indicating frustration or satisfaction of a motive involved in the response to the behavior setting (e.g., "I feel rather bad because I have not performed well in my work" or "I feel rather good because I was successful in my work," which points to the actualization of the achievement motive, be it frustrated or satisfied).

Motive actualization was classified into four broader categories: achievement, activity/sentience, physical comfort, and affiliation. We have excluded the power motive and "higher" motives (Brandstätter, 1994), because in our sample these motives did not significantly differentiate the people and behavior settings.

Multiple Correspondence Analysis (MCA)

Multiple Correspondence Analysis gives an answer to the question whether rows and columns of a contingency table (with more than two kinds of categories) are dependent on each other and how the dependencies can be visually represented in a way that reduces the high complexity of the data. It also facilitates exploratory interpretations of patterns of relationships between the different modalities of categories (e.g., places, activities, persons present) and the different categories within a modality (e.g., leisure, maintenance, and work activities within the modality "activities"). MCA (like correspondence analysis for bivariate contingency tables) compares observed cell frequencies with frequencies expected under the independence assumption and calculates, based on the Chi-square values, scores of deviation from the frequencies expected under the independence assumption. It finds one or more dimensions representing the association between the modalities of a set of variables (Doise, Clemence, & Lorenzi-Cioldi, 1993, p. 114; see also Wickens, 1998).

Whereas Correspondence Analysis (CA) permits an analysis of two kinds of categories (e.g., places and motives), MCA is appropriate for analyzing cross-tabulations of three and more kinds (modalities) of categories. The result can be interpreted with respect to the two dimensions (axes) of a graph on which the coordinates of the different modalities are projected. As Doise et al. (1993) point out, to avoid "certain traps inherent in the objectification of spatial representations," in addition to the visual presentation, some numerical indicators of the analysis have to be taken into account in order to assess the relative contribution of the factor to each modality (RCO: part of the modality for which the factor accounts) and the absolute contribution (CTR: contribution of each modality to the amount of variance explained by the factor). This information is used to interpret and name the factor on the basis of the modalities whose CTR is largest (larger than the mean, the total of CTR being equal to 1000; cf. Table 10.3 in the results section).

MCA also permits us to enter some characteristics of persons, such as social class, sex, age, or education level, into the analysis (cf. Cibois, 1984, p. 130f.).

MCA fits the nature of our data (categorical) well and permits an easier and more intuitive representation of contingencies between the various characteristics of behavior settings and persons' emotional responses to these behavior settings.

Results and Discussion

More about MCA in the Context of the Present Data

The data obtained from 1658 observations were analyzed by means of Multiple Correspondence Analysis (Cibois, 1983). MCA was performed with relative frequencies of all the observations for places, activities, persons present, and actualized motives as active variables and the mood of each of the 11 participants (negative, neutral, and positive mood) as passive variables (for justifying a bipolar mood scale cf. Russell & Carroll, 1999). Observations (at random points of time for the 11 participants) were placed in rows, while places, activities, persons present, and actualized motives, representing active modalities (targets), and passive modalities (momentary mood) were placed in columns (see Table 10.1).

The passive elements do not contribute to factor definition. They are projected onto the axes resulting from an analysis of active elements (Doise et al., 1993).

Table 10.1 Example of the Matrix Submitted to a MCA

Observations	Places			Activities			Persons				Motives			
	Home	Work	Out of home	Maintenance	Work	Leisure	Alone	Relatives	Strangers	Colleagues	Achievement	Activity/sentience	Physical comfort	Affiliation
0001	1	0	0	0	0	1	1	0	0	0	0	0	1	0
0002	0	1	0	0	0	1	0	0	0	1	0	1	0	0
0003	0	1	0	1	0	0	1	0	0	0	1	0	0	0
—	—	—	—	—	—	—	—	—	—	—	—	—	—	—
1658	0	0	1	1	0	0	0	1	0	0	0	0	0	1

The rectangular matrix submitted to MCA is composed of 1658 observations (rows) and 14 modalities (columns): three for places (home places, workplaces, outside-the-home places), three for activities (maintenance, work, and leisure), four for the social settings (alone, with relatives, with strangers, with colleagues) and four for motives (achievement, activity-sentience, physical comfort, and affiliation). As we can see in Table 10.1, the rectangular matrix contains codes "0" or "1" depending on whether the modality was absent or present. This matrix was subjected to a MCA.

In Table 10.2 the eigenvalues of the first nine factors (axes), the percentage of explained variance, and a histogram of the eigenvalue are reported. The first factor has a high eigenvalue. The coefficient of correlation between rows and columns for which the factor accounts, the square root of the eigenvalue, is 0.74. Considering the sharp drop after the second factor in a kind of *scree test*, we examine in more detail only the first two factors, which account for 37% of the variance. To interpret these first two factors, we look at Figure 10.1, on which the coordinates of the 14 different modalities are projected. In this graph, passive

Table 10.2 The First Nine Factors of MCA

Factor	Eigenvalue	Cumulative percentage of explained variance	Histogram of eigenvalue
1	.55	21.8	********************************
2	.38	36.8	**********************
3	.28	47.9	****************
4	.26	57.9	***************
5	.24	67.4	**************
6	.21	75.7	*************
7	.20	83.7	************
8	.17	90.3	**********
9	.13	95.4	********

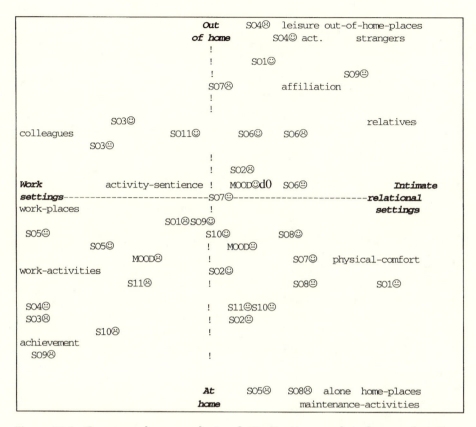

Figure 10.1. Correspondence analysis of 10 situations and 4 classes of motives with mood as illustrative variables.

elements are also projected: the negative mood for each participant (SO1☹, SO2☹ ... SO11☹), the indifferent mood (SO1☺, SO2☺ ... SO11☺) and the positive mood (SO1☺, SO2☺ ... SO11☺). Other supplementary information is given by the centroids of negative mood (MOOD☹), the indifferent mood (MOOD☺), and the positive mood (MOOD☺), representing the average location of these categories across persons.

Table 10.3 provides information that helps to interpret the MCA results.

In the first two columns of Table 10.3, the weight of each modality (WEIGHT: frequency with which each modality is cited) and the inertia (as a measure of dispersion) of each of the modalities (INR: total contribution of each modality to the deviation from independence) are reported. The number represents a percentage (total = 1000) that is all the higher as the modality deviates from independence and thereby helps orient the axes. Table 10.3 also shows the coordinates-ordinates (Coordinates-ord), the relative contributions (RCO: part of the modality for which the factor accounts), and the absolute contributions (CTR: the modality's contribution to the composition of the factor). This information is used to specify and label the axes on the basis of the modalities whose CRT is

Table 10.3 Description of the First Three Factors of MCA

Modalities	Weight	INR	Factor 1			Factor 2			Factor 3		
			Coordinates	RCO	CRT	Coordinates	RCO	CRT	Coordinates	RCO	CRT
Places											
Home	80	68	661	201	63	−953	419	191	−155	11	7
Work	89	64	−1115	679	201	−14	0	0	−121	8	5
Outside home	83	67	567	155	48	932	419	189	295	42	25
Activities											
Maintenance	58	77	717	151	54	−978	281	145	157	7	5
Work	71	72	−1300	658	217	−189	14	7	−41	1	0
Leisure	123	51	414	164	38	563	302	103	−48	2	1
Persons present											
Alone	47	81	403	37	14	−1290	380	206	693	110	80
With relatives	91	64	694	272	79	229	30	13	−582	191	110
With strangers	12	95	518	14	6	1797	165	105	3050	476	407
With colleagues	100	60	−884	516	142	179	21	9	−171	19	10
Motives											
Achievement	40	83	−1059	211	81	−356	24	13	723	99	74
Activity-sentience	63	74	−272	25	8	69	2	1	154	8	5
Physical comfort	73	71	549	122	40	−137	8	4	378	58	37
Affiliation	69	72	274	28	9	297	33	16	−976	360	233

larger than the mean (in this case, the modality that specifies each factor must have a CTR > 1000/number of modalities = 71).

Experience of Situations Represented by MCA

In the first factor, which accounts for 21.8% of the variance, the *work setting* is opposed to the *intimate relational setting*. The work pole aggregates *work activities* (CTR 217) that includes both individual and collective work, *workplaces* (CTR 201), *colleagues* (workshop participants, teachers; CTR 142) and *actualization of achievement motives* (CTR 81). The intimate relationship pole is characterized by the presence of *relatives and friends* (CTR 79). Let us also note that the relative contribution (RCO) indicates that this axis accounts for one-half to almost two-thirds of the variations in the modalities that orient this factor most (work modalities). The latter accounts for almost 64% of the composition of the factor (CRT).

The second factor (which accounts for 15.0% of the variance) represents the distinction between *"home"* and *"outside the home"* settings. The dimension separates situations characterized by the absence of social relationships (*alone;* CTR 206), *at home* (CTR 191), during the performance *maintenance activities* (CTR 145) from *outside-the-home* situations (CTR 189) characterized by *leisure activities* (CTR 103) in the presence of *strangers* (CTR 105). The second factor accounts for 17 to 40% of the variation in the modalities that specify this one.

The third dimension (which accounts for 11.1% of the variance) indicates the opposition between *the need for affiliation* (CTR 233) and the presence of *relatives and friends* (CTR 110) and a sort of *social distance need* expressed by being *alone* (CTR 80) or with *strangers* (CTR 407) and by the *need for achievement* (CTR 74).

Let us turn to Figure 10.1. This graph illustrates a functional connection between the two factors, allowing an overall interpretation of the plane determined by the first two factors. The first consideration concerns the distribution on the plane of the three environmental characteristics chosen as constitutive elements of the concept "behavior setting": activities, places, and persons. Their interrelations allow a classification of the situations that are psychologically meaningful to the study participants. As far as the motives are concerned, the analysis also suggests that the need for achievement is most frequently actualized in work situations. These are situations in which the persons work, performing activities with colleagues, supervisors, or alone. The need for affiliation is more manifest outside the home in the presence of relatives and friends but also of strangers. The need for physical comfort is actualized by doing maintenance activities alone at home. Interestingly, the need for activity/sentience does not contribute to the construction of the factor axis, but, as can be seen in Figure 10.1, it is nearer the work behavior setting outside the home. The greatest opposition between active variables occurs in the second dimension, which allows the differentiation of the situations in which the need for physical comfort is relevant when staying at home, doing maintenance activity alone, from situations in which the need for affiliation is prominent in spending time with relatives in leisure activities outside the home (often in the presence of strangers). The factorial plane, created by the interrelation between the first and the second dimensions, shows the greatest opposition between the semantic space between the upper right part and the lower left part of the plane. This opposition confirms the difference between work environments and leisure environments outside the home. More specifically, this factorial plane describes four different behavior settings. The semantic space extends between the "outside the home polarity" axis and the "intimate relations settings" polarity axis and groups together situations characterized by *"time spent with leisure activities."*

The lower right-hand part of the plane describes a typical situation of *"privacy."* The need for physical comfort is connected with situations in which the participant sleeps, thinks and eats, takes care of himself or others, either alone at home or in other private places. The *"work field"* (the left upper and lower quadrants) comprises *work activities*, workplaces, and *colleagues* with actualization of the *achievement motive* in the lower part and actualization of the *activity-sentience motive* in the upper left quadrant, approaching the location of the affiliation motive.

Mood as a Characteristic of Situations

The three categories of mood are projected onto the plane as supplementary variables the centroids of which are presented by MOOD⊗, MOOD☺, and MOOD☺. Negative mood (MOOD⊗) is closer to variables referring to work (workplaces, work activities, achievement motives), while positive mood (MOOD☺) is closer to the variables that indicate the actualization of affiliation motives and the presence of relatives and friends in leisure settings. Indifferent mood (MOOD☺) is connected with the actualization of the need for physical comfort.

Correspondence Analysis of Emotion Words and Mood

The meaning of negative, neutral, and positive mood becomes clearer if we use a correspondence analysis (CA) of a two-way contingency table with the four adjective quadrants of the mood circumplex (Russell, 1980; Russell & Pratter, 1980) as rows and the three categories of mood as columns. The active (high arousal) positive quadrant (lower left quadrant in Figure 10.2) is made up of *aroused, astonished, excited, delighted, happy, pleased, glad.* The passive (low arousal) positive quadrant (higher left quadrant) is represented by: *serene, content, at ease, satisfied, relaxed, calm, sleepy.* The passive (low arousal) negative (upper right) quadrant reads: *tired, droopy, bored, depressed, gloomy, sad, miserable.* Finally the active (high arousal) negative (lower right) quadrant comprises: *frustrated, distressed, annoyed, afraid, angry, alarmed, tense.* The participants indicated in each diary entry which one of those adjectives came closest to their experienced quality of mood in the moment. Table 10.4 cross-tabulates the 28 adjectives with the three categories of mood. Figure 10.2 presents the results of a correspondence analysis (CA) of the contingency table made up of four groups of adjectives (active positive, passive positive, passive negative, active negative) and three classes of mood (negative, neutral, positive). It shows that the mood category *neutral* lies in the same quadrant as *passive negative.* If one wanted to dichotomize the mood scale, one would separate positive mood from non-positive mood. The rather close correspondence between the mood scores and the valence of the adjectives describing the quality of emotions gives mutual support to the construct validity of both measures.

Individual Differences in the Relationship between Behavior Setting and Mood

When we consider the negative, indifferent, and positive mood in each of the 11 persons, we find individual differences in the dependence of mood on the various behavior settings. In particular, we can observe the large distance between SO1⊗, SO3⊗, SO9⊗, S10⊗, S11⊗ in the lower left quadrant, where most participants are located with negative mood, and SO2☺, SO4☺, SO6⊗, SO7☺ in the upper right quadrant, where some participants show up with positive mood.

SO2 and SO7 (lower right quadrant) feel better when they are in a "private setting" (at home) rather than in a "free-time setting" (out of home). The emotional experience of SO4 and SO6, whether positive or negative, is predominantly

Table 10.4 Mood Descriptive Adjectives Cross-tabulated with Mood Scores

	Mood			Total
	Bad	Neutral	Good	Total
Active positive		13		
1 Aroused	4		103	120
2 Astonished	4		1	5
3 Excited	1	1	72	74
4 Delighted			38	38
5 Happy	1		95	96
6 Pleased		1	101	102
7 Glad			98	98
Passive positive				
8 Serene		1	39	40
9 Content		2	76	78
10 At ease		7	62	69
11 Satisfied		3	62	65
12 Relaxed		10	117	127
13 Calm	1	18	89	108
14 Sleepy	12	30	39	81
Passive negative				
15 Tired	29	54	54	137
16 Droopy	14	18	15	47
17 Bored	14	7	9	30
18 Depressed	21	4	1	26
19 Gloomy	17	5	5	27
20 Sad	26	5	2	33
21 Miserable	6	1	2	9
Active negative				
22 Frustrated	29	5	1	35
23 Distressed	20	8	3	31
24 Annoyed	17	7	4	28
25 Afraid	4		5	9
26 Angry	26	2	3	31
27 Alarmed	9	3	9	21
28 Tense	34	15	39	88
Total	289	220	1144	1653

connected with the leisure setting (upper right quadrant). Finally, the mood of SO5 and SO8 (at the bottom of the lower right quadrant) becomes more positive when one moves from a "private setting" toward a "social setting"; the mood of SO3 shows a positive move from achievement actualization (lower left quadrant) to activity/sentience actualization (upper left quadrant).

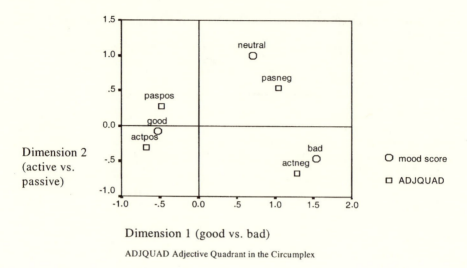

Figure 10.2. Adjectives and mood scores in a circumplex.

Motivational Person-Environment Fit Left for Future MCA Studies

The results suggest that Correspondence Analysis is useful to show the differential influence on mood of behavior settings considered as a combination of places, activities, persons present, and actualized motives.

However, according to the motivational P-E fit hypothesis (Brandstätter, 1994), the intra-individual variation of mood across behavior settings is dependent not only on the characteristics of the setting but also on the *correspondence* between

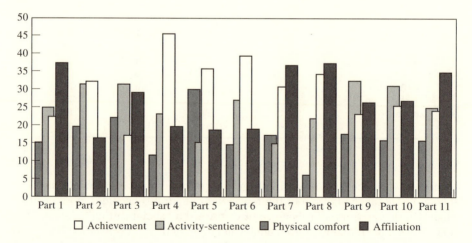

Figure 10.3. Percentages of motive actualization of 11 participants (Part 1 to Part 11).

the reward potential of the behavior setting and the person's motive structure, represented by the ipsative relative frequencies of actualization of the person's motives aggregated over the whole variety of behavior settings encountered by this person. Figure 10.3 gives an idea of the individual differences in the motive profiles.

As yet, we do not have a clear idea about how the motivational person-environment-fit could be analyzed and represented by MCA. In addition to individual mood scores, it will be necessary to get motive importance scores for each participant and motive satisfaction scores for each behavior setting. In our analysis, motive actualization was included in the MCA-design, but not with respect to individual differences, and motive satisfaction (under the condition of motive actualization) was left out of consideration. It will be a task of future studies to integrate the person-environment-fit concept into MCA analyses of person and situation data.

Note

1. For reasons of anonymity, the participants' gender was not recorded.

References

Barton, K. (1986). Personality assessment by questionnaire. In R. B. Cattell & R. C. Johnson (Eds.), *Functional psychological testing. Principles and instruments* (pp. 237–259). New York: Brunner/Mazel.

Brandstätter, H. (1977). Wohlbefinden und Unbehagen. Entwurf eines Verfahrens zur Messung situationsabhängiger Stimmungen [Positive and negative mood. The design of a study for measuring mood changing with situations]. In W. H. Tack (Ed.), *Bericht über den 30. Kongreß der DGfPs in Regensburg 1976* (Vol. 2, pp. 60–62). Göttingen: Hogrefe.

Brandstätter, H. (1994). Well-being and motivational person-environment fit: A time sampling study of emotions. *European Journal of Personality, 8,* 75–93.

Canter, D. (1977). *The psychology of place.* London: Architectural Press.

Cibois, P. (1983). *L'analyse factorielle [Factor analysis].* Paris: PUF.

Cibois, P. (1984). *L'analyse des données en sociologie [Data analysis in sociology].* Paris: PUF.

Csikszentmihalyi, M., & Larson, R. (1987). Validity and reliability of the experience-sampling diary. *The Journal of Nervous and Mental Disease, 175,* 526–536.

Doise, W., Clemence, A., & Lorenzi-Cioldi, F. (1993). *The quantitative analysis of social representations.* Hertfordshire: Harvester Wheatsheaf.

Hormuth, S. E. (1986). The time sampling of experience *in situ. Journal of Personality, 54,* 262–293.

Russell, J. A. (1980). A circumplex model of affect. *Journal of Personality and Social Psychology, 39,* 1161–1178.

Russell, J. A., & Carroll, J. M. (1999). On the bipolarity of positive and negative affect. *Psychological Bulletin, 125,* 3–30.

Russell, J. A., & Pratter, G. (1980). A description of the affective quality attributed to environments. *Journal of Personality and Social Psychology, 38,* 311–322.

Schwartz, S. H., & Bilsky, W. (1990). Toward a theory of the universal content and structure of values: Extension and cross-cultural replications. *Journal of Personality and Social Psychology, 58,* 878–891.

Stokols, D., & Altman, I. (1987). *Handbook of Environmental Psychology*. New York: Wiley.

Sundstrom, E., Bell, P. A., Busby, P. L., & Asmus, C. (1996). Environmental psychology 1989–1994. *Annual Review of Psychology, 47,* 485–512.

Wickens, T. D. (1998). Categorical data analysis. *Annual Review of Psychology, 48,* 537–558.

11

Freedom as Moderator of the Personality-Mood Relationship

Gyöngyi B. Kiss, Erika Dornai, & Hermann Brandstätter

The striving for and experience of freedom are of central importance in human life. Our concern here is not freedom as a characteristic of a social (political) system or as a social value, but the experience of external and internal freedom in the natural surroundings of everyday life. There are situations that offer little restraint, in terms of both physical obstacles and social pressures. In such a situation a person experiences external freedom: If one wanted to, one could leave the situation or do something different within the situation without an effort to overcome physical obstacles and/or without being blamed (punished) by social agents. Thus, the concept of external freedom implies both being able and being allowed to do what one wants to do. There are, on the other hand, situations or activities that one can leave or change without acting against one's personal norms, and feeling guilty. In this case we speak of internal freedom. In this sense, a person, even if experiencing an irresistible impulse to act in a certain way, is internally free to act if the desire is fully compatible with his or her values, that is, if he or she does not have to overcome anticipated feelings of guilt.

Feeling (externally or internally) free does not necessarily imply feeling good, and feeling (externally or internally) restrained by social or personal norms does not necessarily mean feeling bad, because we can like what we ought to do, and we can dislike what we are free to put aside. Nevertheless, we expect a positive correlation between the experience of freedom and subjective well-being, because it is unlikely that we will stay in an uncomfortable situation or continue a disliked activity if we feel (externally and internally) free to move into a more pleasant situation or to engage in better liked activities (cf. Csikszentmihalyi & Graef, 1980). Given external and internal freedom, we may stick to a disliked activity only, if we perceive it as instrumental in helping us obtain later a gratification of higher value. We may also assume that social and personal norms are more often salient in situations and activities that do not match our inclinations and desires. Most people would, for example, prefer leisure to work, if there were no necessity to work (for making a living) and no social pressure to stick to a work schedule. Another example: Helping somebody often entails inconveniences that people would tend to avoid if there were no social and personal norms supporting or enforcing helping behavior.

We are interested (a) in the relationship between external and internal freedom and in the relationship of these two kinds of freedom with personality and value measures, (b) in the influence of external and internal freedom on mood, (c) in how perceived internal freedom moderates the relationship between personality characteristics and value preferences, on the one hand, and subjective well-being (mood), on the other hand.

For studying the antecedents and consequences of experienced freedom, we use the Time Sampling Diary (TSD) (Brandstätter, 1977; 1983). In addition to questions about their momentary mood, their whereabouts, their present activities, and the other persons present, the TSD asks participants for their perceived freedom. The present study is the first in the series of TSD-studies to focus on the distinction between external and internal freedom.

The Concept of Freedom in Social Psychology

In experimental social psychology the concept of perceived (external) freedom has been an important issue in testing *dissonance theory* (Cooper & Fazio, 1984; Festinger, 1957). A person who acts against his or her personal values and norms experiences cognitive dissonance, and discomfort connected with it, only if the act was not provoked by high social pressure (i.e., by low external freedom). According to *attribution theory* (Jones & Davis, 1965; Kruglanski & Cohen, 1973) inferences about a person's dispositions are more likely to be made when his or her behavior is seen as freely chosen.

The concept of responsibility, too, is closely related to freedom of choice (Easterbrook, 1978). Graumann (1994), in a special issue of the *Zeitschrift für Sozialpsychologie* dealing with the social psychology of responsibility, sees responsibility as a relational phenomenon comprising three elements: (1) an actor who is responsible (2) for somebody or something (3) to somebody. In common language, responsibility usually implies the notion of a burdensome duty the intentional violation of which leads to (legitimized) social reprimand and/or feelings of guilt. Obviously, whenever responsibility is an issue, internal and external freedom is restricted. Weiner (1995) applies the concept of responsibility to the negative consequences of a person's act when that act is perceived as controllable (i.e, freely chosen) by him or her, and is performed under circumstances that do not mitigate the blame. One could, of course, also speak of responsibility for the positive consequences of a person's acts. Other authors use the term "responsibility" as a neutral notion with no attached valence to avoid "the overlap between assignment of responsibility and assignment of blame or guilt" (Miceli & Castelfranchi, 1998, p. 296). Most research deals with responsibility for negative consequences only.

In the 1980s, the experience of freedom, primarily in the sense of external freedom, became a topic of interest mainly within the research of volition and action (Kornadt, 1995).

Trommsdorff (1995), in her theoretical reasoning about the experience of freedom of acting, points to the differences between external and internal restrictions and external and internal perspectives. She states that actions occur under certain objective external conditions, including the laws of the physical world as well as social rules, norms, and sanctions. These restrictions can be recognized from the third person's perspective. Restrictions within the individual are evident in his own perception and subjective experiences. These constitute self-commitments and subjective norms. Internal freedom is not visible, it is experienced only from the first person's perspective (p. 305). It is influenced by personal norms, intentions, and desires and affected by emotions.

Using the experience sampling method (ESM), which is similar to our time sampling approach, Csikszentmihalyi and Graef (1980) studied some antecedents and consequences of freedom in a variety of everyday life situations and found that "whenever people feel free, they also wish to do whatever they are doing and vice versa" (p. 413). Emmons and Diener (1986) investigated the stability and consistency of behavior and emotions in both imposed and chosen situations. They found that affect was more consistent and stable within imposed situations, whereas behavior was more consistent and stable within chosen situations. Further, the participants felt more positive and more idiosyncratic emotions in self-chosen than in imposed situations. Extrapolating from the grounded-theory analysis of an interview with a 70-year-old retired professional man, with some health problems, but nevertheless a high level of well-being, Sherrard (1998) found that well-being is most strongly related to the freedom to choose one's activities and to manage one's time.

Hypotheses

In the process of socialization and internalization, social norms are not simply mapped one to one into personal norms, but are selected and modified by the persons according to their innate individual dispositions and, in the course of personal and moral development, according to autonomous decisions that reflect their value priorities and world views. Therefore, even if one does not move into a social environment with different values and norms later, we can reasonably expect only a partial congruence between social and personal norms. *This means that external and internal freedom should be only moderately correlated, and their correlation with value and personality scales should be different to a certain degree (hypothesis 1).*

Feeling good or feeling bad about the present activity can be connected with high or low (internal or external) freedom, although staying in an unpleasant situation is more often connected with lack of freedom than is staying in a pleasant situation.

In nine different TSD-studies performed by Brandstätter and his coworkers, each with between about 2800 and 7100 randomly chosen time points of observation, the correlation between mood and experienced freedom varied between $r = .45$ and $r = .71$, with a median of $r = .56$. The most plausible interpretation of this correlation is that, if people are free, they choose pleasurable situations and activities that make them feel good. Other interpretations would be that freedom is in itself pleasurable irrespective of the chosen activities, or that feeling good is a state that one doesn't want to change and that, therefore, prevents a person from becoming aware of possible restrictions on his or her freedom.

Whatever the functional relationships between the experience of freedom and the experience of good mood may be—a correlation does not tell us what is the cause and what the effect—*we expect for both external and internal freedom again a positive correlation with mood, which should be higher for internal than for external freedom (hypothesis 2).*

To assume that internal freedom is more important for mood presupposes that the participants are more dependent on their consciences than on the perceived social expectations in cases where internal and external norms do not coincide. If a person is internally free to leave a situation or to stay in it, in general the chosen activities will be pleasant, otherwise the person would choose to do something else.

We expected further that personal values and global personality dimensions such as conscientiousness, emotional stability, and extraversion determine, in interaction with environmental conditions, the mood states to a higher degree when freedom, in particular internal freedom, is high than when it is low.

Some situations are predominant in their impact on the participants' mood, whereas other situations are less powerful, giving personality characteristics a higher chance to influence cognition, emotions, and actions. The person is assumed to be in a strong position when the residualized internal freedom score is high. Partialing out the variance of external freedom, that is, predicting internal freedom from external freedom and calculating the residuals, allows to use the residuals as unconfounded, "pure" measures of internal freedom. *We predict that the influence of values and personality characteristics on mood is moderated by the degree of (residualized) internal freedom (hypothesis 3).*

Method

Sample

Participants were 11 doctoral students (nine women, two men) from seven East and West European countries, who attended a EAESP (European Association of Experimental Social Psychology) summer school in the vicinity of Warsaw.

Procedure

We used the Time Sampling Diary (TSD) designed by Brandstätter (1977, 1983). Participants noted their momentary experience in a TSD booklet eight times a day during a period of three weeks: two weeks during the summer school, one week at home. Segments of two hours from 8 A.M. to 12 P.M. had been generated randomly by a computer. Participants had wrist watches, which signaled the preset time when they had to take notes on their momentary experience in the diary. The TSD asked participants about their

- momentary feelings: negative, neutral, positive mood; quality and intensity of emotions;
- behavioral settings: activities; what participants were doing at the signaled moment, places where they were staying, whom they were with;
- attributions of experienced emotions to remembered, perceived, or expected events;
- affected motives (e.g., need for achievement, affiliation, or power); and
- freedom (external and internal) on a 4-point scale.

For the purpose of the present study, situations (behavior settings) were classified into the very broad categories "alone versus with others" and "leisure versus at work."

External freedom was conceived as freedom from physical obstacles or from social pressure (norms, expectations). (The latter means "I can do something else or leave the situation without risking social sanctions.") Internal freedom (freedom from inner obligations or self-imposed duties) was defined by the statement "I can do something else or leave the situation without having to blame myself or feeling qualms of conscience."

Participants also answered an adjective form of the 16 PF Questionnaire (Barton, 1986, p. 255) on a 9-point scale (1 = strongly disagree to 9 = strongly agree) and the list of values by Schwartz (1992) (−1 = opposed to my values to 7 = of supreme importance, later coded into a scale ranging from 1 to 9).

Results

According to hypothesis 1, external and internal freedom are not only conceptually, but also empirically different aspects of freedom. That means, we expect a moderate state correlation between the two facets of freedom and different degrees of correlation with personality and value variables. The state correlation between external and internal freedom across all 1620 observations pooled from the 11 participants is $r = .60$ (Table 11.1). The mean individual state correlation (across the 11 participants) between external and internal freedom is $r = 0.57$, with a standard deviation of 0.18 and a range between 0.27 and 0.80 (Table 11.2).

The Correlation of Internal and External Freedom

As Table 11.1 shows, the correlation coefficients between external and internal freedom on the one hand and personality and value scales on the other hand (correlation of state variables with trait variables), are somewhat different. This means that the data are at least compatible with, although not strongly supportive of the predicted empirical distinctiveness of these two constructs.

Freedom correlated with personality scales. In comparing a state/trait with a trait/trait correlation (left and right side of Table 11.1), one should be aware that a state/trait correlation with observations as units is determined both by intra-individual (state) and inter-individual (trait) variance of mood, external, and internal freedom. As an ANOVA with persons as factor in our sample shows (not presented here), 9%, 9%, and 11% of the total variance of mood, external freedom, and internal freedom, respectively, are explained by individual (trait) differences in mood, external freedom, and internal freedom. Because the personality and value scales represent traits, the intra-individual variance of the momentary TSD-measures is a kind of error variance attenuating the two-level-correlation (level person and level observation time) between personality and value scales, on the one hand, and repeated observations on the other hand. Generally, the following formula (Guilford, 1956, p. 475) should give a reasonable estimate (based on the two-level-correlation) of the correlation between personality and value scales and the averages (per person) of the mood and freedom scores, if the assumptions of classical test theory about the bivariate distributions of the variables are met. In the perspective of classical test theory the formula takes into account that the reliability of a measure increases with test length (Spearman-Brown formula), here with the number of TSD observations averaged, and that validity increases with reliability.

$$r_{y(nx)} = \frac{r_{yx}}{\sqrt{\dfrac{1 - r_{xx}}{n} + r_{xx}}}$$

n number of observations on which the average per person is based
x mood or freedom score
y personality or value score
$r_{y(nx)}$ correlation between personality or value score and the person's average mood or freedom score
r_{yx} correlation between personality or value score and single TSD scores of mood and freedom
r_{xx} reliability of single TSD scores of mood

Among the primary personality scales, social boldness and self reliance have higher (positive) correlations with internal freedom, whereas sensitivity is more closely and negatively related to external freedom. This means that people who perceive themselves as venturesome, uninhibited, and socially bold (Scale H) or as self-sufficient, resourceful, and preferring to make their own decisions (Scale Q2) tend to experience freedom more often, in particular internal freedom. This is true for the raw score as well as for the residualized score of internal freedom. People who score high on sensitivity (Scale I: tender-minded, sensitive, over-protected) experience less external, but more internal freedom than people who score low on sensitivity.

Self-control (negative correlation) is more closely related to internal freedom than to external freedom, whereas the negative correlation with independence (dominance) is somewhat higher for external than for internal freedom. It comes as a surprise that independent (dominant) persons tend to feel less free. This makes sense only if one conceives of independence as "need for independence." A higher aspiration of being independent leads more often to the experience of lack of freedom, in particular of external freedom.

Freedom correlated with value orientations. As to values, benevolence (spiritual life, meaning in life, mature love, true friendship, loyalty, honesty, helpfulness, responsibility, a forgiving nature) and universalism (equality, inner harmony, a world of peace, unity with nature, wisdom, a world of beauty, belief in social justice, broad-mindedness, belief in protecting the environment) are more closely related to internal than to external freedom. Tradition (respect for tradition, detachment from worldly concerns, moderation, humility, submission to life's circumstances, devoutness) shows a negative correlation with external freedom and a slightly positive correlation with internal freedom.

Freedom correlated with mood. According to hypothesis 2, internal freedom and mood are expected to have stronger positive relationship than external freedom and mood. In scoring the mood scales, the participants used, in accordance with the instructions, the neutral category less often ($N = 224$; 13.5%) than the negative ($N = 289$; 17.4%) and the positive categories ($N = 1145$; 69.1%). In order to avoid bimodality in the dependent variable, negative (-1), neutral (0), and positive ($+1$) mood were recoded not-positive (0) and positive (1). Mood is on the average (across participants) actually less closely related to external freedom than to internal freedom (0.23 vs. 0.37) (see Table 11.1).

There are some individual differences in the mood-freedom correlation. For external freedom the correlation is on average 0.24, with a standard deviation of 0.12 and a range between 0.11 and 0.51. For internal freedom the mean correlation is 0.40, with a standard deviation of 0.22 and a range between 0.05 and 0.68. Eight of the 11 participants show a higher correlation of mood with internal than with external freedom (Table 11.2). Therefore, hypothesis 2 is supported by the data.

Internal Freedom Moderates the Influence of Personality and Values on Mood

Hypothesis 3 assumes that personality characteristics and value orientations have a stronger influence on mood in situations with high internal freedom than in those with low internal freedom.

Tables 11.3 and 11.4 show that the predictability of mood from global value dimensions and global personality dimensions, respectively, increases with the residualized internal freedom.

A closer look at the correlation between primary personality scales and mood when residualized internal freedom is low, medium, or high, respectively, shows that in high-freedom situations people who are high on rule consciousness (G+), low on social boldness (H−), low on apprehension (O−), low on openness to change (Q1−), low on self-reliance (Q2−), high on perfectionism (Q3+), and low on tension (Q4−) feel particularly good (Table 11.5). Among the three global personality dimensions self-control has the highest influence on mood when residualized internal freedom is high ($r = .53$ for high, $r = .33$ for medium, and $r = .15$ for low residualized internal freedom).

That the correlation between self-control and mood is moderated by the degree of internal freedom can be shown also by an ANOVA with internal freedom

Table 11.1 Correlation of the Primary and Global Personality and Value Scales with Freedom and Mood

		Observations (N between 1620 and 1658)				Persons (N = 11)			
		External freedom	Internal freedom	Resid-uals	Mood	External freedom	Internal freedom	Resid-uals	Mood
Primary personality scales									
A	Warmth	.01	.08	.10	.11	−.07	.11	.23	.36
B	Reasoning	.09	.09	.05	.07	.28	.26	.16	.21
C	Emotional sta-bility	.17	.15	.04	.03	.67	.53	.23	.06
E	Dominance	−.08	−.10	−.05	.03	−.44	−.44	−.28	.14
F	Liveliness	−.10	−.05	.02	.01	−.42	−.26	−.02	.06
G	Rule-conscious-ness	−.13	−.18	−.13	.11	−.41	−.53	−.46	.36
H	Social boldness	.07	.19	.18	−.05	.18	.49	.60	−.16
I	Sensitivity	−.10	.02	.11	.07	−.43	−.08	.25	.21
L	Vigilance	−.13	−.15	−.08	.02	−.58	−.59	−.39	.10
M	Abstractedness	−.15	−.15	−.07	−.09	−.46	−.39	−.20	−.31
N	Privateness	.07	−.07	−.14	.10	.16	−.24	−.50	.35
O	Apprehension	−.02	−.01	.00	−.12	−.08	−.04	.00	−.41
Q1	Openness to change	−.00	−.06	−.08	−.24	.06	−.06	−.15	−.80
Q2	Self-reliance	.00	.11	.13	−.18	.11	.39	.50	−.61
Q3	Perfectionism	.05	.04	.01	.21	.06	.00	−.04	.69
Q4	Tension	−.13	−.15	−.08	−.26	−.49	−.46	−.29	−.85
	Physical attractive-ness	.13	.10	.03	.20	.34	.20	.03	.66
Global personality scales									
Extraversion		.13	.17	.12	.11	.39	.47	.39	.35
Self-control		−.04	−.10	−.09	.24	−.23	−.38	−.38	.79
Independence		−.15	−.14	−.04	.02	−.65	−.56	−.28	.11
Global value scales									
Benevolence		.02	.12	.12	.01	.26	.46	.47	−.01
Universalism		−.07	.02	.07	−.12	−.00	.23	.35	−.40
Self-direction		−.10	−.03	.03	−.10	−.17	.03	.19	−.37
Stimulation		−.15	−.12	−.04	−.07	−.45	−.32	−.11	−.22
Hedonism		.13	.13	.06	.05	.50	.43	.23	.17
Achievement		.01	.11	.13	.06	.11	.35	.44	.18
Power		−.04	.07	.12	.06	−.16	.16	.38	.18
Security		−.06	.10	.18	−.03	−.20	.26	.57	−.12
Conformity		−.08	.07	.14	.05	−.24	.17	.47	.14
Tradition		−.12	−.01	.08	.00	−.39	−.06	.24	−.00
External freedom		1.00	.60	.00	.23	1.00	.78	.34	.18
Internal freedom		.60	1.00	.80	.37	.78	1.00	.85	.02

Mood (0 = negative or neutral; 1 = positive); Residuals = residualized scores of internal freedom. Only three global factors were derived from a principal components analysis and labeled in analogy to Russell and Karol (1994).

Table 11.2 Number of Observations N, Means M, and Standard Deviations SD of and Correlation r between External and Internal Freedom and Mood (0 = not positive, 1 = positive): Individual Participants

	N	M	SD	Correlated variables	r
Participant 1					
(1) Mood	161	.64	.48	1-2	.27
(2) External freedom	161	3.19	1.01	1-3	.38
(3) Internal freedom	161	2.79	1.13	2-3	.76
Participant 2					
(1) Mood	145	.59	.49	1-2	.11
(2) External freedom	138	3.19	.89	1-3	.18
(3) Internal freedom	133	3.32	.86	2-3	.78
Participant 3					
(1) Mood	160	.68	.47	1-2	.34
(2) External freedom	159	3.03	1.17	1-3	.31
(3) Internal freedom	157	2.97	1.12	2-3	.80
Participant 4					
(1) Mood	145	.83	.38	1-2	.12
(2) External freedom	144	3.26	1.00	1-3	.61
(3) Internal freedom	143	3.01	1.03	2-3	.27
Participant 5					
(1) Mood	134	.73	.45	1-2	.26
(2) External freedom	105	2.53	1.05	1-3	.05
(3) Internal freedom	111	2.46	.92	2-3	.40
Participant 6					
(1) Mood	149	.40	.49	1-2	.23
(2) External freedom	146	2.90	.87	1-3	.28
(3) Internal freedom	144	3.13	.89	2-3	.75
Participant 7					
(1) Mood	168	.89	.31	1-2	.26
(2) External freedom	168	3.50	.73	1-3	.64
(3) Internal freedom	168	3.52	.70	2-3	.56
Participant 8					
(1) Mood	168	.82	.38	1-2	.19
(2) External freedom	168	3.05	.96	1-3	.68
(3) Internal freedom	168	3.37	.87	2-3	.37
Participant 9					
(1) Mood	158	.71	.46	1-2	.12
(2) External freedom	158	3.30	1.17	1-3	.58
(3) Internal freedom	158	2.90	1.22	2-3	.54

Table 11.2 *(continued)*

	N	*M*	*SD*	Correlated variables	*r*
Participant 10					
(1) Mood	163	.76	.43	1-2	.51
(2) External freedom	163	3.69	.74	1-3	.53
(3) Internal freedom	163	3.58	.78	2-3	.46
Participant 11					
(1) Mood	152	.53	.50	1-2	.23
(2) External freedom	152	3.62	.81	1-3	.13
(3) Internal freedom	151	3.66	.75	2-3	.56

(low—medium—high) and self-control (low—high) as factors and mood (coded as 1 if positive, and 0 otherwise) as dependent variable. The mood difference between low and high self control (median split) is .12, .20, and .51 when residualized internal freedom is low, medium, or high, respectively (cf. Tables 11.6 and 11.8). Adding leisure-work as a third factor reveals an additional significant two-way interaction between leisure-work and internal freedom. When internal freedom is low, mood is lower during work (.38) than during leisure (.57). When internal freedom is medium, there is still a small difference in mood between work (.77) and leisure (.81). However, when internal freedom is high, mood is higher during work (.80) than during leisure (.67) Tables 11.7 and 11.8). This could mean that the Ph.D. students who were participating in the summer school were usually in a good mood when they did not feel obliged to work (high internal freedom) but chose to work because of their interest in the subject.

On the other hand, leisure is not always a desired situation (e.g., when one is alone), even if one feels (internally) free to do something different.

Discussion

The meaning of external and internal freedom. Everyday life situations vary greatly in the extent to which persons feel free to stay in or to leave the situation and to continue the present activities or do something else. Generally, higher levels of freedom, particularly of internal freedom, result in better mood. The average individual state correlation between external and internal freedom is $r =$ .57, which is not too high, in order to justify keeping these constructs theoretically apart. The correlations of external and of internal freedom with third variables are somewhat different, too. Although the differences in the trait/trait correlation are not statistically significant ($p > 0.05$)—we do not know any reasonable way of significance testing of a state/trait correlation—they are *post hoc* psychologically meaningful.

Partialing out the covariance of external freedom from internal freedom gives the internal freedom score a clearer meaning. It indicates as a state and as a trait

Table 11.3 Differential Predictability of Mood (0=not positive, 1=positive) from Situational Characteristics (Leisure-Work; Alone-Others) and Global Value Scales

Explained variance	Residualized internal freedom		
	Low (429)	Medium (808)	High (215)
R^2	.03	.03	.02
R^2 change	.10	.14	.40
F change	4.59	13.14	13.99

R^2 represents percentage of mood variance explained by leisure-work and alone-others; R^2 change represents change percentage of mood variance additionally explained by values.

(if aggregated across all observations of a person) self-expression, relative independence of social pressures, and probably low self-monitoring (Snyder & Gangestad, 1986). This interpretation is supported by the correlation of the primary personality dimensions rule-consciousness ($-.13$ and $-.46$), social boldness ($.19$ and $.60$), privateness ($-.14$ and $-.50$) and self-reliance ($.13$ and $.50$) with the residualized internal freedom (state and trait) scores. Less meaningful is the trait correlation of the residualized internal freedom scores with the value dimensions benevolence ($.47$), achievement ($.44$), security ($.57$), and conformity ($.47$) (Table 11.1) However, because no theory-based predictions have been made with respect to which personality and value dimensions should be more closely related to internal than to external freedom, the differences found in this study need cross-validation with new data anyway.

The *moderator effect* of state and trait (residualized) internal freedom with respect to the influence of personality and value scales on mood is quite remarkable. It means (a) that in situations in which a person is in a state of self-expression and independence, mood is determined more by personality characteristics than by the characteristics of the behavior setting; (b) that for persons who are high on the trait self-expression and independence (i.e., high on residualized internal freedom), individual differences in the trait scores of mood (mood ratio, i.e., the relative frequency of feeling good) are clearly dependent on personality and value dimensions. The moderating effect is strongest with the

Table 11.4 Differential Predictability of Mood (0=not positive, 1=positive) from Situational Characteristics (Leisure-Work; Alone-Others) and Global Personality Dimensions

Explained variance	Residualized internal freedom		
	Low ($N = 429$)	Medium ($N = 808$)	High ($N = 215$)
R^2	.03	.03	.03
R^2 change	.05	.11	.31
F change	7.01	35.02	33.02

R^2 represents percentage of mood variance explained by leisure-work and alone-others; R^2 change represents change percentage of mood variance additionally explained by personality dimensions.

Table 11.5 Correlation of (Primary and Global) Personality Scales and Global Values with Mood (0=not positive, 1=positive) when Residualized Internal Freedom Is Low, Medium, or High

		Residualized internal freedom		
		Low	Medium	High
Primary personality scales				
A	Warmth	.04	.12	.16
B	Reasoning	−.11	.19	−.10
C	Emotional stability	−.10	.07	.08
E	Dominance	.20	−.04	−.02
F	Liveliness	.12	−.07	.03
G	Rule-consciousness	−.03	.22	.42
H	Social boldness	−.11	−.05	−.33
I	Sensitivity	−.03	.10	.16
L	Vigilance	.13	−.02	.05
M	Abstractedness	−.10	−.06	−.07
N	Privateness	.04	.20	.16
O	Apprehension	−.05	−.17	−.28
Q1	Openness to change	−.11	−.29	−.48
Q2	Self-reliance	−.25	−.19	−.41
Q3	Perfectionism	.07	.29	.36
Q4	Tension	−.07	−.34	−.44
Physical attractiveness		.07	.25	.28
Global personality scales				
Extraversion		.01	.12	.08
Self-control		.15	.33	.53
Independence		.19	−.06	.05
Global values scales				
Benevolence		−.06	−.04	.17
Universalism		−.13	−.16	−.08
Self-direction		−.07	−.16	.00
Stimulation		.03	−.14	.12
Hedonism		.07	−.03	.17
Achievement		−.03	.05	.22
Power		.07	−.02	.23
Security		.01	−.14	−.02
Conformity		.03	−.03	.24
Tradition		.06	−.08	.21
N		431–469	811–885	218–245

global personality dimension self-control. The correlation with mood states is .15, .33, and .53 when residualized internal freedom is low, medium, and high, respectively (Table 11.5). The differences in the mean mood ratios between low and high self-control persons (high minus low self-control) are .12, .20, .51 for low, medium, and high residualized internal freedom (Table 11.6).

Table 11.6 Mood (0=not positive, 1=positive) as a
Function of Residualized Internal Freedom and Self-
Control

Internal freedom	Self-control	
	Low	High
Low	.41	.53
N of observations	155	276
Medium	.71	.91
N of observations	431	380
High	.44	.95
N of observations	96	121

Some ambiguity in freedom scaling. Finally, we have to draw attention to some
ambiguity in our definition of external and internal freedom of which we were
not aware when we designed the study. It concerns those situations in which one
says, "I am free to leave the situation or to do something different." There are
two possibilities: Either the ongoing activity is not regulated by social or personal
norms as is the case with most (harmless) leisure activities, or the ongoing activity
is perceived as forbidden by some social or personal norms, for example, if a
husband should do some housework just now but prefers instead to violate social
and/or personal norms and to watch TV. In such a situation, the statement "I
could do something different" actually means "I should do something different."
Future studies should clearly differentiate in the instructions given to the participants between "could" and "should"—conditions of external and internal freedom. Evidently, no such ambiguity problem exits when the participants indicate
that they do not feel free (externally or internally), because this unequivocally
means that they feel obliged to stay in the situation or to stick to the present
activity.

The very rich data set of the TSD allows cross-referencing between the different components (or aspects) of the many 'snapshots' of experience in the natural
settings of everyday life. Thus, conjectures arising in the wake of data analysis
can be checked by complementary analyses not planned beforehand. Thinking
further about the distinction between "could" and "should" we can assume that

Table 11.7 Mood (0=not positive, 1=positive) as a
Function of Residualized Internal Freedom and
Activities

Internal freedom	Low	Medium	High
Leisure	.57	.81	.67
N of observations	240	657	128
Work	.38	.77	.80
N of observations	191	154	89

Table 11.8 ANOVA with Leisure-Work, Residualized Internal Freedom (Low—Medium—High), and Self-Control (Low—High) as Factors and Mood (0=not positive, 1=positive) as Dependent Variable

Source of variance	SS	df	MS	F	p
Main effects	47.602	4	11.900	68.885	.000
Leisure-work	.687	1	.687	3.978	.046
Internal freedom	31.321	2	15.660	90.649	.000
Self-control	17.194	1	17.194	99.527	.000
2-way interactions	8.988	5	1.798	10.405	.000
Leisure-work by internal freedom	2.887	2	1.443	8.355	.000
Leisure-work by self-control	.003	1	.003	.020	.888
Internal freedom by self-control	5.874	2	2.937	17.002	.000
3-way interactions	.338	2	.169	.979	.376
Leisure-work by internal freedom by self-control	.338	2	.169	.979	.376
Explained	56.928	11	5.175	29.957	.000
Residual	249.981	1447	.173		
Total	306.909	1458	.210		

mood in situations of high internal freedom is primarily dependent on the satisfaction of "higher motives" (including as an important component the striving for congruence with personal norms and the avoidance of bad conscience) and of the power motive (including the need for self-respect and independence, with its connotation of feeling strong and in control of the situation; for the classification of motives see Appendix B of chapter 2 in this volume).

We have tested this assumption with our data on motive satisfaction, that is, the relative frequency with which a motive is satisfied under the condition of its actualization. With high (residualized) internal freedom, mood is much more dependent on the satisfaction of the higher motives and of the the power motive than with low internal freedom. There is no such difference in the dependence of mood on the satisfaction of the other categories of motives (needs for activity/sentience, achievement, affiliation, and physical comfort). Additional evidence could be provided by comparing the emotion words used in low- and high-freedom situations subdivided according to the valence of mood.

Conclusion

We speak of a state of external freedom if a person can leave a situation or choose a different activity without being hindered by physical obstacles or social pressures. Internal freedom is given if a person does not feel obliged by internalized norms to stay in a situation and/or to continue his or her present activities. With the Time Sampling Diary (TSD) we investigated (a) how external and internal freedom are related, (b) how external and internal freedom influence mood in daily life, and (c) how internal freedom moderates the influence of personality and value structure on mood.

Human beings have to find ways of achieving self-actualization in their daily lives while being influenced by social demands and inner obligations that are present along with their striving for need fulfillment. We have seen that freedom, in particular internal freedom, contributes to subjective well-being and that the participants in our TSD-study live up to their characteristic level of well-being when they feel free of internal and external demands. In those situations, their feelings are more characteristic expressions of their temperament and of their value orientations and less a reflection of situational parameters.

A next step will be to see whether or not only emotions but also the casual attributions of emotions, that is, the events perceived by the participants as causes of their emotions, and the affected (satisfied or frustrated) motives show a larger intra-individual consistency and a larger inter-individual variance in free than in restrained situations. If so, the experience of freedom, as well as its antecedents and consequences, will definitely deserve and possibly attract more systematic theoretical reflections and empirical research.

Finding out which kinds of situations enable people with certain personality structures and value orientations to experience external and internal freedom is not only of theoretical interest but may also be useful as a diagnostic means in different fields of practice such as psychological counseling, education, and personnel management.

There is still another point worth some attention as we conclude this chapter. Throughout the history of humanity, in any region of the world, there have been and still are admirable people, imprisoned because of their faith or political beliefs, utterly deprived of external freedom, who have nevertheless been able not only to keep their human dignity but also to save their "freedom to" (Fromm, 1941) for creating, composing, writing, or, most important, helping their fellow-sufferers. Our study was not directed toward this existential issue of how one can preserve one's freedom of thought and moral integrity (which is not equivalent to our concept of internal freedom but goes beyond it) even under severe restrictions of external freedom. However, we are convinced that this existential and humanistic aspect of freedom deserves more attention in psychological research, and we believe that the TSD-technique is well suited for studying this experience of autonomy of thinking and feeling in conditions of extremely restricted external freedom.

References

Barton, K. (1986). Personality assessment by questionnaire. In R. B. Cattell & R. C. Johnson (Eds.), *Functional psychological testing. Principles and instruments* (pp. 237–259). New York: Bruner/Mazel.

Brandstätter, H. (1977). Wohlbefinden und Unbehagen. Entwurf eines Verfahrens zur Messung situationsabhängiger Stimmungen [Positive and negative mood. The design of a study for measuring mood changing with situations]. In W. H. Tack (Ed.), *Bericht über den 30. Kongreß der DGPs in Regensburg 1976*, (Vol. 2, pp. 60–62). Göttingen: Hogrefe.

Brandstätter, H. (1983). Emotional responses to other persons in everyday life situations. *Journal of Personality and Social Psychology, 45,* 871–883.

Cooper, J., & Fazio, R. H. (1984). A new look at dissonance theory. *Advances in Experimental Social Psychology, 17*, 229–266.

Csikszentmihalyi, M., & Graef, R. (1980). The experience of freedom in daily life. *American Journal of Community Psychology, 8*, 401–414.

Easterbrook, J. A. (1978). *The determinants of free will.* New York: Academic.

Emmons, R. A., & Diener, E. (1986). Situation selection as a moderator of response consistency and stability. *Journal of Personality and Social Psychology, 51*, 1013–1019.

Festinger, L. (1957). *A theory of cognitive dissonance.* Evanston, IL: Row & Peterson.

Fromm, E. (1941). *Escape from freedom.* New York: Holt, Rinehart & Winston.

Graumann, C. F. (1994). Verantwortung als soziales Konstrukt [Responsibility as social construct]. *Zeitschrift für Sozialpsychologie, 25*, 184–191.

Guilford, J. P. (1956). *Fundamental statistics.* New York: McGraw-Hill.

Jones, E. E., & Davis, K. E. (1965). From acts to dispositions: The attribution process in person perception. *Advances in Experimental Social Psychology, 2*, 219–266.

Kornadt, H. J. (1995). Willensfreiheit: Empirische Tatsache und theoretisches Problem in der Psychologie [Freedom of will: Empirical facts and theoretical problems in psychology]. In M. v. Cranach & K. Foppa (Eds.), *Freiheit des Entscheidens und Handelns* (pp. 21–55). Heidelberg: Asanger.

Kruglanski, A. W., & Cohen, M. (1973). Attributed freedom and personal causation. *Journal of Personality and Social Psychology, 26*, 245–250.

Miceli, M., & Castelfranchi, C. (1998). How to silence one's conscience: Cognitive defenses against the feeling of guilt. *Journal for the Theory of Social Behavior, 28*, 285–318.

Russell, M. T., & Karol, D. L. (1994). *The 16 PF fifth edition. Administrator's manual.* Champaign: Institute for Personality and Ability Testing.

Schwartz, S. H. (1992). Universals in the content and structure of values: Theoretical advances and empirical tests in 20 countries. *Advances in Experimental Social Psychology, 25*, 1–65.

Sherrard, C. (1998). Strategies for well-being in later life: A qualitative analysis. *British Journal of Medical Psychology, 71*, 253–263.

Snyder, L. M., & Gangestad, S. (1986). On the nature of self-monitoring: Matters of assessment, matters of validity. *Journal of Personality and Social Psychology, 51*, 125–139.

Trommsdorff, G. (1995). Erleben von Handlungsfreiheit und Restriktionen [Experiencing freedom of action and restrictions]. In M. v. Cranach & K. Foppa (Eds.). *Freiheit des Entscheidens und Handelns* (pp. 302–328). Heidelberg: Asanger.

Weiner, B. (1995). Inferences of responsibility and social motivation. *Advances of Experimental Social Psychology, 27*, 1–47.

Index

Page numbers in *italics* are charts or tables.

Abele, A., 4
ability, 79, 84–86, 90, 92, 118
ability-demand fit, 85–90, 92, 118
achievement
  and Type A, 56–57, 60, 64, 65
  and value-motive congruence, 99,
    102–103, 105, 107
achievement motive
  and housework, 176
  individual differences, 99
  and satisfaction, 104, 105
  and students, 192, 193
action
  decision-related, 84, 85, 86, 87, 88,
    89
  and emotions, 22
  failure-related, 84, 85, 86, 87
  performance-related, 84, 86, 87
  See also energetic resources
Action Control Scale, 78
action orientation
  and reactivity, 75–77, 84–85
  and self-regulation, 84, *86–87,* 90–
    92
  and temperament, 10, 13

actualization
  and action or state orientation, *82–
    83*
  in satisfaction ratio, 79–80
  and self-regulation, 84–85
  and students, 192, 193
  and value-motive congruency, 102–
    104, 107, 109
Adamovic, K., 147
adaptation, 117–118
adaptational outcomes, 113–114
affection, 33–35
affiliation motive
  and housework, 176
  and setting, 35
  and students, 193
  and value-motive incongruence, 102–
    105, 107, 108
Affleck, G., 21
aloneness, 27, 31
ambition, 56
anger
  and Type A, 56
  and unemployment, 153, 158,
    159

anxiety, 58, 91, 92
  and reactivity, 97
arousal
  definition, 116
  and emotions, 27
  and extraversion, 12
  individual differences, 135
  and reactivity, 116–117
  and stimulation, 14
  and values-motive congruence, 11,
    109
  and well-being, 108, 116
Atkinson, J. W., 60
attention
  selectivity, 75, 79, 91
  self-focused, 41
attribution theory, 200
Auhagen, A. E., 31
autonomy, 163

bank employees, 11
Banks, M. H., 148, 158
Barnett, G. K., 163, 167
Barthel, E., 165
Baruch, R., 167
Bastianoni, Paola, 13, 125, 187–198
Becker, P., 4, 148–149
Beckmann, J., 4, 10, 76, 91
behavior
  and freedom, 201
  goal-directed, 21
  and temperament, 8
  and value-motive incongruence, 99
behavioral signature, 9
Bengston, V. L., 166, 180
Bergmann, C., 11, 100
Bermudez, J., 9
Berscheid, E., 20
Bilsky, W., 98
Bird, C. E., 163, 164
Bless, H., 134
body, stimuli from, 59, 62, 67–68
boldness, 204, 209
Brandstätter, Hermann, 3–19, 20–52,
    61, 69–70, 78, 85, 93, 95–112,
    118, 120, 127, 133–146, 150, 160,
    163, 165, 171, 180–181, 187–188,
    196–197, 199–214
Brebner, J., 5, 60
Brief, A. P., 126

cardiovascular activity, 117
Carmelli, D., 56
Castelfranchi, C., 200
Cattell, R. B., 23, 28, 188
charity organization, 35–38
childhood
  and behaviors, 8
  and personality-temperament
    mismatch, 15
  and Type A, 56–57
Ciarrochi, J., 5
Clark, L. A., 7, 158
Clark, R. A., 60
Clemence, A., 189
Cofta, L., 56, 57, 58, 120
cognition
  and control, 115
  and mood, 133–134
  and self-regulation, 75–76
  and values, 98
Cognitive-Affective Personality
    System, 9
cognitive control, 115
cognitive dissonance, 200
Cohen, G., 167
Cohen, M., 200
coherent stability, 9
commercial students, 35
commuting, 12, 164–165, 168, 171,
    174–180
competence, 115
competition, 56, 60, 65–66
component process model, 22
conflict, 56
congruence
  and action orientation, 10, 13
  and personality integration, 13
  temperament and type A, 13
  and Type A, 9–10, 13, 69
  See also value-motive congruence
conscience, 13, 202
conscientiousness
  and experience, 8
  and self-regulation, 85, 89
consistency, 26, 60, 64–65
control
  cognitive, 115
  of emotions, 79, 90
  modes of, 75–76
  of stimulation, 97

and Type A, 58–62, 64–67
volitional, 74–76
See also environment control;
   motivational control
Cooper, H., 113
Cooper, J., 200
coping, 55, 114–115, 126
coping resources, 58, 59, 60
coronary heart disease, 56, 59
Costa, P. T., Jr., 114
couples
   married, 31–35
   unmarried, 31–32
crane drivers, 139–143
creativity, 134
criticism, susceptibility to, 59, 67
Cronbach's alpha, *102*, 106
Csikszentmihalyi, M., 3, 20–21, 25,
   199, 201
culture, 98–99

Davidson, R. J., 5
Davis, K. E., 200
decision-making, 10
   and freedom, 204
   and mood, 134
   and parents, 167
   and self-regulation, 10, 77, 79, 85,
   88, 91
defensive mechanisms, 99
demand-ability fit, 85–90, 92, 118
DeNeve, K. M., 113
details, 79
Diener, E., 4, 21, 201
difficulty, of task, 91, 115
discouragement, 79
discrepancies, 77
dissonance theory, 200
distraction, 91
Doise, W., 189
dominance
   and experience, 8
   and freedom, 204
   and marital relationships, 34
Dornai, Erika, 13, 100, 199–214
Dörner, D., 5, 21, 22
Dunn, D. S., 41
Džuka, Jozef, 12, 147–162

Easterbrook, J. A., 200
ecological approach, 8–9

Ekman, P., 5
electronic devices, 42
Eliasz, Andrzej, 3–19, 55–73, 77, 96,
   97, 100, 116, 117, 127
Elliot, A., 14, 99
Emmons, R. A., 4, 21, 201
emotional stability
   and freedom, 201, 202
   and interaction with others, 31
   and marital relationships, 34–35
   and situational demands, 14
   and temperament, 8
   and unemployment, 153–154, 159
emotions
   categories, 27
   component process model, 22
   control of, 79, 90
   and goals, 4–5, 21
   in human interactions, 27
   integrative function, 4–5, 22
   versus mood, 5
   and neuroticism, 96
   and personality, 5–8
   and reactivity, 97–98
   and self-regulation, 75
   and unemployment, 158–159
   vocabulary for, 38–39
Endler, N. S., 9, 77
endurance, 85, *89,* 116
energetic resources, 115, 116–117, 126
environment
   fit with, 9, 14, 28
   and self-regulation, 75, 79
   and volition, 78
   See also organizational demands;
      settings; situations
environment control
   and action or state orientation, 84,
   91
   and Type A, 10, 59, 61
Epstein, S., 98, 117
Ericson, R. J., 166
experience
   and behaviors, 8
   fragmentation, 42
Experience Sampling Method, 25
extraverts
   and arousal, 12
   and emotions, 7
   and freedom, 202

extraverts (*continued*)
  and interaction with others, 31
  and leisure *versus* work, 31, 135,
    136, 140–141
  and marital relationships, 33–34
  and performance, 143
  and positive emotions, 96
  and reactivity, 93 n.1
  and risk, 135–144
  and self-regulation, 91
  and temperament, 8
  and unemployment, 12, 14, 153–
    155, 159
  well-being, 143
Eysenck, H. J., 12, 33, 91, 96, 120,
  135, 143
Eysenck, M. W., 58, 120, 135, 143

failure
  analytical thoughts, 79
  feelings of, 15, 21, 38, 77
  and state orientation, 92
  See also action, failure-related
family, 31, 159–160, 164–168, 171–
  173, 180
  See also parents; relatives
Farris, A., 165
Farthofer, Alois, 12, 107, 133–146
fathers, 167
fatigue, 27
Fazio, R. H., 200
fear, 21, 27, 153
Feather, N. T., 98
Festinger, L., 200
Fiedler, K., 134
Filipp, G., 38–39
flexibility, 67, 77
Folkman, S., 58
Forgas, J. P., 5
Försterling, F., 58, 59
Fraccaroli, F., 149, 159
Franzkowiak, P., 148
freedom
  and dominance, 204
  and emotional stability, 201, 202
  and extraversion, 202
  internal, 13, 201–202
  and mood, 13, 199–213
  and workplace, 99–100

Friedman, M., 56, 60
friends, 27, 31
Fromm, E., 213
Frost, T. F., 59
frustration, 35–38, 62
Fünfgelt, V., 165

Gangestad, S., 209
Gaubatz, S., 26, 38
gender differences
  and couple relationships, 32
  emotional vocabulary, 9, 38–39
  and failure attribution, 38
George, J. M., 126
Gerstel, N., 165, 166, 167, 179
Glass, D. C., 59, 67
Gluchman, V., 159
goals
  and emotions, 4–5, 21
  self-concordant or self-discordant,
    14
  and self-regulation, 10
  and social setting, 27–31
  and Type A persons, 56–57
Goldstein, H., 16
Graef, R., 199, 201
Graumann, C. F., 200
Gray, J. A., 77
Griffin, D., 4
Gross, H., 165, 166, 167, 179
Gross, J. J., 114
Grossman, M., 38–39
Guilford, J. P., 204

Hajjar, V., 149, 159
happiness
  and person-environment fit, 6, 27–
    31
  philosophical question, 42–43
  versus satisfaction, 95
having one's way, 85, *89*
Heady, B., 7
health, somatic, 68, 123–124, 148, 158–
  159
hedonic tone, 120, 125
Helmreich, R. L., 56
Hepburn, L., 120
Hesse, F. W., 134

Hettema, P. J., 77
hostility, 56
housework, 156, 159, 163–164, *172*, 174–178
Houston, B. K., 56, 60
Hull, J. G., 41–42
Hunter, J. E., 118
Hunter, R. F., 118
husbands, 32–35, 181

impatience, 56
incentives, 107, 108
independence, 204, 209
individual ability profile, 85
individual differences
    and achievement motive, 99
    and freedom, 203–204, 213
    optimal arousal, 135
    and well-being, 115, 116–117, 125
    See also intra-individual differences
information
    discrepancies, 77
    and mood, 134
    and self-regulation, 10, 75, 77, 85, 91
insecurity, 59
integration, 4–5, 13, 15
integrity, 213
intelligence
    and adaptability, 117–118
    and coping, 115
    and mood, 125
    and new workplace, 11, 121–122, 125
interaction
    with colleagues, 192
    and mood ratio, 123
    with other people, 9, 27, 31, 107
    with relatives, 193
    and Type A individuals, 60, 61
    and unemployment, 154–156, 157, 158, 159
    See also relationships; support
interactionism, 27
internal states, 41–42
interventions, 109
intra-individual differences, 196–197
introverts
    and marital relationships, 33–34

and reactivity, 93 n.1
and risk, 12
and unemployment, 12, 153–154, 159
and well-being, 143
and work *versus* leisure, 135, 140–141
irritability, 56, 59

Jackson, P. R., 148, 158
Jenkin's Activity Survey, 56, 62
Johnson, J., 41–42
Johnson, R., 5
Jones, E. E., 200
Journal of Personality, 21
joy, 27
judgment, 133–134

Kahneman, D., 114, 116
Kanner, A. D., 58
Karner, G., 167
Karoly, P., 41
Kessler, R. C., 167, 181
Ketelaar, T., 114, 143
Kieselbach, T., 148
Kirchler, E., 12, 15, 31–32, 149, 163–182
Kiss, Gyöngyi B., 13, 100, 199–214
Kleinová, R., 147
Klonowicz, Tatiana, 11, 97, 113–129
Kornadt, H. J., 201
Kozma, A., 149
Kraft, D., 47
Kruglanski, A. W., 200
Kuhl, J., 10, 74–76, 78, 91, 92, 93, 134
    See also Action Control Scale

Larsen, R. J., 4, 7, 21, 114, 125
Larsen, R. L., 114, 143
Larson, R., 3, 21, 25
Lazarus, R. S., 5, 58
Le Blanc, A., 149, 159
leisure
    and freedom, 208
    at home, 81, 90, 91
    at home *versus* out of home, 194–195
    of housewives, 163–164, 165, 174–175, 181

leisure (*continued*)
    and introverts and extraverts, 31,
        135, 136, 140–141
    and personal interactions, 31
    and self-regulation, 84
    and students, 193
    and temperament, 81
    and unemployment, 156–157
Lersch, Philipp, 15, 22
Levine, S., 4
Lewinsohn, P., 95, 96
Liske, D. J., 41
logit transformation, 152
Lorenzi-Cioldi, F., 189
Lowell, E. L., 60
Lucas, R. E., 21

Machalová, M., 147
Macklin, E. D., 165, 180
Magnusson, D., 77
Mancini, Tiziana, 13, 125, 187–198
Mann, J., 134
marriages, 32–35, 165–182
Marszał-Wiśniewska, Magdalena, 10,
    74–94
Maslow, A. H., 99
Matthews, G., 91
McClelland, D. C., 60, 98, 107
McCrae, R. R., 7, 96, 114
McFatter, R. M., 7, 159
McLeod, J. D., 167
media, 158, 159, 160
Melton, R. J., 134
men
    in couple relationships, 32–33, 180
    emotional vocabulary, 38–39
    and failure attribution, 38
Metcalfe, J., 15
Meyer, G. J., 7, 143
Miceli, M., 200
military, 35–38
Mischel, W., 8–9, 15, 60, 125
mobility
    definition, 77, 117
    and motivational control, *88*
    in new workplace study, 11, 121–
        122, 125, 126
    and satisfaction ratio, 81–84
    and self-regulation success, 91
    and volition, 84–85

Mohr, H. M., 148–149
mood
    and cognition, 133–134
    definition, 95–96, 134–135
    versus emotion, 5
    and freedom, 201–202, 205–211
    and high risk work, 142
    and intelligence, 125
    introverts and extraverts, 140–141
    and mass media, 160
    personality effect, 12
    and reactivity, 97
    of students, *191,* 194–197
    and unemployment, 153–157
    variability, 120, 122–123, 125
    of wives, 12, 32–35, 165, 171, 174–
        181
    at work, 100
    See also well-being
mood ratio, 123, 140–141
mothers
    and children, 164
    mood, 12
    and power motive, 178–180
    and stress, 167
    and unemployed youth, 159–160
motivational control, 75, 77, 84, 85,
    88, 89, 91–92
motives
    of control, 61–62, 64–65, 67
    definition, 21
    and organizational climate, 35–38
    and person-environment fit, 27–
        31
    physical needs, 59, 62, 65, 67–68
    self-value, 59, 62, 64–65, 67
    and Type A, 58–59, 61–62
    versus values, 11, 98
    See also achievement motive;
        affiliation motive; power, as
        motive; task motives
motive structure, 28
Multiple Correspondence Analysis,
    13, 16, 188–192

Navon, D., 114, 116
need-offer fit, 85
negative emotions, 27
neuroticism, 7, 91, 96, 97

obstacles, 21
Ochel, A., 164
operator, steel plant, 137–138
Orendi, B., 163
organizational climate, 35–38
organizational demands, 114–115, 118
Orientation to Work Values Inventory, 100

parents, 15, 56–57, 164, 167
  See also mothers
Parkes, K., 114
partners, 15, 31–32
passivity, 77
Pavlov's Temperament Inventory, 62, 78
Pearlin, L. I., 149
Pelzmann, L., 149
performance
  and arousal, 116
  and mood, 143
persistence, 60
personality
  and congruence, 13–14
  and emotions, 5–8
  and freedom, 202, 203–211
  and interaction with others, 31
  and mood, 12, 202, 205–208
  of steel plant workers, 140
  versus temperament, 7–8, 15
  variables, 8–9
  and well-being, 96
personal resources
  allocation, 126
  and arousal, 116
  background, 113–114
  energetic and structural, 115–118, 126
  for organizational fit, 121–127
personal strivings, 10, 21, 56
person-by-situation fit, 12
person-environment fit
  energetic and structural resources, 115
  and happiness, 6, 27–31
  as hypothesis, 14
  and self-regulation, 76
personnel selection, 38

person-organization fit, 118–127
Pervin, L. A., 5, 76
Peuckert, R., 164
physical comfort, 175
physical health, 68, 123–124, 148, 158–159
physical needs, 59, 62, 67–68
pilots, 142
Pina, D. L., 166
Piotrkowski, C. S., 166, 167
Pleck, J. H., 166
Pončáková, K., 147
positive emotions, 27
positive feelings, 79
power
  as motive, 102, 102–103, 107, 108, 109
  and reactivity, 109
  and value and motive congruence, 11
power motive
  and child care, 178–179
  and housework, 175
  and organizational climate, 35–38
Pred, R. S., 56
Prescott, S., 3, 21, 25
prestige, 107
Price, V. A., 59
pride, 22
prison, 35, 213
privacy, 193
privateness, 209
process approach, 9
procrastination, 91
psychosomatic disorders
  and new workplace, 11
  and stimulation control, 97
  and Type A, 58
  and value-motive incongruence, 99
punishment, 77

rationality, 35
Raven's Advanced Progressive Matrices, 119
reaction time, 91
reactivity
  and action versus state orientation, 77
  and arousal, 116–117

reactivity (*continued*)
   and cardiovascular activity, 117
   definition, 116
   and emotion control, 90
   and excitation, 93 n.2, 126 n.1
   low and high, 55, 77, *82–83*, 90, 97
   and neuroticism, 97
   and personal resources, 115
   and power motive, 109
   and satisfaction, 81–84, *82–83*, 98
   and self-regulation, *82–83, 89*
   and Type A, 9–10, 56–60, 64, 69
   and value-motive congruence, 11, 99, 104, 105, 107, 109
   and workplace, 11, 100, 121–122, 125
relationships
   marital, 9, 32–35
   social, 27, 107
   students, 192, 193
   unmarried couples, 31–32
   See also interaction
relatives, 27, 31, 193
   See also family
relaxation, 27
Rerrich, M. S., 163, 180
resourcefulness, 204
resource theories, 114–115
responsibility, 200
reward potential, 28, 196–197, 199–200
Reykowski, J., 98
Ridley, 148
rigidity, 67, 68
risk
   and achievement, 60
   and extraverts, 135–144
   and health, 68
   and introverts, 12
   and mood, 134
Rodler, Christa, 12, 163–182
Rogers, C. R., 96, 99
Rosenman, R. H., 56, 60
Ross, C. E., 163, 164
routine tasks, 21
Rückert, D., 163
ruminant thoughts, 76, 77
Russell, J. A., 27, 194
Rusting, C. L., 7, 134, 135

sadness, 21, 27, 153, 158, 159
safety, 142
Sanders, A. F., 125
satiation, 27
satisfaction
   and affiliation value, 107
   versus happiness, 95
   measuring, 3–4
   and motive, 104, *105, 106, 108*
   and power value, 107
   with self-regulation, 90
   in Type A study, 62
   and Type B, 57
   and value-motive congruence, 107–109
satisfaction ratio, 80, 81–82, 85, *86–87, 88, 89*
Scheier, M. F., 115
Schimmack, U., 4
Schmidt, F. L., 118
Schneewind, K. A., 23, 28
Schooler, C., 149
Schröder, G., 23, 28
Schwartz, S. H., 98, 203
Seifert, K.-H., 11, 100
self-awareness, 41
self-control, 204, 205–208, 209–211
self-esteem, 67
self-expression, 209
self-regulation
   abilities for, 10
   and action or state orientation, 84, *86–87*
   bank employee study, 78–90
   Kuhl theory, 74–76
   and temperament, 81–85, 90–91
self-reliance, 209
self-sufficiency, 204
self-value, 59, 62, 64–65, 67
sensitivity, 97
settings, 35, 187–197
Shack, J. R., 7, 143
Sheldon, K. M., 14, 99
Sherrard, C., 201
Shoda, Y., 9
siblings, 31
situational demand, 85, *89*
situations
   and emotional stability, 14, 125
   and freedom, 13

and settings, 187–197
social, 27
and value-motive congruence, 99, 107, 108
See also ecological approach; leisure; person-by-situation fit; workplace
Smith, C. A., 5
Smith, T. H., 148–149
smoking, 74, 75
Snyder, L. M., 209
socialization agents, 10
See also volition
social pressures
and dissonance, 200, 202
and freedom, 13, 211–213
and high-reactives, 57, 97
and unemployment, 149
and values, 98–99, 201–213
social relationships, 27, 107
and unemployment, 154–156, 157, 158, 159
social situations, 27–31
social support, 166
socio-economics students, 35
somatic health, 123–124
Somatic Symptoms Checklist, 120
Spearman-Brown formula, 26
Spence, J. T., 56
Spies, K., 134
stability coefficients, 26
Stafford, E. M., 148
state orientation
and reactivity, 75–77, *89*
and self-regulation, 84, *86–87, 88, 89,* 90, 91, 92
and temperament, 10–11
state/trait correlations, 203–204
statistical analysis, 16, 80–81, 102–106
steel workers, 11
stimulation
and arousability, 14
control of, 97
and extraverts, 135
physical, 59, 62, 67–68
and reactivity, 77, 91
and self-regulation, 75, 91
and Type A, 55, 58, 59
Stones, M. J., 149

Stößel, U., 148
strangers, 31, 193
Strelau, J., 7, 55, 57, 69 n.1, 77, 78, 90–91, 93 n.2, 97, 107, 116, 117, 125
Strelau Temperament Inventory, 102, 119
Strelau Temperament Inventory—Revised. *See* Pavlov's Temperament Inventory
stress
and commuting, 167
and mothers, 167
and reactivity, 58, 60–61, 67, 97
and value-motive incongruence, 109
See also risk
strivings, 10, 21, 56
structural resources, 115, 117–118, 126
students, 31–38, 187–197, 208
success
and ability, 90
analytical thoughts, 79
feelings of, 15, 21, 38
Suh, E. M., 21
Super's Work Value Inventory, 11, 100
support
from colleagues, 38
for family, 167
perceived by wives, 166, 178–180
and self-regulation, 79
Sutton, S. K., 114
Swan, G. E., 56

task difficulty, 91, 115
task motives, 58–59, 61, 63–64, 69
temperament
and action or state orientation, 13
and leisure, 81
versus personality, 7–8, 15
and satisfaction, 90
and self-regulation, 81–84, 90
and transactional relations, 5
and Type A, 13
versus volition, 10
See also mobility; reactivity
temperament-volition coherence, 10, 78, 91–92
Tennen, H., 21
tension, 153, 158, 159, 165

Thomae, H., 42
Thomas, A., 7
Tiggemann, M., 148
time pressure, 56, 58, 60, 134
Time Sampling Diary
  advantages, 13–14, 39–41
  assumptions, 21–23
  background, 8, 20–21
  coding instructions, 45–48
  method, 23–25, 41
  reliability, 25–26
  shortcomings, 15–16, 41–42
  subject instructions, 43–45
trait approach, 8–9
transactional relations, 5
triumph, 21–22
Trommsdorff, G., 201
Tversky, A., 4
Type A
  and body, 59, 62, 67–68
  and control, 58–59, 61–62, 64–65, 67
  and criticism, 67
  description, 55–56
  and reactivity, 9–10, 56–68, 69
  and temperament, 13
  workplace type study, 61–68
Type A behavior pattern (TABP), 70
  n.2
Type B, 57

unemployment
  and emotional stability, 153–154,
    159
  and introverts, 12, 153–154, 159
  long and short term, 12, 150–160
  in Slovak youth, 147, 150–160
  in Western countries, 148, 149
  of wives, 32

value-motive congruence
  and arousal, 11, 109
  definition, 96
  deprivation, 98–99, 108
  and power, 11
  and reactivity, 11, 99, 104, 105, 107,
    109
  study method, 100–101
values
  and freedom, 13, 202, 205–211

versus motives, 11, 98
  of unemployed youth, 159
Van Harrison, R., 118
Veenhoven, R., 95
Vetter, August, 22
vocabulary, 38–39
volition
  Kuhl theory, 74–76
  and mobility, 84–85
  See also temperament-volition
    coherence
Vonkomerová, R., 147

Wagner, W., 32, 165, 180
Wakker, P. P., 42
Warr, P., 148
Watson, D., 7, 158
Wearing, A., 7
Weiner, B., 200
well-being
  and arousal, 108, 116
  classification, 95
  in couple relationships, 32
  extraverts and introverts, 143
  and freedom, 201
  of housewives, 164, 165, 166, 175–
    181
  and mood variability, 11, 120
  in new workplace, 11
  and personality, 96
  and person-environmental fit, 27–31
  and Type A, 58
  See also congruence; mood
Wickens, C. D., 114, 189
Wicklund, R. A., 41
will power, 85, 89
Wilson, H. G., 59
Wilson, T. D., 41–42
Wilson, W., 99
Windischbauer, A., 149, 160
Winefield, A. H., 148
Winter, D. G., 98
wives
  of commuting husbands, 12, 167–
    180
  employed and unemployed, 32
  moods, 32, 34–35
women
  in couple relationships, 32
  emotional vocabulary, 38–39

and failure blame, 38
See also wives
work
  and freedom, 208
  and introverts, 135, 140–141
  and students, 192, 193
  See also housework
workers
  bank employee study, 78–90
  eager, bright, and poor, 121–122,
    123–125
  in high risk jobs, 12, 135–144
  mood attributions, 38
  morale, 126
  See also unemployment
work-home, 85, 193
workplace
  adjustment to new, 9–10, 38, 113–
    128
  and extraverts, 31, 135–144

and family, 165–166
and motives, 99
and personal interaction, 31
and reactivity, 100
and self-regulation, 84, *88, 89,* 90,
  91–92
and students, 193
and Type A individuals, 60, 61, 63–
  64, 67
and value-motive incongruency,
  100, 105
and volitional properties, 91–92
work psychology, 163
Work Values Inventory, 11, 100
Wrześniewski, K., 56, 58, 97

Yerkes-Dodson law, 116

Zalewska, Anna M., 11, 76, 95–112